History, Imagination and the Performance of Music

History, Imagination and the Performance of Music

Peter Walls

THE BOYDELL PRESS

First published 2003
The Boydell Press, Woodbridge

ISBN 1 84383 005 1

The Boydell Press is an imprint of Boydell & Brewer Ltd
PO Box 9, Woodbridge, Suffolk IP12 3DF, UK
and of Boydell & Brewer Inc.
PO Box 41026, Rochester, NY 14604–4126, USA
website: www.boydell.co.uk

A catalogue record for this book is available
from the British Library

Library of Congress Cataloging-in-Publication Data
Walls, Peter.
  History, imagination, and the performance of music / Peter Walls.
    p. cm.
Includes bibliographical references (p.   ) and index.
  ISBN 1–84383–005–1 (alk. paper)
  1. Performance practice (Music)   2. Music – Performance.   I. Title.
ML457.W34 2003
781.4'3 – dc21   2003001924

This publication is printed on acid-free paper

Typeset by Joshua Associates Ltd, Oxford

Printed in Great Britain by
The Cromwell Press, Trowbridge

Contents

Illustrations

Music examples

Tables

for Alison

Preface

In 1983 the Taverner Consort and Choir marked their tenth anniversary by hosting a weekend symposium on performance practice. For me personally, this was a landmark event. At it I presented a paper on the performance implications of 18th-century violin fingering, and this was to become my first article on a performance practice topic.

A few months later an *Early Music* editorial drew attention to the fact that the publicity for the Taverner symposium had stated ('wearily' according to the editor, Nicholas Kenyon), 'We shall not waste time discussing the nature of authenticity.'[1] At that time I shared in the other participants' impatience (rather than 'weariness', I think) with such questions. It seemed that we all knew why we wanted to do performance practice research and that we had a reasonably sophisticated understanding of the limits of its applicability. As time went on, however, I became increasingly frustrated at the assumptions about aims and motivation that are projected onto those involved in performance practice research or onto those who wished to draw on such research in their performance. For that reason, I was very glad to be given the opportunity afforded by Magdalen College's Waynflete lectures for 2000 to take a critical look at the issues. My Waynflete lectures form the core of this book. Having had this stimulus to think through and address the intellectual rationale for performance practice research and its application, I can say that any residue of impatience or weariness has been well and truly driven out by a sense of the value of an increased awareness of the aesthetic complexity of questions in historical performance practice. Consequently, the performance practice course I have taught since 2000 has aimed for a considerably increased level of continuous, reflexive critique than in previous years. My hope is that academic colleagues, performers, and students who read what follows will be similarly encouraged in dealing with historical performance matters to think about the philosophical ramifications of what they do and why they do it.

I am indebted to Anthony Smith, the President of Magdalen College, and to the other Fellows at Magdalen for the invitation to give the Waynflete Lectures and for their hospitality during the six months I spent there with them as a Visiting Fellow. In particular, I would like to thank Dr Bojan Bujic for his help in the organisation of the series and especially for his encouragement and interest. Before, during, and after the lectures I was stimulated by fruitful discussions with friends and colleagues. In this regard, I would especially like to mention Dr Peter Allsop, Dr Bonnie Blackburn, Michael Lowe, Dr Richard

---

[1] *Early Music* 12 (1984), 2.

Maunder, Andrew Parrott, Professor John Rink, Professor Eric Stanley, Professor Brian Trowell, Dr Susan Wollenberg and Professor Neal Zaslaw. I have tried, as appropriate, to incorporate their suggestions and to respond to their queries (or protests) in this published version (though that is not to say that I now expect their acquiescence in all that I say here). Professor John Butt read a draft of the book and provided many helpful suggestions. I was helped (in retrieving material I had left 12,000 miles away) by Dr Samantha Owens and Roy Carr at the Victoria University School of Music in Wellington. Dr Inge van Rij kindly checked my German translations and steered me towards some interesting Brahms material. I am grateful to Dr Warren Drake for telling me about the Wagner letter cited in chapter 5, to Sonya Monosoff for alerting me (some years ago) to the interest of Heinrich Dessauer's edition of the Mendelssohn Violin Concerto in E minor reproduced as illus. 6.2, to Douglas Mews for keeping me supplied with the Bach organ scores I needed in writing chapter 7, to Uri Golomb for sending me details of the Harnoncourt B minor Mass recording referred to in chapter 3 and to Usha Bhana for carrying out numerous small tasks as a research assistant. Sarah Martin kindly directed me towards the programme Sforzando Pro (used in analysing the recorded examples discussed in chapters 6 and 8). I would like to thank Bruce Phillips for facilitating this volume and Caroline Palmer and her colleagues at Boydell & Brewer for all their assistance. For the lectures themselves in Oxford I was assisted by Dr Ian Gibson in the compilation of recorded examples and by Bill Lees, the obliging administrator of Magdalen's Grove Auditorium. I must also record my thanks to the Rector and Fellows at Exeter College, Oxford (where I had been a graduate student) for making me feel so welcome there and, in particular, for electing me to a visiting fellowship in the term following the period of the Waynflete lectureship. I would like to acknowledge the invaluable support of the Marsden Fund (administered by the Royal Society of New Zealand) and of my faculty leave committee at Victoria University of Wellington.

Finally, I must thank my wife, Kathryn, for her support and her forbearance in listening to various drafts of what you are about to read.

1. Introduction

My hope in this volume is to contribute to a more sophisticated understanding of the rationale for performance practice research and historically-oriented performance. In the process, I visit a few of the hot spots where attempts to reconcile notions of historical fidelity with the exigencies of contemporary performance have produced conflict of various kinds.

The debate to which these essays contribute has had some very unsettling effects. Performers have been factionalised; there has been mutual suspicion between modern and period instrument players. Within the latter group there has been further dissension around opposing views of what constitutes historical fidelity. By its very nature, any performance which, as it were, declares an interest in historical conditions has a more or less explicitly academic dimension. But academic discussion surrounding historical performance issues has often exacerbated this discord – not just by a normal healthy failure to agree on historical truth but by calling in question the whole nature of the enterprise. In this series of essays, I have tried to disentangle some of the issues. I write as someone who values performance practice research in itself and who has long been convinced of its importance to performers. But throughout, I have emphasised the need to distinguish between the effort to determine historical truth and the attempt to follow through on that in contemporary performance.

I am, clearly, very much concerned with what is often called 'authenticity'. It need hardly be said that this term is highly problematic and that it has had a chequered history. 'Authentic' was a word less used in relation to the performance of early music in the first half of the 20th century than we might expect.[1] It does not appear in Dolmetsch's *Interpretation of Music of the 17th and 18th Centuries* (1915), nor in Schering's 1931 volume on historical performance practice.[2] Thurston Dart occasionally used it in a relative sense,

---

[1] In 19th-century Germany there was a prolonged debate about the 'authentic' way of performing the music of Palestrina. As James Garratt pointed out at the Royal Musical Association conference held at the University of Southampton in April 2000, authenticity (the term was used) vied with what was described as 'necessary anachronism' – the adaptation (by Liszt, Wagner and others) of old church music to fit modern taste. No other repertory seems to have been the focus of quite such a sustained discussion of authenticity – perhaps because getting the *stylus a capella* right seemed a matter of liturgical importance rather than a question of purely musical taste.

[2] Arnold Schering, *Aufführungspraxis alter Musik* (Leipzig, 1931).

writing, for example, that 'medieval music . . . can never be brought to life with the same authenticity that should characterise performances of baroque music'.[3] Dart may have been the first person to enclose the word in quotation marks ('scare quotes' as they have come to be called) as a way of indicating his own scepticism about the concept: 'Meanwhile our unfamiliarity with the harpsichord, with its proper balance with other instruments, and its playing technique turns many present-day 'authentic' performances of old music into mockeries.'[4] In 1980 *The New Grove* absorbed the word (once again qualified by 'scare quotes') into its definition of 'Performing Practice':

> A term adapted from the German *Aufführungspraxis.* . . . As applied to Western music, it involves all aspects of the way in which music is and has been performed, and its study is of particular importance to the performer concerned with 'authentic' style.

Robert Donington, though, had no qualms about embracing the concept, nor even about reinforcing its dogmatic overtones in ways bound to make hackles rise. He announced in the 1989 revision of *The Interpretation of Early Music* that

> The first assumption [underlying the original 1963 edition of this book], that we can best serve early music by matching our modern interpretation as closely as possible to what we know of the original interpretation, may be called *the doctrine of historical authenticity* . . . This [doctrine] is in better standing today than ever before . . .[5]

This is an extraordinary statement. By 1989, the idea of historical authenticity in performance, far from being 'unquestionably respectable' as Donington put it, was very much under scrutiny. Five years earlier, *Early Music* had embarked on what it called a 'discussion' of 'The Limits of Authenticity' with uniformly sceptical contributions from Richard Taruskin, Daniel Leech-Wilkinson, Nicholas Temperley, and Robert Winter.[6] And in 1988, the journal's then editor Nicholas Kenyon published a symposium entitled *Authenticity and Early Music* which proved to be influential in fuelling debate on motivation and intentions. Taruskin was again one of the contributors and in 1995 republished his chapter along with a number of other combative essays in *Text and Act*. The conceptual issues were taken up by philosphers interested in aesthetics – most fully by Peter Kivy in *Authenticities* (1995) and most provokingly by Roger Scruton in *The Aesthetics of Music* (1997).[7] Through the 1980s and 90s serious debate about the aims, methods and assumptions of both performance practice scholars and early music performers permeated musicological journals.

[3] Thurston Dart, *The Interpretation of Music* (London, 1954), p. 16.
[4] Ibid., p. 162.
[5] Robert Donington, *The Interpretation of Early Music*, revised ed. (London, 1989), p. 37 (my italics).
[6] *Early Music* 12 (1984), 3–25.
[7] Peter Kivy, *Authenticities: Philosophical Reflections on Musical Performance* (Ithaca and London, 1995); Roger Scruton, *The Aesthetics of Music* (Oxford, 1997).

In the introduction to a recent compendium of essays on current trends in musicology, Nicholas Cook and Mark Everist express general agreement with Richard Taruskin's view that historically-informed performance is 'in essence a modernist phenomenon' while adding (in a footnote) 'Modernist, and – as an intellectual concept, perhaps – exhausted.' The note continues: 'It was originally intended to include a chapter on historically informed performance, but it proved impossible to find an author who could feel that there was something useful that could be said beyond a summary of conclusions of arguments current in the 1980s.'[8] I'm afraid I read this as something of a challenge. A continuous interrogation of the basis for adopting certain approaches in either research or performance is always going to be necessary. It would, I believe, be a great pity if the discussion were now thought to be closed since it seems to have got stuck ('exhausted!') at a rather unsatisfactory point.

What, in fact, were the apparently definitive 'conclusions' to emerge from the debates of the 1980s? Cook and Everist do not elaborate, but something like the following can be inferred from the literature on the subject:

1. that the goal of authenticity in performance is fatally flawed; a comprehensive authenticity is impossible since various aspects of the concept are incompatible with each other. (According to this view, successfully recreating the sound world of, for example, a work by Bach is likely to obstruct rather than facilitate an audience's experiencing something like the emotional impact intended by Bach and/or originally felt by audiences in Cöthen or Leipzig in the 1720s and 30s.)

2. that – presuming that historically-authentic reconstruction were possible – historical listening is not. (We cannot escape the fact that we already know the music of Brahms, Berg, and Birtwistle and that that knowledge colours our apprehension of earlier music.)

3. that to conceive of pre *c.* 1800 music in terms of aesthetically-autonomous musical 'works' is anachronistic (and therefore inauthentic); and as a corollary, to present music in concert that was composed for a totally different purpose (as an element in a liturgy, for example) is intrinsically inauthentic.

4. that performance that strives for historical authenticity is itself historically circumscribed and thus inescapably subjective and unreliable; consequently any proper evaluation of the significance or value of such performance goals must be contextualised (i.e. restricted) in this way.

5. that period-instrument performances privilege what is essentially a modernist taste for such features as transparent textures, light and buoyant rhythms, clarity of articulation and energy over attributes like weight and richness of sound, and depth of feeling.

[8] N. Cook and M. Everist, eds., *Rethinking Music* (Oxford and New York, 1999), p. 12.

6. (even worse) that such performances involve the suspension of musical judgement and imagination in favour of the observance of instructions gleaned from historical sources.[9]

Debate on these issues – far from being exhausted – may only just have begun. In this volume, I consider each of the points just summarised, not in every case with the aim of rebutting them outright, but in the hope at least of promoting a less glib evaluation of historical performance practice.

One of the complications of addressing the kind of issues represented by the six putative 'conclusions' listed above, is that they emanate from musicians and scholars with very different reasons for objecting to what they think is going on in the early music world. It may be helpful to consider briefly what points of view are represented here since addressing them in the essays that follow involves me in some inevitable, but I hope not too disconcerting, changes of focus.

Broadly speaking, there are three groups whose views need to be taken into account. First, there are those who for one reason or another simply do not like period-instrument performance. At their most sympathetic, their attitudes reflect a kind of generation gap where some whose tastes were formed before about 1970 feel that the directions taken by period-instrument performers have interfered with the enjoyment and appreciation of early music. Paul Henry Lang is an eloquent spokesperson for this group:

> As the exploration and restoration of the authentic performance practice of earlier music became an important branch of musicology, all of us felt like discoverers glimpsing through the fog the shores of an unknown land, marvelling at the new vistas opened by scholarship. To the extent that the study of performance practice by scholars has opened new insight into what is vaguely called old music, it has indeed been a most welcome spur to fruitful activity both in education and in practice; but to the extent that the new discipline attempts to structure and regiment the whole experience of musicians concerned with pre-romantic music, it may now actually be impeding the revival of old music. The refusal to make any concessions to contemporary musical sensibilities tends toward elitist music making which, however engrossing and valuable, cannot reach beyond restricted audiences.[10]

The second group (of which Richard Taruskin has been the most prominent and influential representative) adopt a more complicated stance. They profess an allegiance to historical performance practice but accuse many of its (other) practitioners of a kind of quaint naivety. Taruskin's criticisms of those involved

---

[9] '. . . the hard-line [pro-authenticity] attitude at least generated some interesting objections: that they were using data to limit choices, and replacing creativity with blank antiquarianism; or on the contrary that they were tacitly imposing artistic decisions of a very definite kind, viz. the impersonal and hygienic ideals of Stravinskyan neo-classicism; and that this fanatical respect for authorial intentions is, anyway, a legacy of a *romantic* prestige given to the unique artist and his inviolable work': Tom Lubbock, 'The Early Early Show', *The Independent* 20 September 1988.

[10] Paul Henry Lang, 'Performance Practice and Musicology', in *Musik, Edition, Interpretation: Gedenkschrift Günter Henle*, ed. M. Bent (Munich, 1980), p. 315.

in period-instrument performance are simultaneously forthright and elusive. On many issues, I find myself wanting to invoke his writings in support of my own position – and yet there is a fundamental underlying difference in outlook. As an example of what I mean, consider the following:

> Empirical science, as all the world knows, claims to be "value-free". But art is not, and performance must not be. The adoption of the doctrinaire empiricist, positivist, and unprincipled stance of scientific research when investigating performance practice can be pernicious, leading in extreme cases to an evasion of responsibility, something distressingly close to a musical Eichmann defense. I have in mind the perpetration of musical results the performer himself regards as unattractive, in the belief that that's how it was done, like it or not ('I was just following orders'). There have been notable recent instances of this in Bach performance, where the situation is exacerbated by the knowledge that Bach himself did not like certain aspects of his own performance practice, notably involving the size and quality of his choir in Leipzig. Still more disturbing is the 'scientific' pressure to keep up with the state of research, whatever one's personal predilections. I know of more than one instance in which performers of Renaissance and Baroque music have followed practices of which they were not personally convinced either historically or esthetically for fear that otherwise they might be suspected of ignorance.[11]

It is impossible to accuse Taruskin of not approving of good performance practice research or of disliking performances that attempt to incorporate such research. The attitude here is ostensibly one of merely placing certain caveats around these activities. I agree unreservedly with the first two sentences in the excerpt quoted. Yet many of Taruskin's adjectives here are prejudicial – the clearest case being 'unprincipled' (with its connotations of immorality) rather than a more neutral term. ('Disinterested', for example, would make the point more clearly that the ideal being alluded to here is research carried out without a pre-determined agenda.) The nuance of immorality is continued in his use of the Eichmann metaphor. This is more than just prejudicial; it is an offensive way of characterising those who wish to try out what has been learned through research in their performance.

Who, in any case, are these musicians Taruskin knows who have adopted some practice without any conviction about its historical truth or aesthetic worth? This is not a question that should need answering since in every branch of music we all from time to time encounter incompetence, stupidity, deficient musicianship and ignorance – but we don't usually attempt to argue from such local disappointments to generalise about the whole enterprise.[12] More importantly,

---

[11] R. Taruskin, *Text and Act* (New York and Oxford, 1995), pp. 61–2, n. 17.

[12] Charles Rosen, commenting on Taruskin's contribution to the Kenyon symposium, describes him as writing 'brilliantly and at the top of his voice' but observes that 'his most crushing arguments are often reserved for opinions that no one really holds': Charles Rosen, 'The Benefits of Authenticity', originally published in *The New York Review of Books* in 1990, and reprinted in *Critical Entertainments* (Cambridge, Mass., and London, 2000), p. 204.

the passage conflates the activities of research and performance in a way that undermines the value of both.

The third broad grouping is of those committed to period-instrument performance and who, though untroubled by the broader questions of the underlying philosophical rationale, scorn approaches conspicuously different from their own. (Chapter 3 in this volume examines some specific instances of this.)

Why has the question of the applicability of performance practice research become the site of such vigorous, even acrimonious, debate? To begin with, the debate has never been a normal academic discussion, confined to those directly involved in research and performance projects. It is, in fact, hard to think of any other area in music in which what managers have taught us to call the 'stakeholders' are so numerous or so varied. Performers, musicologists, instrument makers, music critics, journalists, concert promoters, record company producers, and – last but not least – audiences all have an interest.

The interested parties appear, superficially, to be talking about the same issues. The larger picture, however, is of distinct, but overlapping and intersecting discourses driven by divergent motives and values. Sometimes, these are of a quite meretricious kind, nothing more or less than commercial advantage (the attempt to ensure that a particular product has a competitive edge). But where this is so, its proponents often manage to harness the more sincere (and sometimes more naive) ideals of performers, scholars, and their audience or readership.

Let me explain what I mean with one recent example. At the beginning of 2000 (the 250th anniversary of Bach's death), Sir John Eliot Gardiner with the English Baroque Soloists and various choirs embarked on a 'Bach Cantata Pilgrimage' backed by Deutsche Gramaphon. The printed programme distributed at individual concerts in the series was silent on the contentious question of the numbers of performers Bach expected (about which more in the next chapter); but it did recommend the series to audiences on the basis of other kinds of historical fidelity. An introductory note reads, 'No musical ensemble has ever previously attempted to perform all of Bach's surviving church cantatas within a single year on the appropriate day, nor to replicate, as it were, the weekly musical preparation leading to performances of these extraordinary works.'

This sort of rhetoric is perversely misleading. First, this venture has some quite well-known antecedents.[13] More significantly, however, Bach's extant cantatas are drawn from what was once at least three annual cycles, so the idea of performing them all within a twelve month period is speciously historical. And to claim that this project allowed the musicians involved to replicate the weekly musical preparation leading to performances is palpable

---

[13] Emmanuel Music in Boston, for example, have been working their way through Bach cantata annual cycles (presented as part of the liturgy) on a nearly weekly basis for thirty years. They cover thirty-eight cantatas each year.

nonsense. Who could possibly believe that having London-based freelance musicians speeding from one European centre to another to perform these concerts has anything at all in common with a rehearsal regime embedded in the routines of a stable community in Leipzig in the 1720s? And what, anyway, would be the point? We are given no indication as to how this might affect the final result – the performance.

The programme claimed more of this kind of spurious uniqueness in the form of a testimony from one of the singers in the choir who wrote excitedly (and no doubt sincerely) of singing in the Nikolaikirche in Leipzig 'where precisely *these* cantatas were performed in *these* days of the year, in *this* church' (his emphases, not mine). In what sense is this musically important? (There was a joke doing the rounds in the mid 1970s – one which, fortunately, has less of the ring of truth about it now – that the Italians' notion of authenticity was to perform something in the right city.) I would not wish to deny the possibility – likelihood even – that musicians will learn something by performing works in the venues for which they were originally written. What precisely they will learn needs spelling out, however, if this is not to be seen as just another claim for a rather pointless dimension to authenticity. The Nikolaikirche, to pick up on the singer's example, was so extensively remodelled in the years following 1784 that its acoustic now cannot be taken as a reliable indication of what Bach and his musicians experienced.

Promotional material for concerts or recordings, and the popular journalism associated with it brings discussion of historical performance practice into arenas where it can seem rather incongruous. After all, many of the approaches adopted in the last century to the study of music have been controversial, but few have attracted general interest. Subscribers to *Country Life* are unlikely ever to find within its covers articles about the value of Schenkerian analysis for performers, whereas they have been treated to Anne-Sophie Mutter's erstwhile scorn for the scrawny sound of baroque violins. The serious musicological and aesthetic debate is surrounded (often invaded) by a more populist one. This succeeds in complicating the issues in a multitude of ways – most damagingly by giving performers and their promoters a vested interest in overstating the value and authority of what they do through simplistically attacking the validity of other approaches.

A sense of quasi-moral exclusivity seeps through in the evangelistic overtones of expressions like the 'Early Music movement' and the 'Early Music Revival' (the title of a book by Harry Haskell). We have already encountered Donington's '*doctrine* of authenticity' (see above, p. 2). This sort of imagery now has a long history. Over thirty years ago, Theodor Adorno complained that 'Today . . . under the unholy star of Historicism, the performance of Bach has assumed a *sectarian* aspect. Historicism has incited a *fanatical* interest . . .'[14] Those who feel themselves to be on the outside of a cult reach for metaphors of

---

[14] T. W. Adorno, 'Bach Defended against his Devotees', in *Prisms*, trans. S. and S. Weber (London, 1967), p. 142. This article was originally written in 1951.

religious conformity as a way of characterising what they see as its prescriptiveness; hence, Frederick Neumann, fulminated, 'The way the authenticists make the use of period instruments the object of a categorical imperative, hence an issue of morality, reveals a cultist trait of their movement; and this in turn explains the zealotry with which some of their followers demand conformance and condemn any questioning of their dogmas.'[15] Charles Rosen uses a related metaphor, writing 'during the past two decades . . . the "Early Music" movement has taken on the character of a crusade'.[16] As we can see, assertions of authenticity – or, often, just the assumption that such assertions are implicit in certain kinds of musical behaviour – provoke defensive reactions.

Hence, the area also became associated with militaristic imagery. My favourite example comes from Haskell's book. Writing on the spread of period-instrument performance around the world, Haskell provides a classical example: 'Steady if less spectacular gains have been registered in France, Switzerland, Canada, Belgium, Spain, Italy and Denmark, and early music beachheads have been established as far afield as Buenos Aires, Rio de Janerio, Santiago, Vancouver, Toronto, Sydney and Wellington.'[17] (One imagines freedom fighters from local early music societies rushing on stage to saw the legs off the Steinway.)

Demonising of 'the other' continues. Sir Roger Norrington, in the preface he contributed to Clive Brown's excellent book on 18th- and 19th-century performance practice, invoked an array of metaphors to ridicule those who have kept their distance from historically-informed performance:

> By the time this book has become a classic tool of eighteenth-and nineteenth-century performing practice, it will be hard to believe that there were once musical professionals whose fear of the kind of knowledge it contains urged them to scorn the historical movement. It will be hard to explain that such 'flat-earthers' called an informed approach to music 'flummery', 'exoticism', or 'learning to play out of tune'.[18]

This seems less like war than playground stone-throwing; but it contributes nothing to an atmosphere of receptivity for the kind of research it purports to recommend. Hard-hitting logical debate is to be welcomed, but all too often in discussions of historical performance practice shallow metaphors have taken the place of reasoned arguments.

---

[15] Frederick Neumann, *New Essays on Performance Practice* (Ann Arbor and London, 1989), pp. 29–30. See also p. 24, 'This requirement [the use of a lower pitch standard] is to the authenticists beyond debate, self-evident, a true article of faith because they fervently believe that the spirit of a work is indissolubly linked with its original sound. Is this dogma incontestable?'

[16] Rosen, 'The Benefits of Authenticity', p. 201.

[17] H. Haskell, *The Early Music Revival: A History* (London, 1988), pp. 168–9. For other examples of military imagery see Taruskin, *Text and Act*, p. 92 and n. Taruskin's essay, 'The Pastness of the Present and the Presence of the Past', was first published in Nicholas Kenyon, ed., *Authenticity and Early Music* (Oxford and New York, 1988), pp. 137–207.

[18] Preface to Clive Brown, *Classical and Romantic Performing Practice 1750–1900* (Oxford, 1999), p. viii.

Promotional material and the like is, by nature, ephemeral. Of more enduring consequence are the internal tensions evident in the development of performance practice as a sub-discipline in musicology. Arnold Schering opened his *Aufführungspraxis alter Musik* in 1930 with a definition of what he called 'the general problem':

> The question 'How was old music performed?' can be motivated by two kinds of interest. On the one hand, it can be driven by a purely scientific thirst for knowledge . . . On the other hand, it can be prompted by the particular aim of trying to realise in sound some or other old music.

He then adds, 'That both aims can be pursued together goes without saying . . .'

But does it? True, on the face of it, performance practice is very much an applied branch of musicology.[19] But, as I shall argue, there are dangers in seeing performance practice research as necessarily applied research – that is, research justified purely by its outcome in practice. In my ideal world we might pursue research into historical performance as if driven by a 'purely scientific thirst for knowledge' and then, as a distinct process, consider what to do (or what not to do) with what has been discovered. All too often the lines between historical research and its application have become blurred in ways which diminish the value of the research without adding compensating value to the performance.[20]

In different ways, the concept of authenticity has been the stumbling block for each of the three groups whose attitudes are outlined above.[21] And the philosphical problems inherent in this concept account for at least half of the very negative set of 'conclusions' sketched in above. Many have tried to replace the word 'authentic' with other less inflammatory terms. The most favoured has been 'historically informed', which gives rise to the acronym 'HIP' (for 'historically-informed performance'). Taruskin objects to this one on the grounds that it fails the 'invidious antonym' test. (Who wants to be called

---

[19] Denis Stevens, in his unbalanced and misleadingly titled *Musicology: A Practical Guide* (London, 1980), calls the section on performance practice (over half the book) 'Applied Musicology'.

[20] Leon Plantinga would clearly agree. In *Beethoven's Concertos: History, Style, Performance* (New York and London, 1999), p. 281, he writes: 'The questions "What were performances of Beethoven's music like in his own time?" and "How should that music be performed these days?" . . . are best seen as two separate ones that may be related in complex ways and for which none should presume to prescribe a rule. But surely we may also interest ourselves in that first question, quite apart from its connection with the second. We may wish to look into early nineteenth-century performances of Beethoven out of simple historical curiosity.' See also Carl Dahlhaus, *The Foundations of Music History*, trans. J. B. Robinson (Cambridge, 1983), p. 62: 'We can immerse ourselves in the past and reach a sympathetic understanding of it without necessarily wishing to recreate it – though obviously music historians will feel an urge to communicate their discoveries to the world of music lovers.'

[21] 'Authenticity – like monetarism and alternative comedy – is one of those overdone terms which leading exponents do not now remember personally ever having used': Lubbock, 'The Early Early Show'.

'historically uninformed'?) Taruskin himself proposes (and uses) 'authenticist' which, he says, is to 'authentic' as 'helenistic' is to 'helenic'. But while we might stand in awe of Alexandrian civilisation, helenistic is nevertheless fake-helenic. 'Authenticist' as a term denies even the possibility of historical truth (which, of course, is precisely Taruskin's aim in deploying it).

Except when quoting or alluding to the views of others, I favour the neutrality of 'period-instrument' as a descriptor – though that involves asking readers to make allowances for the fact that I am not talking exclusively about instrumental music. Even so, this seems less distracting than trying to cope with the endless disclaimers that must be placed around any of the other available terms.

This book is about the relationship between performance practice research and actual performance. Its title, *History, Imagination and the Performance of Music* began as an attempt to accommodate 'Imagination' within the otherwise misleading 'HIP' acronym. (At one point I considered calling the book *Historically Inspired Performance*.) Admittedly, the advocates of the phrase 'Historically Informed Performance' (who doubtless wished to dissociate themselves from the implication of naivety that adhered to the notion of authenticity) never intended to exclude musical flair but, as we shall see, they have often enough been charged with exactly that. The argument promulgated in my title and developed below is that being historically informed shapes and stimulates the imagination.

Performance practice research is, however, more than an important imaginative resource. It is a vital key to our understanding the very incomplete record represented by musical notation. And, as already noted, research into historical performance practice has – and ought to have – a life of its own as a legitimate scholarly activity separate from its application in performance. This autonomy is in the final analysis a crucial guarantor of its usefulness to performers.

Chapter 2 is primarily historiographical. Through a (selective) reception study of attempts at authenticity in the Bach G minor Adagio for solo violin I seek to demonstrate the difficulty of sifting out (historically determined) personal tastes in performance. Or, to put this another way, the essay illustrates the way in which historical recovery has often been thwarted by preconceptions about such things as notions of expressiveness.

Chapter 3, constructed around a series of case studies that all deal with the appropriate resources for particular repertories, again argues for the need to recognise that performance-practice research and the application of performance-practice research to actual music-making are distinct activities. The blurring of boundaries here has often, as they say, produced more heat than light. The fourth chapter resulted from my continuing to pull one of the threads from the preceding essay. The results are tantalisingly insubstantial. In looking at early printed editions of violin sonatas it is very clear that they are constructed with performance in mind, yet they still refuse to tell us how to behave. I trust nevertheless that the essay illustrates the intrinsic interest of primary source material even where it refuses to divulge all we would like know about how it was used in performance.

Chapter five, after considering the applicability of the concepts of fidelity to composers' intentions for music before *c.* 1800, sets out to suggest a justification for historically-informed performance as, ultimately, a matter of musical literacy – an ability to read a score in a richly-contextualised way. The argument is illustrated in chapter seven through the use of 19th- and 20th-century examples. The choice of period here was driven partly by the lure of being able, through recordings, to hear performances that shorten the gap between completion of the score (as an intentional object) and its realisation. But it is also illuminating to be able to consider the views of highly articulate and sophisticiated musicians for whom the *Werktreue* concept (in its full-blown post-Kant, post-Hoffman form) seemed axiomatic.

The last section of chapter 6 explores the idea of fidelity to composers' intentions as a performance ideal from a different angle. In a series of brief case studies, it considers the way in which the circumstances surrounding the first performances of various operas make it impossible ever to determine what, in the end, the composer would really like to have heard.

Chapter 7 examines transcription from a variety of perspectives, all designed to elucidate the relationship between the essence of a composition and the specific sound world (instrumental timbre and strength) evoked in performance. Chapter 8 tackles the commonly-voiced idea that period-instrument performers resign their musicianship, imagination, and judgement in favour of submitting to sets of rules.

With the conspicuous exception of those discussed in chapter 6, most of the music examples included here are oriented towards 17th- and 18th-century string playing – a consequence of the fact that most of my own research in performance practice has been in this area. In this context, however, they are intended to facilitate a discussion of more general questions. The lectures on which this book is based were illustrated in part by my own playing but more particularly by recorded examples. (Sometimes, the particular recordings used have been indicated.) The process of revising these lectures for publication has mostly been a matter of making sure that the points made about particular pieces of music made sense when read without aural illustration. Otherwise, I have tried to keep my alterations to a minimum since I wanted to preserve the sense that these were short, 'direct speech' interventions in a fascinating but unruly area that embraces historical musicology, aesthetics, semiotics, critical theory, organology, reception studies and more.

2. Escaping tradition, embracing history

When we examine the development of the interest in performance practice, it is apparent that the horizon of expectations (expressed usually as the prevailing orthodox performance style) has generally coloured the interpretation of historical evidence. I shall explain what I mean here by sampling changing notions about the performance of the Bach works for solo violin, concentrating in particular on the opening Adagio of the G minor Solo Sonata, BWV 1001 (illus. 2.1). I choose this movement only because others before me have been rash enough to use it to illustrate their hypotheses about how violins and bows worked in the 18th century.

The movement immediately poses certain obvious questions for the performer. How are the fast notes (the demisemiquavers) to sound? How much, if any, vibrato is appropriate here – particularly on the sustained notes? Is any other kind of expressive inflection called for? How are the chords to be played?

The last of these questions is the one that has elicited the most curiosity. In the 19th century, these chords seemed to speak of grandeur, and the violin was thought scarcely equal to the task. Both Mendelssohn and Schumann provided piano accompaniments to make good its inadequacies. Schumann used the full resources of the piano to thicken out the chords (illus. 2.2).[1] Four-note chords in the violin are reinforced by eight-note chords marked *forte* and *tenuto*. The bass line (sometimes merely implicit in the original) is emphatically spelled out in left-hand octaves (enhanced occasionally by, for example, the substitution of a 6/3 for a root-position chord).

A related view of movements like this survived in the notion that the violin was being asked to evoke the majesty and polyphonic assurance of Bach's organ works. In 1941 Paul Henry Lang waxed lyrical on the subject:

> It is the spirit of the organ which is expressed everywhere, in the cantata-symphonies and in the wondrous polyphonic sonatas for unaccompanied violin . . . Thus if we wish to penetrate the gigantic yet graceful, dark yet warm-toned, cathedral of Bach's lifework, we must pass by the main portal. It is through the side door of the sacristy that we must enter, and as we pass through the mystic

---

[1] *Sechs Sonaten für die Violine von Johann Sebastian Bach mit hinzugefügler Begleitung des Pianoforte von Robert Schumann* (Leipzig: Breitkopf & Härtel, [1853]).

dark of the winding staircase to the friendly and intimate organ loft, we shall find the place that was the closest to his heart . . .[2]

Organs are, of course, unafraid of big chords.[3]

One response early in the 20th century to the idea that chords should be chords was the development of the so-called 'Bach bow'. This took as its starting points, first the observation that violin bows in the first half of the 18th century had out-curving sticks and second, the assumption that Bach must have wanted chords to sound like chords – something that the modern (Tourte-style) bow is ill-equipped to do. In 1904, in an influential article called 'Disappearing Traditions of Bach's Age', Arnold Schering published his convictions about the bows Bach had in mind for the solo sonatas:

> The hair of the violin bow in Bach's time was only loosely fastened (without a screw) to the stick and it was given a tighter or looser tension at the player's discretion by means of the thumb. As a result, the free use of the wrist and consequently of 'sprung' bowings was restricted to a minimum, but by the same token there was much greater scope for the playing of double stops. A series of chords, of the kind found in the G minor and C major Fugues, in the Chaconne, and in the Prelude to the Fifth Sonata are clumsily performed these days because the bow has to be dragged across from the lower strings, whereas in earlier times the hair of the bow was momentarily loosened so that it curved over the upper strings thus removing any harshness . . . We can only regret that with these bows a good part of the marvellous effect of old music is irrecoverably lost.[4]

The basic concept that this repertory demanded an exaggeratedly out-curved bow in order to realise up to four-note chords satisfactorily gained currency. In 1915 Saint-Saens pronounced in a lecture 'On the Execution of Music, and Principally of Ancient Music' at the San Francisco exhibition that

---

[2] Paul Henry Lang, *Music in Western Civilization* (New York, 1941), p. 504.

[3] Peter Williams, commenting on the opening of his hypothetical violin version of the so-called D minor Toccata and Fugue writes, 'an 18th-century composer would have found that violin version perfectly rhetorical in its own right; only the generations after Beethoven have confused rhetoric with noisy power', 'BWV565: A Toccata in D Minor for Organ by J. S. Bach?' *Early Music* 9 (1981), 335.

[4] 'Die Haare des Violinbogens waren zu Bachs Zeiten nur locker (ohne Schraube) an der Stange befestigt und wurden vom Daumen der rechten Hand nach Belieben fester oder lockere gespannt. Der freie Gebrauch des Handgelenks und der 'springenden' Bogen stricharten schränkte sich somit auf ein Minimum ein, wofür dem doppelgriffigen Spiel ein weiter Raum zur Entfaltung geschaffen wurde. Akkordverbindungen, wie sie in der G moll und C dur-Fuge, in der Chaconne, im Präludium der 5. Sonate, stehen, werden heute mühsam durch Zurückwerfen des Bogens auf die tieferen Saiten hervorgebracht, während ihnen früher durch augenblickliches Lockerlassen der Haare – so daß sie sich über dem dünnen Saitenbezug wölbten – jegliche Härte genommenwurde. Bachs vielstimmige Fugen und namentlich Sätze wie das Siciliano der G moll Sonate, welchem selbst bei vollkommenster Ausführung durch moderne Geiger immer ein technischer Schlakenrest anhaften wird, finden aus dieser Praxis heraus ihre Erklärung, und wir können nur bedauern, daß mit ihr ein gut Teil der großartigsten Wirkungen alter Violinmusik unwiederbringlich verloren gegangen ist.' A. Schering, 'Verschwundene Traditionene des Bachzeitalters', *Bachjahrbuch* 1 (1904), 113.

Illus. 2.1 J. S. Bach, Sonata in G minor for Solo Violin, BWV 1001, first movement, Adagio (autograph); Berlin, Staatsbibliothek Preußischer Kulturbesitz, Mus. Ms. Bach 967 Bl. 1r

Illus. 2.2 J. S. Bach, Sonata in G minor for Solo Violin, BWV 1001, first movement, Adagio, from *Sechs Sonaten für die Violine von Johann Sebastian Bach mit hinzugefügler Begleitung des Pianoforte von Robert Schumann* (Leipzig: Breitkopf & Härtel, 1853), bars 13–22 (© Copyright 2002, Bodleian Library, University of Oxford)

In the time of Bach and Handel the bow really deserved its Italian name of *arco*. It was bent like an arc, the hairs constituting the cord, the great flexibility of which enabled it to press firmly upon (*enveloper*) the strings of the instrument and make them return simultaneously. It seldom left the strings, only doing so in very rare cases and at given indications.[5]

5　Camille Saint-Saens, 'The Execution of Classical Works: Notably those of the Older Masters', *The Musical Times* 56 (August 1915); reprinted *The Musical Times* 138 (October 1997), 32.

Andreas Moser tried to set the record straight in 1920, but by then the idea had firmly taken root.[6]

Schering's article had been read with approval by Albert Schweitzer who included a close paraphrase of the passage quoted above in his *J. S. Bach*.[7] Schweitzer championed the development of the so-called 'Bach bow' which had a wildly out-curved stick and a mechanical attachment on the frog so that players could adjust the tension of the hair with their thumbs. This was seen as a kind of cooperation with history – using modern technology to encourage the natural tendencies of old bows. Schweitzer's enthusiasm for the idea was very much in line with his championing of re-invented baroque organs that incorporated mechanical 'improvements'.

The 'Bach bow' was taken up by a number of violinists, notably Emil Telmanyi who recorded the Bach Solo Sonatas and Partitas using this remarkable piece of pseudo-restoration. The results were grotesque. The simultaneous onset of three- and four-note chords at the opening of the D minor Chaconne, for example, and the elimination of the inflection which is the inevitable consequence of crossing the strings to pick up each new chord produces a sound which is strongly reminiscent of a rather deficient accordion. Amazingly the concept has still not entirely disappeared, despite the fact that the historical hypotheses underlying the design of the Bach bow have long since been discredited: a recording of the Solo Sonatas and Partitas played by Rudolf Gähler using such a bow was released as recently as 1998.[8]

Arnold Dolmetsch, that key figure in the growth of interest in historical performance practice, did not endorse the 'Bach bow' as such – but the same impulses that led to its development were quite strongly there in his work. What he had to say about early bows in 1915 involved some rash generalizations about their physical properties, though he stressed their ability to deliver an articulate staccato more than their capacity to play chords:

> The old violin bow was only about 20 inches long. Its stick was curved outwards, like a shooting bow. It was thick at the base, and finished in a delicate point, and had in consequence great firmness, lightness, and very little momentum . . . A sharpness of accent and clearness of phrasing were obtainable for which the "staccato leggiero" of the Tourte bow affords no compensation. The writer, after considerable experience in playing with the old bow, has no hesitation in pronouncing it preferable to the modern bow for playing the old violin music.[9]

[6] See A. Moser, 'Zu Joh. Seb. Bachs Sonaten und Partiten für Violine allein', *Bach-Jahrbuch* 17 (1920), 52ff.

[7] See Albert Schweitzer, *J. S. Bach*, trans. E. Newman, 2 vols. (Leipzig, 1911; repr. New York c. 1966), i. 209. Schweitzer's study first appeared as *J. S. Bach: le musicien poète* (Leipzig, 1905) and then in an enlarged German translation of 1908 on which Newman's English translation is based.

[8] Johann Sebastian Bach, *Sonatas and Partitas for Solo Violin*, performed by Rudolf Gähler 'Violine mit Rundbogen', Arte Nova Classics 74321 67501 2.

[9] Arnold Dolmetsch, *The Interpretation of Music of the 17th and 18th Centuries* (London, 1915), p. 454.

But Dolmetsch, no less than the proponents of the 'Bach bow', seems to have believed that Bach must have wanted chords sounding as chords. His approach to the problem was, however, primarily via a theory about bridge design (though the arched bow was supposed to help). We learn about this from a tribute written by a young Robert Donington in 1932:

> As a result of some most important researches and experiments, the fittings of the Dolmetsch violins and of violins restored by him depart appreciably from recent traditions, and approach closely the original principles of the old violin-makers. The bridge in particular is much less arched than is usual at present, so that the distance between the level of each string is reduced to the minimum; greater accuracy of bowing is thus demanded, but neatness and precision in crossing the strings is greatly facilitated, and three-part chords or counterpoint can be simultaneously maintained. Many early sonatas for the violin, including the famous unaccompanied suites of J. S. Bach, cannot be really satisfactorily performed with the highly-arched bridge now in use . . .[10]

There is, in fact, absolutely no evidence to support the idea of flatter bridges – especially not by the 1720s. This speculation about bridge shape is a different route to the same musical results as the 'Bach bow'. In each case, history is being constructed to fit preconceptions current in the first half of the 20th century about how the music should sound. Here, a misplaced notion about the way chords should sound was made to override historical evidence while being presented as if it were exactly that.[11]

No other violin compositions have prompted so many theories about the way old violins and bows must have been set up. This is doubly ironic. First, these pieces are (notwithstanding a significant number of antecedents) quite atypical of violin repertory.[12] To construct hypotheses about bow and violin construction on the basis of the Solo Sonatas might seem like the tail wagging the dog. Second, Bach is not supposed to need this. A commonly-expressed view has been that Bach, as the colossus whose conceptions stride across such considerations as specific instrumental or vocal sonorities, can be exempted from the kind of resuscitation through period-instrument therapy that – in particular – French baroque composers are thought so desperately to need.[13] Even Howard

---

[10] Robert Donington, *The Work and Ideas of Arnold Dolmetsch* (Haslemere, 1932), p. 12.

[11] Another extraordinary manifestation of the conviction that Bach was indicating musical ideas beyond the capacity of an ordinary violin is the string-quartet arrangement by Max Rostal of the Adagio from the G minor Sonata, printed as an appendix to his edition of the sonatas (Leipzig: Peters, 1982). What this arrangement really demonstrates is just how inappropriate it is to think of this movement as implying (consistently at least) four-part polyphonic writing.

[12] There is a significant repertory of unaccompanied violin music before Bach – notably by Thomas Baltzar (in GB-Ob Mus. Sch. 573), J. P. von Westhoff (a suite for violin 'sans basse continue' and six partitas, 1696), Biber (Passacaglia, *c.*1676), and J. G. Pisendel (unaccompanied sonata, ?1716). Telemann's Fantasias *senza basso* were composed shortly after BWV 1001–6.

[13] Haskell, *Early Music Revival* (p. 183) writes 'a strong case can be made that a stylish performance of, say, an overture by Lully is more dependent on the sonorities of period

Mayer Brown (who was well known for his enthusiastic interest in period-instrument performance) wrote that 'The truth – although it may seem controversial to say so now – is that it is more acceptable to play Bach's music on modern instruments than Rameau's for it can be argued that authentic sonorities and old playing techniques are less important in the one than in the other, and that therefore the essential nature of Bach's music can emerge in a performance that translates the original into modern terms.'[14] This is essentially an intelligently tempered version of the old idea that Bach was ahead of his time, making demands that instrument development would only catch up with later, an idea so beautifully encapsulated in the 19th century by Phillip Spitta's notion that the piano 'floated in the mind of Bach'.[15]

Many of the earlier misconceptions about bows and bridges were corrected by David Boyden in his *History of Violin Playing*, published in 1965. But while this book was a major contribution to the literature on performance practice, the accompanying recording with examples played by Alan Loveday is a curiosity which simply confuses the picture. Boyden has Loveday playing various passages intended to illustrate the difference in the basic sound of baroque and modern violins and in the technical and expressive devices appropriate to

---

instruments than a performance of a Bach orchestral suite. Bach's music is intrinsically more abstract than Lully's, less tied to a specific sound-world and set of instrumental techniques.' Neumann, predictably, pursues this argument even further (though note the shared use of the expression, 'a strong case'): 'There are, it is true, some compositions of that period [pre-1750] that are thoroughly idiomatic for a certain instrument, perhaps the clavecin pieces of d'Anglebert, Couperin, and Rameau, which might lose some of their character by transfer to the modern piano . . . The case is different for Bach. The essence of the music lies in its line, not in its colour . . . But regarding works for the solo clavier, a strong case can be made for the proposition that they gain musically and do not lose their soul by being transferred to the modern piano. In view of the supremacy of line and indifference to colour, the spirit of Bach's music stands to be enhanced, not denatured, by the modern piano's potential of giving his phrases plasticity in three-dimensional space.' *New Essays*, p. 27. Whether or not Neumann is justified in writing of Bach's 'indifference to colour' is a topic that is explored in chapter 7 below.

[14] Howard Mayer Brown, 'Pedantry or Liberation? A Sketch of the Historical Performance Movement', in Kenyon, ed., *Authenticity*, p. 30.

[15] Phillip Spitta, *Johann Sebastian Bach* (trans. C. Bell and J. A. Fuller-Maitland), 2 vols. (New York, 1951), ii, 44; quoted by Robert Morgan, 'Tradition, Anxiety, and the Musical Scene' in Kenyon, ed., *Authenticity*, p. 68. The idea that composers would surely have wished to take advantage of developments in instrumental design comes through in an 1829 review of a performance in Chester of the Mozart re-orchestration of *Messiah*: 'Handel himself would in all probability have made [such additions] had some of the wind instruments been in use in his day, and if any had been in the state of perfection to which our modern performers have brought them. I take it for granted that [*Messiah*] will now never again be heard but in its improved condition.' *The Harmonicon* vii/1 (1829), p. 255; quoted by Howard Smither, '*Messiah* and Progress in Victorian England', *Early Music* 13 (1985), 340. And on the piano see also Rosen, 'The Benefits of Authenticity', p. 216: 'The proper question now is: which instrument will deliver Bach's original conception to the public most adequately? The piano is clearly more capable of setting details in low relief than either the harpsichord or organ.'

each. But the differences are, for the most part, barely perceptible – except that the 'early violin' sounds rather thin in the hands of someone not totally comfortable playing it. Loveday's 'baroque' version of the G minor Adagio has the effect of denying a latitude that is there in the historical evidence while, at the same time, it illustrates the difficulty of making a break from received tradition in performance. This example was included on the recording explicitly to illustrate chordal playing, but it is noteworthy that there is very little difference between the 'modern' and 'baroque' versions when it comes to the other questions posed at the beginning of this chapter.

Vibrato, in particular, is an area where personal taste – that is, preconceptions conditioned by current fashion about what constitutes an expressive perform-ance – has often become the arbiter in assessing historical evidence. This tendency can be seen in the work of Robert Donington where historical insight and (culturally acquired) musical preferences became progressively more confused. In 1963 he published *The Interpretation of Early Music* which, by his own account, was the product of twelve or more years' work. Donington's method in this still very useful volume was to provide copious quotation from original sources organised around key issues with fairly minimal commentary. But Donington followed this with other books addressed directly to performers where the ratio of source-quotation to comment shifted sharply in favour of the latter.[16] The effect was to make Donington's own musical preferences loom larger in successive publications – eventually all but obliterating the historical evidence he imagined to be supporting his case.

This can be illustrated by reviewing what Donington had to say about vibrato in each of these books. Comment in *The Interpretation of Early Music* was brief and to the point:

> From the middle of the baroque period until the generation of Kreisler, there was controversy whether the instrumental vibrato should be used (in the modern way) more or less continuously as a means of enlivening the tone, or intermittently as a specific ornament. But that it was used throughout the baroque period, there can be no doubt at all; nor have we any reason to suppose that it was then a novelty.[17]

Donington then goes on to present apposite and quite substantial quotations from Mersenne (1636) through to Carl Flesch (1939). At three points he interleaves further succinct comment, once simply to clarify a matter of terminology. Finally, he summarises his own opinions:

> In truth a continuous vibrato always is musically justifiable provided it is adapted to the degree of intensity which the music momentarily requires. Totally vibrato-less string tone sounds dead in any music. It is just as much an illusion to think that early performers preferred it as to think that early singers preferred a 'white'

---

[16] First *A Performer's Guide to Baroque Music* (London, 1973), then, *String Playing in Baroque Music* (London, 1977), and finally *Baroque Music: Style and Performance* (London, 1982).

[17] Page 167. Both this and the next passage quoted remained unaltered in the revised 1989 edition (p. 232).

tone. Sensitive vibrato not only can but should be a normal ingredient in performing early music.[18]

This view is not actually supported by the evidence he has just presented. But at least the source material is there to speak for itself and it occupies considerably more space than Donington's personal convictions.

In the *Performer's Guide to Baroque Music* (published ten years later), there is still a balance between quotation and comment – though the quotations have now been reduced to single sentences woven into an argument that concludes with the judgement that the baroque period countenanced two distinct types of vibrato, a 'conspicuous vibrato' used as ornament, and an 'inconspicuous vibrato' which, he writes, '. . . was taken for granted as the natural enlivening of string tone, of vocal tone, and to some extent of wind tone, and which though variable in extent is never altogether absent'.[19] As a general statement about baroque practice, this is completely indefensible. But Donington was clearly incapable of imagining an expressive vocabulary that was not in accord with his own instincts.

By 1977, when he wrote *String Playing in Baroque Music* (addressed to string students generally rather than to baroque specialists or academics), historical source material was being more conspicuously manipulated to support his own taste. This book had an accompanying lp in which Donington enlisted the help of Sir Yehudi Menuhin to demonstrate his ideas about stylish baroque playing. Menuhin played four versions of the opening of the slow movement of the Bach D minor Double Concerto to illustrate Donington's ideas about the appropriate use of vibrato (ex. 2.1).[20] The first version was said to show the disastrous result of misapplying to Bach the sort of 'thick intensity' appropriate, for example, in performing Sarasate's Gypsy Airs. The result – as intended – sounds absurd. But then, introducing the second version, Donington writes, 'if we take out all the passion from the tone, all the vibrato from the colouring, all the intensity from the line, we fall into an opposite extreme which is just as disastrous. This is purity carried to a fault, and we can hear . . . how weak it sounds.'[21] And so it does. But then, how could it be otherwise since it is a kind of aural caricature presented by musicians whose starting point is that such an approach will not work? Since Donington's commentary unquestioningly equates vibrato with passion and intensity, Menuhin was hardly likely to discover other routes to expressing these emotional qualities in the thirty seconds or so that it took to record this brief exercise. The performance, one might say, lacks any authenticity.

[18] Page 170.
[19] Donington, *Performer's Guide*, p. 87.
[20] There is a fascinating recording of this work made in 1915 by Kreisler and Efrem Zimbalist which seems to pinpoint a change in the attitude to vibrato. Both violinists had studied with Leopold Auer, though Kreisler traced his own intensification of vibrato back to Henryk Wieniawski (1835–88). In the D minor Concerto slow movement, Zimbalist has only a hint of a very narrow vibrato; at the beginning of bar 3, Kreisler enters with a continuous and much wider and more fluid-sounding vibrato.
[21] *String Playing in Baroque Music*, p. 108.

Ex. 2.1 J. S. Bach, Concerto in D minor for Two Violins, BWV 1043, second movement, Largo ma non tanto, bars 1–3

The commentary moves on to the third rendition:

> There is, however, a different kind of intensity, not thick, but glowing, which has the necessary baroque transparency and inwardness, as may be heard beautifully [in the following example]. The stroke is slower, the vibrato is narrower, but the focus of the line could not be keener, and the tone is spun to the finest tension. The baroque bow was used, but modern stringing.

Each of the first two recorded examples had been cut off abruptly in the middle of bar 2. Now, with this third example, Menuhin continues on into the first violin entry as well, and the track ends with a graceful fade.

Finally, the passage is played, according to Donington,

> in the same (right) style, but using gut strings on the Guanerius violin in addition to the baroque bow. The difference is solely in the colouring . . . Gut strings may appeal very much to some players (they do to me) and they bring us nearer to the baroque colourings. On the other hand, they do not condition the style, and they are therefore not essential to good baroque performances.

All of this adds up to be a remarkable case of a well-informed musicologist allowing personal hunches about 'purity' and 'the right style' to override all other considerations.

But Donington was not alone in using personal taste as a yardstick for assessing the validity of historical evidence. Frederick Neumann even felt that the exercise of this kind of judgement was essential. He argued that, given the limitations and the fallible character of 18th-century theoretical sources, precepts derived from them must not be allowed to overrule musical judgement. Expressions like 'musical common sense' crop up again and again in his work. Neumann even made the extraordinary claim that 'we have good reason to assume that no fundamental change has occurred in the aesthetics of performance . . . We are therefore on fairly firm ground in assuming the basic identity of an informed cultivated taste of today with the one Mozart expected to encounter in his audiences.'[22] Which 'informed cultivated taste' did he have in mind? His own allegiances were very much with the orthodoxy he had learned as a violinist from Ševčík, Flesch, Rostal, and Busch. His approved ways of spreading a four-note G major chord in the Mozart 'Dissonance' Quartet, for example, are all variants on the two-top notes-on-the-beat approach – a method first described in Spohr's *Violinschule* of 1832 (see ex. 2.2).[23]

Ex. 2.2 Frederick Neumann's suggested ways of spreading a chord in Mozart, String Quartet in C major (the 'Dissonance'), K 465; from *Ornamentation and Improvisation in Mozart* (Princeton, 1986), p. 172

It is relatively easy to illustrate the subjectivity of the views of writers like Robert Donington, David Boyden, and Frederick Neumann. From the vantage point of the 21st century they stand out against a background of quite a different set of attitudes. Neumann, at least, was well aware of swimming against the tide – and, I suspect, even enjoyed the role of cantankerous reactionary.

In many ways, what I am pointing out here is no more than a very clear-cut case of a phenomenon that has been much commented upon in recent years – the way in which writers of history inevitably bring their own contemporary cultural contexts with them. In performance practice studies it has been an unusually straightforward matter to relate authors' tastes, cultural heritage, and prejudices to what they write as 'research'. Leo Treitler has written about more general manifestations of these distorting factors in the work of music

---

[22] F. Neumann, *Ornamentation and Improvisation in Mozart* (Princeton, 1986), p. 5.

[23] 'In executing four-part chords, the bow is placed firmly on the lower two strings right at the heel and then brought with a strong pressure over to the top two strings with the stroke steadily continued right to the point . . . Although the two lower notes are written in crotchets, they should be held for no more than a semiquaver.' ['Bey dem vierstimmigen Accord . . . wird der Bogen dicht am Frosch fest auf die beyden tiefsten Saiten gesetzt, dann mit einem starken Druck auf die beyden höchsten herabgerissen und nun ruhig auf diesen bis zur Spitze fortgezogen. Obgleich die beiden tiefsten Noten als Viertel geschrieben sind, so darf der Bogen doch nicht auf ihnen verweilen und ihre Dauer höchstens die eines Sechzehntels betragen.'] Louis Spohr, *Violinschule* (Vienna, 1832), p. 147.

historians: 'We do not on the whole like to confront the historicity of the truths we hold or of the ways we have of coming by them. We do not like to acknowledge that, as historians, we are within history.'[24] One response to this predicament might be to retreat into the anarchic relativism of the deconstructionists. Taruskin is effectively doing this in his insistence on seeing what he calls authenticist performance as a modernist phenomenon. I prefer Treitler's sense of the value of attempting, at least, to engage with a real historical past while 'working with a sensitivity to the interests and conventions that are embodied in the models that we have inherited and the habits that we have acquired'.[25] The process of trying to filter out the prejudices of our own context, of escaping received tradition, is made far more difficult if we fail to keep a sense of the distinction between historical enquiry (that is, performance practice research) and the project of translating that into performing style.

I want now to return to the Bach G minor Adagio mentioning some aspects of the historical context that seem to me relevant or helpful in approaching a performance of this movement. One way of looking at the relationship between the florid line and its harmonic (chordal) support is to relate it to the performance expectations surrounding other kinds of Adagio movement. The Adagio that opens the G minor Sonata in Corelli's Opus 5 (1700), for example, has a melodic line which is extremely simple – bare, even (see illus. 2.3(a)).[26] It is clear, however, that Corelli, and others who performed these sonatas, improvised – or pretended to improvise – florid decoration on this framework. The best known model is the edition published by Etienne Roger in Amsterdam in 1710 with graces purportedly by Corelli himself (illus. 2.3(b)). If we imagine violinists decorating the melodic line in this way – and providing their own realisation of the figured bass in the form of chords – then we get something which starts to look quite like the Bach Adagio. So that might give us a clue as to how to approach the little notes – not as earnestly-measured details but as something that might sound like improvised gestures. And perhaps thinking of the chords as a continuo part realised by the soloist might influence the way these, too, are played.

The image of the violin imitating the organ in this movement might be offset by some less powerful instrumental parallels. According to his pupil, Johann Friedrich Agricola, Bach 'often played [the solo violin pieces] on the clavichord . . .'[27] (Not, I hasten to add, that I am suggesting that the tiny sound of a clavichord is incapable of evoking grandeur – just that it does not and could not do it through strongly-voiced block chords.) Another of his pupils, Johann Christian Weyrauch, arranged the Fugue from the G minor Sonata (though not the Adagio) for lute. The closing bars, which recall the Adagio, might suggest

[24] Leo Treitler, *Music and the Historical Imagination* (Cambridge, Mass., 1989), p. 4.
[25] Ibid., p. 359.
[26] Such an approach is suggested in Jaap Schröder and Christopher Hogwood, 'The Developing Violin', *Early Music* 7 (1979), 160–1.
[27] See H. T. David and A. Mendel, eds., *The Bach Reader* (New York and London, 1972), p. 447.

Illus. 2.3 Arcangelo Corelli, Sonata in G minor, Op. 5, No. 5, Adagio
(a) from *Sonate a Violino e Violone o Cimbalo* (Rome, 1700)

(b) from *Sonate a Violino e Violone o Cimbalo . . . ou l'on a joint les agréemens des Adagio de cet ouvrage, composez par Mr. A. Corelli, comme il les joue* (Amsterdam, 1710)

something other than block chords – at least if we bear in mind that the lute provided the paradigm for the *style brisé* (ex. 2.3).[28] An even more relevant analogue here might be the late 17th- and early 18th-century chordal repertory for viola da gamba.

Ex. 2.3 J. S. Bach, Sonata in G minor for Solo Violin, BWV 1001, second movement, Fugue, final two bars (© **Copyright** *J. S. Bach: Neue Ausgabe sämtliche Werke* (Kassel and Basle, 1954–)

But what else can be said about ways of playing chords on a violin? Quantz (1752) writes that in playing chords 'the lower strings must not be held . . . they must be struck quickly one after the other'.[29] There are, in fact, numerous chords in 18th-century violin literature that must be arpeggiated, not because of the characteristics of the bow but because of the way the notes lie on the instrument. Occasionally, however, 18th-century composers specified with three-note chords at least that they did not want them arpeggiated.[30] In other words, the possibilities for which some form of historical sanction could be claimed ranges from something as close to block chords as the violin could ever produce through to chords broken one note at a time.

Among a number of recordings of the Bach solo violin sonatas that give me considerable pleasure I wish to select just two – by Rachel Podger and Sigiswald Kuijken – to consider what can be said about their proximity to what Bach might have expected or (better still) wanted to hear.[31] Both treat the sweeps of fast notes in ways that suggest an affinity with that improvisatory tradition mentioned above. Both vary their treatment of chords in ways consistent with the historical evidence. The same could be said of their inflection of long notes, the use of the 'messa di voce' as (borrowing from vocal practice) it has come to be called. Both use vibrato, too, in ways that fit within the scale of historical possibilities. But the latitude in each of these areas is enormous (something that I will address in chapter 8) and, in fact, Kuijken and Podger each produce performances that are quite distinctive. This is at least partly because each of these violinists has made a different set of decisions about what we might think of as preliminary questions.

To elaborate: firstly, what precise design of bow is most appropriate for these

[28] The Fugue also exists in a D minor version for organ (BWV 539).

[29] J. J. Quantz, *Versuch einer Anweisung, die Flöte traversiere zu spielen* (Berlin, 1752); trans. E. R. Reilly as *On Playing the Flute* (London, 1966), p. 227.

[30] See Peter Walls, 'Strings', in H. M. Brown and S. Sadie, eds., *Performance Practice: Music after 1600* (London, 1989), pp. 55f.

[31] For Rachel Podger, see Channel Classics (CD) CCS 12198 (1999) and for Sigiswald Kuijken (LP) Deutsche Harmonia Mundi 1C 3LP 157 (1983).

works? Since bows before the 19th century are nearly all unsigned and undated, history does not yield any easy answers here. The bows in, for example, the Hill Collection in the Ashmolean Museum illustrate the diversity of shapes before the Tourte bow's standardising influence. Secondly, should the violin be held under the chin, on the collar bone, on the breast, or even lower? All of these positions can claim historical endorsement, yet the particular choice will affect the sound of the instrument itself and, inevitably, the performer's implementation of 18th-century advice about such matters as bow inflections and vibrato. In other words, two performances of this Adagio might score equally well on a checklist of features (the stylistic appropriateness of the treatment of chords, long notes, flourishes of short notes etc.) but sound quite different from each other because of a different set of answers to some very basic questions about violin playing.

While, too, I would defend my checklist as providing a relevant set of considerations for anyone interested in being historically-informed about the performance of this repertory, it would be folly to claim for it any kind of comprehensiveness. Just as Donington found a basic sound without vibrato inconceivable, it is not unlikely that there may be other features of 18th-century violin performance that have become as unimaginable within our horizon of expectations as the fourth to forty-second dimensions that we are now told give shape to our universe.

Performance practice, as an academic discipline, can throw considerable light on what a performance of the Bach G minor Solo Sonata in the early 1720s in Cöthen might have been like. It can establish within fairly broad limits what kind of bows would have been available and how the violin would have been set up. It can clarify how violinists would have approached certain technical problems – such as the performance of chords, the choice of fingerings and so on. It can suggest stylistic affinities that might in turn assist in clarifying the implications of the notation. All of these matters are part of the historical record – and are no less so just because, on the one hand, there are gaps and, on the other hand, because what is offered must be expressed as a range of possibilities rather than a single factual statement. (Often, this information is most simply expressed in negative terms, as a list of features in modern performance that would have been unknown in the 18th century.)

While history tends to offer alternatives, performances have no option but to commit to a single solution. That is why the very concept of demonstration recordings of the kind released with the Boyden and Donington publications is inherently dangerous. But they do illustrate in a wonderfully magnified form the folly of ever trusting that a particular performance or recording could have exemplary status. The expression 'definitive performance' can only ever be rhetorical. It might be possible in theory to create a kind of 'flow chart' for performers who aspire to be historically informed. It would begin with the most basic decisions they must make (which bow to take out of the violin case, for instance) and follow through with the consequences of that to the next level of conscious choice (how do you hold that bow?) and so on through all the other contingent options. One could imagine (impossibly) the flow chart converging in identical higher-level decisions about the specific musical features of the work to be performed but nevertheless pointing to utterly distinctive performances because of the 'decisions' that preceded and followed that band of agreement. The flow chart would necessarily stop, or at least become too complicated, where the mostly unconscious, intangible aspects of musicality – there in every single performance (including bad ones) – take over. The problem, of course, is that the model cannot proceed as an orderly set of unprejudiced decisions since the decisions are inevitably affected by the musical backgrounds of the performers. (The Boyden and Donington recordings illustrate that much more obviously than they do their stated objectives.) At nearly every point in the flow chart there will be for individual performers what in computerese is called a 'default option' (though with some performers the anxiety of influence might encourage an equally unreliable rejection of habitual practices).

Both Podger and Kuijken would doubtless wish to argue (as I do myself) that the use of period instruments and an interest in historical performance practice bring musical benefits to their playing. I am not so sure that either of them would make claims to 'authenticity'. In the final analysis, what all of this demonstrates is the need to distinguish between the genuine historical insights brought by performance practice studies and their function in performance. This is a theme that will be pursued further in the next chapter.

3. Measure for Measure or As You Like It?

During a brief visit to London in 1998, I managed to see *As You Like It* at the new Globe theatre followed, the next day, by *Much Ado About Nothing* performed by Cheek-by-Jowl at the Strand Theatre. The Strand has a proscenium arch, boxes, stalls, and circle disposed exactly as one would expect of a theatre built in 1905. The *Much Ado* production there set out to break down the Stanislavskian fourth wall: actors leaped off the stage into the boxes, ran up and down the aisles, and declaimed lines from somewhere under my feet in the stalls below. Yet, somehow, the whole thing seemed contrived, tired, and uninvolving (alienating, even). By contrast, the Globe's *As You Like It* was a revelation. For all that there were aspects of that production that were demonstrably unhistorical, the sense of an intimate, direct relationship between actors and audience that seemed to follow from the physical space itself was thrilling.[1]

From the point of view of musicians with an interest in historical perform-ance, the insights prompted by the use of the Globe as a performing space were only to be expected. As others have pointed out, presenting Shakespeare in a replica of the theatre he wrote for and worked in with all the implications that that has for acting styles and the audience-actor relationship has strong parallels with what was happening in early music about twenty-five years ago.[2]

But this chapter is not about Shakespeare; its title is intended only to introduce the question of selectivity in the application of historical evidence. As we have seen, performance practice tends to be regarded very much as an applied branch of musicology – an area where historical research and per-

---

[1] In 2000 I saw *Hamlet* at the Globe and was both extraordinarily moved by the production's powerful engagement with its audience and made to realise more vividly than ever before the self-referential aspects of this great tragedy. I note that the programme for their highly-successful 2002 *Twelfth Night* describes it as probably their most authentic production to date. (They'll learn.)

[2] See Tess Knighton's editorial in *Early Music* 24 (1996), 548–9. The parallels work even further back: the theatre at the Folger Shakespeare Library in Washington is to the New Globe what the Dolmetsch harpsichord is to the exquisitely-made historical copies we now enjoy. Samuel Baron, director of the (modern instrument) New York-based Bach Aria Group, observed in 1982, 'You don't have to reconstruct the Globe Theatre to present a meaningful Shakespeare performance.' (Quoted by L. Dreyfus, 'Early Music Defended against its Devotees: A Theory of Historical Performance in the Twentieth Century', *Musical Quarterly* 49 (1983), 307.)

formers' imagination converge. And yet, as I shall argue, it can be distorting to assume that there must be an exact fit between what we can establish about historical performance and what we do as performers.

My sense that this argument needed to be spelled out was sharpened when, in 1996, an article I wrote at the request of *Early Music* surveying existing recordings of Corelli's Opus 5 was attacked in the next issue for not having castigated the performers whose recordings I had discussed for their various unhistorical practices. My critics – John Holloway, David Watkin, and Lars Ulrik Mortensen – were on the brink of releasing (as 'Trio Veracini') their own complete recording of Opus 5. Their contributions to *Early Music* made the claim, at least implicitly, that their performances would come closer to Corelli's intentions than any existing recordings had done.[3]

As it happens, none of them was able to point to a single historically invalid practice that had gone unnoticed in my article – but, as I said in my reply to *Early Music*,

> My own awareness of unhistorical practices in what I heard on the recordings was offset first by a genuine admiration for what performers like Elizabeth Wallfisch and Monica Huggett have achieved which made me reluctant to use them as whipping persons, and second by a growing sense of the limitations of complete recordings as musicological documents . . .
>
> Research in historical performance practice is not about providing the thought police with heavier batons. The way listeners (including historically-aware listeners) respond to a performance is a matter of taste rather than ethics. And, of course, a direct relationship between performance practice research, actual performance, and listeners' responses cannot be forced. If performers (and listeners) are to feel stimulated (rather than threatened) by performance practice research, they must be given the freedom not to adopt certain historical practices as part of their own vocabulary, at least for the time being.[4]

That, as such letters tend to be, was a rather blunt summary of my views. Here I want to expand on those ideas by exploring the possible responses of performers to what we can ascertain about historical conditions for three repertories: Corelli violin sonatas again, and (more briefly) choral works by Vivaldi and

---

[3] See J. Holloway, 'Corelli's Op. 5: Text, Act . . . and Reaction', *Early Music* 24 (1996), 635–40; D. Watkin, 'Corelli's Op. 5 Sonatas: "Violino e violone *o* cimbalo"?', ibid., 645–63; L. U. Mortensen, ' "Unerringly tasteful"?: Harpsichord continuo in Corelli's Op. 5 Sonatas', ibid., 665–79. My own article had appeared as 'Performing Corelli's Violin Sonatas, Op. 5', *Early Music* 24 (1996), 134–5.

[4] *Early Music* 25 (1997), 172. I was interested to see my police metaphor resurfacing in a discussion by Bruno Nettl of the relationship between musicology and creative musicianship: 'The fact that musicologists are themselves musicians, but perhaps not among the best, may have something to do with attitudes among performers and composers: musicologists, they believe, should be supporting them and their efforts, but in practice act as a kind of police, requiring them to toe the line in their knowledge of insignificant music and in their adherence to authentic performance practice.' ('The Institutionalization of Musicology', in *Rethinking Music*, ed. Nicholas Cook and Mark Everist (Oxford and New York, 1999), p. 300.)

Bach. What these case studies have in common is a concern with resources; each deals with the implications for performers of the question 'Who was originally involved in performing this music?'

We start with Corelli's Opus 5, the *Sonate a violino e violone o cimbalo* – 'Sonatas for Violin and Cello or Harpsichord'.[5] Thirty years ago there seems to have been consensus on the latitude with which phrases like 'violone o cimbalo' should be treated. Robert Donington, taking his cue from F. T. Arnold, confidently stated that 'Titles such as "Thorough-Bass for the Harpsichord or Violoncello" *etc.*, are to be taken in the sense of "and/or".' He added, 'No doubt the "or" was for commercial reasons; it encouraged amateur buyers who might not muster the complete complement of instruments.'[6] At the time of my Opus 5 survey for *Early Music* I was feeling uneasy about such assumptions and wrote:

> Increasingly . . . scholars have been troubled by the lack of either linguistic support or hard historical evidence for such an interpretation. Tharald Borgir, Sandra Mangsen and Peter Allsop are in agreement about the inappropriateness of applying a practice recommended half a century later by C. P. E. Bach to 17th-century Italian repertory. While the picture is far from clear, particularly in relation to solo sonatas from the very end of the century, there is nevertheless more evidence for taking Corelli's title-page literally than for the conventional keyboard-plus-cello solution.[7]

Holloway and his colleagues seemed not to notice this expression of a point of view with which they clearly agreed. Instead, they chastised me for my reluctance to condemn out of hand performers not brave enough to record the entire twelve sonatas with only one instrument at a time on the bass line. I suppose I must be very counter-suggestible, but their articles have driven me to the defence of those who still prefer the combination of a melodic bass-line instrument with another – organ, archlute, or harpsichord – capable of providing a realisation. So I want to revisit the issue. But I wish to repeat at the outset that it is clear to me that performing Corelli sonatas with just cello or harpsichord on the bass line is emphatically an option endorsed by history. (Some of the evidence I am about to consider provides support for, particularly, David Watkins's case.) My aim here is to argue that this was not the one and only correct path. In other words, it cannot have been unthinkable in Corelli's lifetime (or even in his specific milieu) to have performed these works with a range of different provisions for the bass line.

Before we start, it is worth just taking a moment to consider a couple of preliminary matters, starting with the implications of a (supposed) direction to

---

[5] 'Violone' here may be taken as a synonym for 'violoncello'.
[6] Donington, *Interpretation of Early Music*, p. 361. For F. T. Arnold, see below, p. 36.
[7] Walls, 'Performing Corelli's Violin Sonatas', 135. See also Tharald Borgir, *The Performance of the Basso Continuo in Italian Baroque Music* (Ann Arbor, MI, 1987); Sandra Mangsen, 'The Trio Sonata in pre-Corellian Prints: When Does 3 = 4?', *Performance Practice Review* 3 (1990), 138–64; and Peter Allsop, *The Italian 'Trio Sonata' from its Origins until Corelli* (Oxford, 1992), pp. 39ff.

use *only* harpsichord *or* cello. This is not like saying 'harpsichord or archlute', or perhaps 'violone or viola da gamba'. Harpsichord and cello are very different instruments – in timbre, attack, sustaining power, and in their capacity to provide a harmonic realisation. That in itself should give us pause before concluding that Corelli was being narrowly prescriptive rather than trying to suggest the open-ended versatility of the publication by indicating that these sonatas can be played with either of the two bass-line instruments most likely to be at hand.

We need also to bear in mind the kind of information that the composer – or often, probably, the publisher – wished to convey to users of a printed edition. Modern orchestral players are not puzzled by any apparent ambiguity when confronted with a part marked 'violoncello or contrabass', because it is clear why that form of words has been used. Nobody in their right minds would take it to mean that, say, Mozart's 'Jupiter' Symphony K 550 should be performed with only one double bass or one cello. The designation quite clearly means 'this printed part *may be used by* cellists or double-bass players'. Here, what all orchestral musicians know already doesn't need explaining, though it is not inconceivable that that there will come a time when it *will* need clarification. The problem now is to judge whether equivalent assumptions were made in the 18th century about the interpretation of the wording on title pages.

Corelli's other collections of chamber works prove interesting in this context. The two sets of *Sonate da camera a tre* (Opp. 2 and 4) comprise three part books and are described on their title pages as being for 'doi violini, e violone, o cimbalo'. In other words, the basso continuo is described exactly as in Op. 5. The *Sonate a tre* Opp. 1 and 3 (which we would now describe as *sonate da chiesa*, though this is not a term used by Corelli) both have 'doi violini, e violone, o arcileuto, col basso per l'organo' (two violins, and violone or archlute with a bass for the organ). These publications have four part books.[8] Thus it seems that Corelli favoured having organ plus a melodic instrument (cello or archlute) for the 'church' sonatas but just harpsichord *or* cello for the chamber sonatas.

Now since the first half of Opus 5 consists of church sonatas and the second part of chamber sonatas, there is perhaps just a little encouragement here for thinking that Corelli might have tolerated players who wished to assign at least the sonatas of Part I to more than one player – and even to have substituted organ for the harpsichord designated on the title page.

Once these collections were published outside Italy this bass-line configuration underwent some changes. An edition of the Op. 4 Sonate da camera published in Antwerp in 1692 changed the 'or' to 'and' (though it still had only three part books). When Pierre Mortier published both sets of chamber sonatas (Opp. 2 and 4) in Amsterdam in 1705 he added a fourth, 'organo' part book.[9] Hence, there may have been a different understanding by Corelli's contemporaries in Northern Europe about what constituted appropriate bass line instrumentation.

---

[8] This description is a standard formula; see, for example, G. P. Franchi, *La cetra sonora; sonate à trè, doi violini, e violone, ò arcileuto, col basso per l'organo* (Rome, 1685).
[9] The 'violone' part was also renamed 'violoncello'.

What about other composers? Many publications use general phrases like 'col suo basso continuo'. But by far the most common formula is that found on the Corelli Op. 5 title page – or some variant of it ('clavicembalo ò violoncello', 'spinetta, ò violone' etc.) In such cases we are back with the same questions: (1) When, if ever, could 'or' have meant 'and'?; and (2) Could there be an implied preference for the first named in these pairs of alternatives?

While our primary concern here is with sonatas for one violin, the fact that standard expressions of this kind are used to describe the bass line across quite a wide range of ensembles suggests that a genre-specific explanation of the significance of a phrase like 'violone ò cimbalo' will not do. In other words, we should be cautious about being too insistent about bass line instrumentation for the 'duo sonata' (not a 17th-century term) if the same explanation cannot be applied to larger ensembles where the bass is similarly described (though see the description of Mascitti Op. 1 below for an instance of genre-specific discrimination in bass-line instrumentation).

It is interesting to consider the implications of genre here. The inadequacy of the standard terminology (particularly 'trio sonata') for Italian chamber-music ensembles in this period has been pointed out often enough.[10] Italian practice in the 17th century (even then not properly understood outside Italy) was to designate pieces à 2, à 3 etc. by the number of melodic lines disregarding any basso continuo part. Thus, a sonata à 2 might describe a piece for two violins and basso continuo or it might indicate a piece for one violin and a bass instrument (with or without basso continuo). Recent thinking about the implications of this for bass lines tends towards the general rule (one that finds some support in the provision or otherwise of more than one bass-line part) that if the description (à 1, à 2 etc.) does not specify a bass-register part then there is no call for more than one instrument to supply the continuo line.

But this descriptive system does not seem to work out quite as neatly as one might hope. To begin with, Corelli's ensemble sonatas Opp. 1–4 appear not to fit since all are described as 'sonate a tre' despite the differing numbers of part books and the different numbers of instruments listed on the title pages. The more I examine actual compositions, the less reliable this rule seems to be since,

---

[10] Most recently and emphatically by Peter Allsop, *The Italian 'Trio' Sonata from its Origins until Corelli* (Oxford: Clarendon Press, 1992). See also N. M. Jensen, 'Solo Sonata, Duo Sonata and Trio Sonata: Some Problems of Terminology and Genre in 17th-Century Italian Instrumental Music', *Festskrift Jens Peter Larsen* (Stockholm, 1972), 73–101. Jensen writes (p. 80): 'No treatise on thorough-bass from the Italian area in the 17th century is known to me which prescribes the obligatory use of a reinforcing string-bass or other instrument together with the continuo part's chord-playing instrument insofar as few-voiced instrumental music is concerned . . . the need for an independent melody bass in Italian chamber music of this time only appears when, in addition to the part book for the thorough-bass player, there is a separate printed bass part.' Steven Zohn gives some indication of the ambiguities that are nevertheless inherent in this system of terminology in 'When is a Quartet not a Quartet?: Relationships between Scoring and Genre in the German Quadro, ca. 1715–40', *Johann Friedrich Fasch und sein Wirken für Zerbst*, Fasch-Studien 6 (Dessau: Anhaltische Verlagsgesellschaft, 1997), 263ff.

more often than not a separate melodic bass line part turns out to be distinguished only by occasional elaborations of the continuo part in some, but not all, sonatas in the collection. Sporadic elaboration of this kind does not, in my view, constitute a genuinely independent voice. The lack of precision about whether a bass-register part is truly independent or a slightly-varied continuo line seems to extend into the system of describing compositions according to the number of voices. (But more of that in chapter 4.)

Ex. 3.1 Bartolomeo Laurenti, *Suonate da camera à violino e violoncello* (Bologna, 1691): Introduttione Settima, opening

It seems impossible on the basis of examining the many works that have some affinity with Corelli Op. 5 to give an absolutely unequivocal and universally applicable answer to the basic questions about bass line numbers (though I stand by the statement quoted above from my 'Performing Corelli's Violin Sonatas' article). First, and importantly, there are a few publications that do not offer the alternative of a keyboard at all, such as the 1691 set of *Suonate da camera a violino e violoncello* by Corelli's fellow-Bolognese, Bartolomeo Laurenti. The cello part is entirely without figures (so it seems no realisation was expected or wanted).[11] Yet this publication has to be taken seriously as an

---

[11] The absence of figures does not exclude the possibility of a realised bass line. The Purcell autograph song book at the Guildhall Library, London, has no figures for songs which

Illus. 3.1 Arcangelo Corelli, *Sonate a violino e violone o cimbalo*, Op. 5 (Rome, 1700), Sonata 1, opening

analogue for Op. 5; some movements seem quite closely related in style to Corelli Op. 5. One notes the alternation of Adagio and Presto passages above sustained pedal notes in the 'Introduttione Settima' (ex. 3.1). This is strikingly similar to the opening of the first sonata in Op. 5 (illus. 3.1).

When the violinist Niccolò Cosimi (who was on friendly terms with Corelli) left Rome in October 1700 to spend three years in the service of the Duke of Bedford he insisted on bringing the cellist, Nicola Haym, with him. Cosimi's meticulously-kept financial diary makes it clear that the two played together (always in private households) and were joined for repertory requiring two violins by Gasparo Visconti (a Corelli pupil).[12] The final two sonatas in Cosimi's *Sonate da camera a violino e violone o cembalo*, Op. 1 (London, 1702) seem almost to presuppose performance by two (unaccompanied) string players. Sonata No. 11 in F major, especially, has a bass line which often participates in an equal-voiced duo with the violin and, at such points, it is without figures and quite often written in the tenor clef (ex. 3.2).[13]

If Cosimi is a clear-cut case of a musician who seems to have favoured (or at least found convenient) the 'violino e violone' option, one of his English pupils, Sir Anthony Cope, provides an apparently unambiguous instance of playing this

---

appear in *Orpheus Britannicus* with figures. For that matter, the Roger (and Walsh) editions of Corelli Op. 5 are completely without figures for the graced adagios. See my 'Performing Corelli's Violin Sonatas', p. 136.

[12] See L. Lindgren, 'Nicola Cosimi in London, 1701–1705', *Studi musicali* 11 (1982), 229–48 and 'The Accomplishments of the Learned and Ingenious Nicola Francesco Haym (1678–1729)', *Studi musicali* 16 (1987), 252ff.

[13] Tenor clef does not, in itself, rule out the possibility of keyboard performance. Figured bass treatises recommend that keyboard players master all the clefs as an aid to transposition (which is seen as an essential part of the accompanist's art). See Lorenzo Penna, *Le primi albori musicali* (Bologna, 1672), Book III, chapter 16, and Francesco Gasparini, *L'armonico pratico al cimbalo* (Venice, 1708), trans F. S. Stillings as *The Practical Harmonist at the Harpsichord* (New Haven and London, 1963), p. 94. On the other hand, Gasparini seems to have assumed a keyboard plus a melodic instrument on the bass lines of his *Cantate da camera a voce sola*, Op. 1 (Rome: Mascardi, 1695); see Borgir, *Performance of the Basso Continuo*, p. 42.

Ex. 3.2 N. Cosimi, *Sonate da camera a violino e violone o cembalo*, Op. 1 (London, 1702): Sonata No. 11 in F, second movement, Allegro, bars 59–69

repertory using 'violino e cembalo'. Cope wrote to Cosimi from Hanover in 1705 reporting that 'The queen of Prussia who plays the harpsichord very well has done me the honour several times of accompanying me in a sonata, which is truly my favourite pastime.'[14]

Where the option of one instrument or another is offered a wide range of possibilities seems to be envisaged. At one extreme, Peter Allsop has demonstrated that for some composers 'o' implied, not an even-handed choice, but a preference for the first of the offered alternatives. He cites Bononcini's note in his *Arie a violino e violone over spinetta* (1671): 'one should bear in mind that the violone will produce a better effect than the

---

[14] 'La Regina di Prussia che suona benissimo del Cembalo mi fa l'honore qualche volta d'accompagnarmi una Suonata, che è veramente il mio più gran spasso.' Quoted by Lindgren, 'Nicola Cosimi', p. 232n.

spinet since the basses are more appropriate to the former than to the latter instrument'.[15] Corelli's pupil, Michele Mascitti (*c.* 1664–1760) provides further encouragement for regarding a single instrument as appropriate for the bass line in solo violin sonatas. His arrival in Paris in 1704 was signalled by the publication of his Opus 1 – a publication that proclaims its Corelli connections even in the way its frontispiece derives from the beautiful engraving that prefaces Op. 5. Mascitti's volume compresses the Corelli oeuvre. There are nine solo sonatas (three of the *da chiesa* type and the rest specifically called 'da camera') and three sonatas à 3. His title page envisages a different bass line treatment for the larger ensemble: *Sonate a violino solo col violone ò cemballo e sonate a due violini, violoncello é basso continuo.* (Thereafter, even in his 1711 Opus 4, which contains a similar mixture of sonatas for one and two violins, he abandoned the particularity of the Op. 1 bass line description.)

But the broader picture is far from simple. In 1656 Cazzati's Op. 18 had appeared offering the possibility of both a harmonic and an optional melodic instrument on the bass line: *Suonate à due violini, col suo basso continuo per l'organo, & un'altro à beneplacito per tiorba, o violone.* F. T. Arnold mentioned Vivaldi's *Suonate da camera a 3*, Op. 1, of 1705 and Giuseppe Valentini's *Idee per camera*, Op. 4, of 1706 as instances where the title pages said 'or' and the parts themselves said 'and'.[16] Pietro Sanmartini's *Sinfonie a due violini, e liuto, e basso di viola*, Op. 2 (Florence, 1688) provides a particularly interesting case where the relevant part says 'or' while the title page not only says 'and' but omits any reference to the 'organo' part included in the set.

There are, in fact, quite a number of cases where title pages and the designation of specific part books provide different information about bass line instrumentation. Often this is just a matter of the title page taking a continuo presence for granted. Cazzati's *Sonate a due istromenti cioè violino e violone*, Op. 55 (Bologna, 1670), for instance, describes itself as being for 'two instruments, namely violin and violone' but has a separate basso continuo part marked 'Organo, ò Tiorba'. A few other cases of this kind are shown in table 3.1.

Luigi Taglietti's *Suonate da camera*, Op. 1 (Bologna, 1697) has a part book designated 'violone o spinetta' which has two staves labelled 'violoncello' and 'cembalo' respectively.[17] His Op. 6 *Pensieri musicali a violino, e violoncello col basso continuo* has separate cello and basso continuo parts (with the cello occasionally having an elaborated version of the bass line).[18] Some publications simply say 'and'. Tomaso Antonio Vitali's Op. 4 collection of sonatas for solo

[15] See P. Allsop, *Arcangelo Corelli: New Orpheus of our Times* (Oxford, 1999), p. 121.

[16] F. T. Arnold, *The Art of Accompaniment from a Thorough-bass as Practised in the XVIIth & XVIIIth Centuries* (London, 1931), p. 329.

[17] *Suonate da camera à tre due violini, e violoncello, con alcune agguinte à violoncello solo* (Bologna, 1697). I am grateful to Richard Maunder for drawing my attention to this publication.

[18] See Borgir, *Performance of the Basso Continuo*, p. 43.

Table 3.1 Publications with different bass-line designations on title page and part-books

1670   M. Cazzati, *Sonate a due istormenti, cioè violino, e violone* (Bologna, 1670): parts (i) violino o cornetto, (ii) violone, (iii) organo o tiorba

1676   G. Colombi, *Sonate a due violini con un bassetto viola se piace*, Op. 4 (Bologna: Monti, 1676): parts (i) violino primo, (ii) violino secondo, (iii) bassetto viola, (iv) basso continuo

1678   G. B. Viviani, *Sonate à violino solo* (Venice, 1678): parts (i) violino, (ii) 'Organo o Gravicembalo'

1678   G. B. Viviani, *Sinfonie, arie, capricci, alemande, corrente, gighe, introduttioni, sarabande, etc. per violino solo* (Rome, 1678): parts (i) violino solo, (ii) organo o gravicembalo

1679   G. B. Viviani, *Suonate à tre, due violini e viola* (Venice, 1679): parts (iii) viola (p. 23 running title 'viola, ò tiorba'), (iv) organo

1683   G. B. Vitali, *Balletti, correnti, e capricci per camera à due violini, e violone* (Modena, 1683): part (iii) violone o spinetta

1684   D. Gabrielli, *Balletti, gighe, correnti, alemande, e sarabande, à violino, e violone, con il secondo violino à beneplacito* (Bologna, 1684): part (iii) violone o spinetta

1685   P. Albergati, *Balletti, correnti, sarabande, e gighe, à violino e violone, con il secondo violino à beneplacito* (Bologna, 1685): part (iii) violone o spinetta

1686   P. Albergati, *Sinfonie à trè istromenti, col basso per l'organo* (Bologna, 1686): parts (i) violino primo, (ii) violino secondo, (iii) violoncello, (iv) organo, (v) violone o tiorba

1686   G. Torelli, *Sonate à tre stromenti con il basso continuo*, Op. 1 (Bologna, 1686): parts (i) violino 1, (ii) violino II, (iii) violoncello, (iv) tiorba o violone, (v) organo

1688   P. Sanmartini, *Sinfonie a due violini, e liuto, e basso di viola*, Op. 2 (Florence, 1688): parts (i) violino primo, (ii) violino secondo, (iii) liuto o basso di viola, (iv) organo

1693   G. Buoni, *Divertimenti per camera a due violini, e violoncello*, Op. 1 (Bologna, 1693): parts (i) violino primo, (ii) violino secondo, (iii) cembalo

1693   G. Buoni, *Sonate a due violini, e violoncello, col basso per l'organo*, Op. 2 (Bologna, 1693): parts (i) violino primo, (ii) violino secondo, (iii) bassetto, (iv) organo

before 1696   A. Veracini, *Sonate da camera à violino solo* (Modena, no date): parts (i) violino solo, (ii) cimbalo o violone

1703   N. Haym, *Dodeci sonate à trè cioè due violini, e violone ò cembalo*, Op. 1 (Amsterdam, 1703): parts (i) violino primo, (ii) violino secondo, (iii) violone o leuto [fully figured]

1704   N. Haym, *Sonate a tre due violini, flauti, violoncello e basso continuo per il cembalo*, io. 2 (Amsterdam, 1704): parts (running headings) (i) violino primo [Sonatas 1–9] violino solo [Sonatas 10–11] flauto primo [Sonata 12], (ii) violino secondo [Sonatas 1–9] violoncello [Sonatas 10–11] flauto secondo [Sonata 12], (iii) violone o leuto

violin (published the year after Corelli's Op. 5), for example, specifies 'violoncello, e cembalo' for its bass line.[19]

Once we spread the net a little wider – to Italian-style music appearing in other parts of Europe – then it seems even less likely that composers had a prescriptive attitude to bass-line instrumentation. Johann Walther's *Scherzi* for solo violin (published in 1676) offer a bass line 'for organ or harpsichord but which may also be accompanied by viola [da gamba] or lute'.[20] Nicola Matteis's *Ayres*, parts 3 and 4, appeared in 1685 with a bass line for 'Base Viol *or* Harpsechord' while a second edition published two years later offers 'Bass-Viol *and* Harpsechord'. (Moreover, it is interesting to reflect that Matteis was the author of a treatise on the use of the guitar as a continuo instrument.[21] If we take the view that title pages are prescriptive then we must conclude that he never expected his *own* music to be accompanied by guitar. Given that the *Ayres* contain a number of pieces in which the guitar is evoked, this would seem almost perverse.) Perhaps more interestingly (since it is quite obviously modelled on Corelli Op. 5), Geminiani's Opus 1 appeared in 1716 in London as *Sonate a violino, violone, e cembalo*, while subsequent editions with English title pages (the first dated 1719) have *XII Solo's for a Violin With a Through Bass for the Harpsichord or Bass Violin*.

The only account of Geminiani actually performing a violin sonata – supposedly when making his debut at the English court in about 1714 – has him accompanied by a single distinguished colleague:

> Geminiani had been in England a short time, during which he had published and dedicated to baron Kilmansegge his Opera prima, consisting of those twelve Solos for the violin, which will be admired as long as the love of melody shall exist, and the king was desirous of hearing them performed by the author, who was the greatest master of the instrument then living; Geminiani was extremely pleased with the thought of being heard, but was fearful of being accompanied on the harpsichord by some performer, who might fail to do justice both to the compositions and the performance of them: in short, he suggested to the baron a wish that Mr. Handel might be the person appointed to meet him in the king's apartment; and upon mentioning it to his majesty, the baron was told that Handel would be admitted for the purpose, and he attended accordingly; and upon expressing his desire to atone for his former misbehaviour, by the utmost efforts of duty and gratitude, he was reinstated in the king's favour.[22]

---

[19] *Concerto di sonate a violino, violoncello, e cembalo*, Op. 4 (Modena, 1701). Bernado Tonini's *Baletti da camera a due violini, e violetta, & cembalo* (Venice, 1690) has part books for violins 1 and 2, violetta, and cembalo. The copy in the Austrian National Library, Vienna, has a manuscript 'Violone' part as well.

[20] *Scherzi da violino solo con il basso continuo per l'organo ò cimbalo, accompagnabile anche con una viola ò leuto* (Leipzig and Frankfurt, 1676).

[21] N. Matteis, *The False Consonances of Musick or Instructions for the Playing a true Base upon the Guitarre* (London, 1682).

[22] Sir John Hawkins, *A General History of the Science and Practice of Music* (1776), 2 vols. (London, 1963) ii, 358–9.

That story – recounted by Sir John Hawkins sixty years after the event – seems *ben trovato* rather than true (especially since it draws on the now-discredited idea that Handel's relationship with the King had been strained by the composer's failure to return to Hanover). But on the face of it, Geminiani was accompanied by harpsichord alone – but in repertoire for which the first edition title page offers 'violone e cembalo'.

How can we deduce more about Corelli's own attitudes in all of this? Little is known about the gestation of the Opus 5 sonatas but it seems likely that – like the Opus 6 Concerti grossi – they included revised versions of earlier compositions. There is a letter from Corelli to Count Laderchi dated 13 May 1679 in which he promises to write a sonata in which 'the lute will have equal status to the violin'. The promised sonata (which may eventually have found a place in Opus 5) was sent off three weeks later with a note to say that violone would work just as well as lute.[23] The second letter suggests a certain relaxedness about the instrumentation of the bass line (though admittedly in each case Corelli is suggesting a single instrument).

But starting to think of the Opus 5 sonatas as perhaps having a history parallel to that of Opus 6 leads us back towards the idea that one of the main strategies of title pages was to make the works seem attractive to as large a segment of the market as possible. The 1714 Opus 6 title page stresses that you do not need an orchestra to perform these compositions – they will work well as trio sonatas. It is clear that Corelli went to considerable trouble to adapt the concerti so that they would, in fact, be musically self-sufficient if played by two violins and cello.[24] Rudolph Rasch has pointed out that Corelli's contract with the Amsterdam publisher Etienne Roger for Opus 6 shows that he had quite an astute business sense. He also suggested that the Opus 5 publication was a private edition undertaken speculatively by Corelli and marketed by him.[25] This might lead us to expect that the Opus 5 title page is offering minimum requirements rather than prescribing strict limits.

Altogether we are dealing with quite a confused situation here. If performers are seeking permission from historical precedent for what they do, then (as I see it) this gives them a lot of latitude. It partly depends how narrowly they set their focus. It would be possible to argue, as Peter Allsop does, that, as examples of the 'relatively new genre of unaccompanied duo', Corelli's first choice of instrumentation in Op. 5 would have been to have no realized continuo accompaniment'.[26] Obviously, though, Corelli at least countenanced (and

[23] See A. Cavicchi, 'Corelli e il violinismo bolognese', *Studi Corelliani. Atti del Primo Congresso Internazionale (Fusignano 5–8 settembre 1968)* (Florence, [1972]), p. 39; also Allsop, *Corelli*, pp. 121f.

[24] On Corelli's revisions, see P. Walls, 'Geminiani and the Role of the Viola in the Concerto Grosso', in *Liber Amicorum John Steele: A Musicological Tribute*, ed. Warren Drake (New York, 1997), pp. 386f.

[25] Rudolph Rasch, 'Corelli's Contract: Notes on the Publication History of the Concerti Grossi . . . Opera Sesta [1714]', *Tijdschrift van de Koninklijke Vereniging voor Nederlandse Muziek Geshiednis* 45.ii (1996), 92.

[26] Allsop, *Corelli*, p. 121.

may even have preferred) harpsichord as a substitute – and my guess is that he would not have ruled out either other single-instrument possibilities (archlute, for example) or the combination of several (violoncello *and* harpsichord etc.) That, as I say, is just a guess and can't be anything more. What is certain, however, is that many of his contemporaries – and particularly those living outside Italy – assumed such a range of options.

There are at least two dimensions to the historical problem in the Corelli case. First, there is the issue of Corelli's own preferences. Can we be confident that the description of these sonatas as being for violin and 'violone or harpsichord' was, in fact, intended to be prescriptive rather than a commercially-shrewd indication of minimum resources? In other words, did Corelli really think that harpsichord or cello were the only acceptable options and clearly preferable to any of the other available possibilities – archlute, theorbo, chamber organ, or – dare I mention it – a combination of two or more instruments? But even if we were to agree that Corelli meant exactly what he said and only what he said, we are still left with the problem of deciding what jurisdiction the composer had over his publications. In other words, did those who purchased Opus 5 in Amsterdam or London read these title pages in the same way as violinists in Rome? Obviously not. If we are going to accuse modern players of unhistorical practices, my guess is that we would be on very shaky ground unless we insist that the only 'right' performances of Corelli sonatas are ones that mimic exactly what Corelli would have done (with his associates Lulier *o* Pasquini) in Rome in 1700.

At this point I would like to return to Trio Veracini's recording. It does contain some very attractive playing and I have quite enjoyed listening to it. I commend their willingness to test the musical possibilities of a strict interpretation of the 'violone ò cimbalo' rubric and for realising that accepting this kind of discipline can provide a spur to creativity. My quarrel is entirely with the authority they wish to claim for their approach and the confidence with which they dismiss the alternatives.

As might have been expected, Trio Veracini's liner notes made claims very much in line with the players' contributions to *Early Music*:

> This is the first recording to present the music entirely on violin with *either* violone *or* harpsichord . . . What is unique about this recording is that the specified instrumentation is applied *with* the continuo-realisation practises [*sic*] of the time. Thus the discreet tinkling harpsichord so beloved of many of today's critics is replaced by the fullblooded textures of late-17th and early 18th century Italian practise [*sic*]; indeed, the version of Sonata 3 in C with harpsichord is presented here with the realisation as written down by Antonio Tonelli (1686–1765).[27]

---

[27] Corelli, *12 Sonate a violino e violone o cimbalo, Op. 5*, Trio Veracini, Novalis 150 128–2. Andrew Manze and Richard Egarr's complete Op. 5 is, for my taste, the most musically-satisfying single-instrument recording to date (and Manze's introductory essay provides an intelligently-argued apologia for their approach); HMU 907298.99 (2002).

Well, this is quite something – but, as with so many recordings that make such claims, it seems driven by a dangerous blend of opportunism and naiveté. From one point of view, the project is manacled by a reverence for historical sources which, in fact, push the strictly two-at-a-time trio further away from their objective of letting us hear these works as Corelli played them. We read in their notes, for example, that a notable aspect of the Tonelli realisation of Sonata 3 'is the harmonisation of the pedal note before the final chord, despite the *Tasto Solo* marking in the original'. Well, who should they obey then: Corelli or Tonelli? (Holloway and Mortensen of course opt for Tonelli.)

There are other instances of Trio Veracini being led astray by not-quite-relevant sources. In the slow movements of Sonata No. 11 in A major, Holloway uses the Matthew Dubourg ornamentation. This is as an outstanding English example from *c.* 1740 of the grotesque over-elaboration in this kind of florid 'improvisation' which became prevalent as the 18th century wore on.[28] Corelli's line is all but lost. I much prefer Elizabeth Wallfisch doing her own more modest, but infinitely more musical, decoration. Hers seems totally in keeping with the Roger/Corelli model in the way that, far from obliterating the original line, it seems to enhance it.[29]

Ex. 3.3 Arcangelo Corelli, *Sonate a violino e violone o cimbalo,* Op. 5: Sonata No. 10 in F, third movement, Sarabanda (Largo), bars 1–8

Presenting all of these sonatas with only harpsichord or cello as continuo involved them in some difficult choices. In the case of the Folia variations the decision proved too hard – we get two versions, one with harpsichord and one with cello. What we are dealing with here is a new puritanism. But what about the idea that here, for the first time, we are listening to the continuo practices of the time? In the Sarabanda from Sonata No. 10 in F (performed with just

---

[28] 'Corelli's Solos Grac'd by Doburg', MS in private hands; see Neal Zaslaw, 'Ornaments for Corelli's Violin Sonatas, Op. 5', *Early Music* 24 (1996), 99.

[29] Corelli, *12 Sonate a violino e violone o cimbalo, Op. 5,* Locatelli Trio, Hyperion CDA 66381/2.

harpsichord on the bass line) the rests in the continuo part are filled in with chords and the repeat of the first section is assigned to solo harpsichord, without violin (ex. 3.3). While I do not particularly mind them doing either of these things I do object to being told that this is how it meant to be.

The performances of sonatas in which just cello has been deployed on the bass line are predicated on the notion that the (figured) bass line needs realisation. There is very little evidence that, historically, this was the case. Admittedly, Roger North boasted that he became 'a complete, ready, and dextrous thro-base man' on the bass viol (but that was in another country and besides, full chords are more idiomatic on that instrument than on the cello). More to the point perhaps, the *Concerti per camera à violino, e violoncello solo* (Modena, 1697) by the virtuoso cellist Giuseppe Jacchini includes a few simple figures in the violoncello part, apparently implying that these bass lines should be realised (unless, like some of the examples in Table 3.1, the title page does not spell out the complete range of instrumental realisations envisaged by the composer). The earliest discussion of the cello's capacity to provide an harmonic realisation of bass lines comes in Baumgartner's cello treatise published in the Hague in the 1770s and Baumgartner was dealing with the comparatively static and spacious bass lines of operatic recitative.[30] The cello realisations on the Corelli recording are (not surprisingly) fairly minimal compared to the very saturated chords in all the sonatas recorded with harpsichord.

Ex. 3.4 Arcangelo Corelli, *Sonate a violino e violone o cimbalo,* Op. 5: Sonata No. 11 in A, second movement, Allegro, bars 1–8

And now for an observation based on a combination of expediency and personal taste. There are many situations in which it will be desirable (for

---

[30] J. B. Baumgartner, *Instructions de musique, théorique et pratique à l'usage du violoncelle* (The Hague, *c.* 1774).

practical or for musical reasons) to play one of these sonatas with just cello or harpsichord. But there are, too, musical advantages in using both a melodic instrument and one capable of providing a satisfactory realisation (not the cello!). The first Allegro of Sonata 11 in A major has thematic material alternating between solo violin and bass line (ex. 3.4).[31] Here, a melodic bass instrument can concentrate on the dialogue with the violin while the naturally-chordal instrument takes care of the harmonic realisation.

It is folly to claim (or to accept) a status equivalent to a complete edition for any recordings. A performance is inescapably an interpretation – act not text, to use Taruskin's terms. Performers have no way of indicating alternative 'readings', so to speak, in a critical apparatus. Moreover, the conditions under which we listen to recordings (potentially subjecting ourselves to the entire Op. 5 in a single sitting) are completely unlike any historical listening situation (Corelli with one, two, maybe four companions presenting a sonata as part of a varied offering at one of Queen Christina's or Cardinal Pamphilii's academies). Furthermore, there are many factors in determining whether a performance works or not which have nothing to do with source-awareness (tonal quality, subtleties of phrasing, technical mastery . . .).[32]

Whatever Corelli wanted in relation to his bass lines, he could have had – whether that meant one instrument or six. The other two issues I want to touch on in this essay introduce a slightly different kind of question since they both involve situations in which composers were providing for existing and institutionally-restricted resources.

We can only speculate about what Vivaldi might have regarded as an ideal performance of one of the sacred works he wrote for the Ospedale della Pietà. In recent years Michael Talbot, Faun Tannenbaum, and others have made us face up to the fact that the Venetian *ospedali* really did manage with only women performers – and this, of course, included the choral works.[33] A significant part of this repertoire is for an SSAA choir, but many works – especially those written for the Mendicanti and the Pietà – are scored SATB. There are three possible ways

---

[31] Note that in the original 1700 edition, the bass line in bars 5–8 of ex. 3.4 is written in the tenor clef (compare ex. 3.2).

[32] As a postscript, it is interesting to note that, even by the time C. P. E. Bach was recommending a harpischord plus cello solution, the matter was not fixed. Quantz, *On Playing the Flute*, writes (p. 252): 'In a trio the keyboard player must adjust himself to the instrumentalists that he has to accompany, noting whether they are loud or soft, *whether or not there is a violoncello with the keyboard*, whether the composition is in a galant or elaborate style, whether the harpsichord is loud or soft, open or closed, and whether the listeners are close by or at a distance . . . *If* the keyboard player has a violoncellist with him, and accompanies soft instruments, he may use some moderation with the right hand . . .' (my italics).

[33] See Michael Talbot, 'Tenors and Basses at the Venetian *Ospedali*', *Acta Musicologica* 66 (1994), 123–38. Talbot (p. 123n) refers to unpublished dissertations by J. M. Whittemore and F. Tannebaum. I heard Dr Tannebaum give a paper on this subject at the Biennial Baroque Conference held in Durham in 1992.

in which this might have been done: first, by training selected women to sing bass lines at pitch; second, by having the tenor lines sung at pitch by contralto voices while the bass lines sounded an octave higher; or thirdly (and most probably) by having both bass and tenor lines sung an octave above written pitch. In the second and third of these possibilities, the sung bass line would most often act like a 4′ stop on an instrument above the same line sounded at pitch by the instrumental accompaniment. But this is not always the case. To take just one example, the 'Et in terra pax' from the better-known of Vivaldi's settings of the Gloria (RV 589) has a vocal bass line that is independent of the instrumental bass line (ex. 3.5). Sung entirely with women's voices, Vivaldi's pairs of imitative entries rising from bass to soprano come out sounding like a simple repeat.

A significant number of works from the choral repertory for the Venetian *ospedali* were re-scored for situations outside Venice. Hasse's C-minor *Miserere*, for example, was written for the Incurabili in the 1730s with an SSAA chorus which was changed to SATB when the work was later adapted for the Katholische Hofkirche in Dresden.[34] It seems probable that Vivaldi would have been pleased to have works like the Gloria performed with a mixed choir. If I am right, the issue helps bring into focus a question about what really are the ideal forces. It is undoubtedly interesting and instructive to replicate as far as possible what the composer expected to hear; but ultimately it makes better sense to strive musically for something which lives up to the composer's vision of how something might sound (not, as we shall see in chapter 4, that it is an easy matter to determine what that might be). And the province of the musicologist surely embraces both the task of discovering actual historical conditions and the attempt to relate this reality to an ideal.

But this is not easy. Real and ideal groups of singers for Bach sacred works presents us with a rather more complicated question. The debate on this has been going on since November 1981 when Joshua Rifkin first outlined to the American Musicological Society his hypothesis that Bach's choral compositions were conceived for solo voices who, at specific moments in certain works, would each be reinforced by a ripieno singer.[35] Since then more and more musicologists and performers (not to mention musicologist-performers) have been drawn in to what now looks set to become a thirty years war. I would like to offer a few ('brief yet highly necessary') observations on the debate.

The latest round of skirmishes in this particular battle was set off by the

---

[34] Talbot, 'Tenors and Basses', p. 127.

[35] Rifkin was prevented from giving the complete version of his paper at the AMS meeting. The following year he published a shorter article outlining his views, as 'Bach's Chorus: A Preliminary Report', *Musical Times* 123 (1982), 747–54. This provoked a response from Robert L. Marshall, as 'Bach's Chorus: A Preliminary Reply to Joshua Rifkin', *Musical Times* 124 (1983), 19–22. The full version of Rifkin's 1981 paper has now been published as Appendix 6 in Andrew Parrott, *The Essential Bach Choir* (Woodbridge, 2000); Appendix 7 ('Twentieth-Century Discussions of Bach's Choir') and the Bibliography provide a comprehensive list of contributions to this debate.

Ex. 3.5 Antonio Vivaldi, Gloria RV 589, 'Et in terra pax', bars 9–16

unhappy coincidence of having Ton Koopman's prospectus, as it were, for his complete Bach cantata recordings appear in *Early Music* between the same covers as articles by Joshua Rifkin himself and Andrew Parrott reaffirming the case for one-singer-per-part.[36] Koopman saw the Rifkin/Parrott contributions as undermining the value of his recordings – inevitably, since he, like Trio Veracini, very firmly subscribes to a position which would claim for complete recordings the status of Denkmäler. He writes that the Harnoncourt/Leondhardt cycle of Bach cantatas recorded in the 1960s have 'rightly been declared a historic document' and sets out at some length the provisions made to ensure scholarly respectability for his own set. This seems to have involved Professor Christoph Wolff from Harvard, a veritable army of research students from the University of Utrecht, a large number of facsimiles of pre-1800 Bach sources, and a copious supply of coloured felt-tip highlighters for marking up the Neue Bach Ausgabe. It is no wonder that Koopman felt aggrieved at then implicitly being accused of getting the basic resources wrong.[37]

But, actually, nobody seemed to be happy. Andrew Parrott, having written what I would regard as an impeccable piece of musicology which manages to be both lively and quite objective in tone, immediately returned to *Early Music* to voice anguish at the 'decidedly shaky musicology' informing the Koopman recordings. His quarrel was not just with Koopman and his associates but with what he saw as a kind of indifference exhibited by the musicological community at large. He cited from the same issue of *Early Music* as the Koopman piece, a positive review of a *St Matthew Passion* recording which, according to its author, Malcolm Boyd, embodied 'current orthodoxy' in its use of sixteen voices for each of the two choirs. Parrott's frustration was palpable:

> What is the innocent reader to make of all this? (Thus far, the scholarly silence has been deafening.) Unquestionably, the consensus hitherto has been that Rifkin's arguments are 'unconvincing' – and that the current orthodoxy (three or four voices per part) remains historically acceptable . . . But is mere acknowledgement of continuing 'controversy' all we can expect? Certainly, by itself this would be counterproductive; it would serve to undermine confidence in musicology (as a tool for the historically aware), and instead promote even greater reliance, in these

---

[36] Ton Koopman, 'Recording Bach's Early Cantatas', *Early Music* 24 (1996), 604–19; Andrew Parrott, 'Bach's Chorus: A "brief yet highly necessary" Reappraisal', ibid., 551–80; Joshua Rifkin, 'From Weimar to Leipzig: Concertists and Ripienists in Bach's *Ich hatte viel Bekümmernis*', ibid., 583–603.

[37] See Taruskin, *Text and Act*, p. 61, n. 16: '. . . sound recording . . . offers the possibility of permanence to a medium that had formerly existed only "at the moment". Most historical reconstructionist performances aspire at least tacitly to the status of document, if not that of Denkmal. When the performance is recorded, the aim usually becomes explicit (witness the slogan of the SEON series of historical recordings: "Document & Masterwork"). No less than the score, the performance is regarded as a "text" rather than as an activity, and this creates another pressure toward the elimination from it of anything spontaneous or "merely" personal, let alone idiosyncratic.' See also Joseph Kerman, 'The Byrd Edition – in Print and on Disc', *Early Music* 29 (2001), 109–18.

purely factual matters, on good old-fashioned personal taste and individual musical instinct?[38]

What interests me here is the phrase 'a tool for the historically aware'. Of course performance practice research must function as a resource for historically-aware performers. But what seems to be implied here – and in many other places – is rather stronger than that. Performance practice research is not really being viewed as a tool (an available resource) but as a binding statute. That is exactly what performers seem most afraid of and the fear presents a huge obstacle in the way of dispassionate evaluation of relevant scholarship. John Eliot Gardiner, having nailed his colours to the mast with a choir of 5–4–4–4 for his 'Bach Cantata Pilgrimage' (see above, p. 6f.) responded with what could fairly be described as paranoid hysteria when questioned about the Rifkin/Parrott case:

> 'That's all so irritating', says Gardiner. 'Those who have hijacked that area of musicological research and scholarship – and hijacking is not too strong a word for it – have dictated the agenda and taken things to a position of brute positivism. They look at things in such an absurdly minuscule fashion that they lose the overall picture. Much of the old scholarship may have been imprecise but it was informed by a truer spirit; that has been thrown overboard. Bach's relationship with his texts, his concerns for symbols and to align himself with the Lutheran orthodoxy in Leipzig, have been forgotten by the fashionable, introspective, self-serving world of modern musicology . . .'[39]

One might wonder how positivism can be brutish or even why modern musicology should be thought 'introspective' let alone 'self-serving' on these matters. The most striking assertion here, though, is that imprecise scholarship might have a greater claim on truth than accurate research. It is hard to escape the conclusion that by 'truth' Gardiner means something like 'nostalgia' which, as Carl Dahlhaus observed, 'may possibly kindle an interest in history; but it can only hinder this interest by making further refinements by increased knowledge appear not just unnecessary but even harmful'.[40]

Now, as it happens, I am totally persuaded by the Rifkin/Parrott argument (which has now been very fully and lucidly expounded in Parrott's *The Essential Bach Choir*). Let us for the moment anyway assume that their case has been proven beyond reasonable doubt. What are (would be, if you prefer) the implications of this for performers?

First, without getting involved in its actual arithmetic, Bach's famous 1730 *Entwurff* (the 'Brief yet highly necessary outline of a properly-constituted church musical establishment') reveals a pragmatic musician trying to do something about inadequate resources in the face of a not-very-sympathetic controlling administration.[41] I find this picture of Bach both moving and, in a

---

[38] Andrew Parrott, 'Bach's Chorus: Who Cares?', *Early Music* 25 (1997), 297.

[39] A. Stewart, 'Sir John in Love', *Early Music Today* 8.4 (2000), 18.

[40] Dahlhaus, *Foundations*, p. 5.

[41] The text and translation of the *Entwurff* is given as Appendix 3 of Parrott's *Essential Bach Choir* (pp. 163–70).

way, inspiringly familiar. Working (normally) in Wellington (rather than in London, Amsterdam, New York, or Sydney), the question is never 'What singers and players will I call upon to do such and such a work?' but 'Can we do this work and, if so, how?' In such circumstances the vision of Bach tackling monumental works with a very small team of musicians is, to say the least, encouraging.

But now I am in danger of confusing the issue. It is not Bach the pragmatist putting a performance together as best he could that need concern us, but Bach the composer having his vision moulded by available resources. Providing more than eight singers for a performance of the B minor Mass might not be enhancing it; it might instead be doing violence to the conception, which was tailored to fit the constraints (if you like) of the situation. We might, for example, compare Stravinsky preparing to write *L'Histoire du Soldat* at the end of World War I: 'So we worked at our task with great zest, reminding ourselves frequently of the modest means at our disposal to carry it to completion. I knew only too well that so far as the music was concerned I should have to be content with a very restricted orchestra.'[42] Knowing that circumstance dictated that he was now having to think in terms of a much smaller ensemble than for *Le Sacre du Printemps* would provide no justification for bumping up the numbers when performing *The Soldier's Tale* or even *Pulcinella* (where, at least, sections rather than solo players are indicated).

It is interesting just to examine one of the moments in the B minor Mass where the Rifkin hypothesis really makes a conspicuous difference. As Rifkin explained about the transition from the 'Domine Deus' to the 'Qui tollis',

> Modern performances underscore the shift from two parts to four with a shift from solo to choral forces; yet the parts show no trace of such a differentiation. The tenor bears the heading *Duetto* at the start of the 'Domine Deus', which confirms that Bach intended this number for two soloists. But at the 'Qui tollis' – which follows without so much as a double bar – no further marking appears . . . He could scarcely have anticipated anything but a performance by five solo voices.[43]

Rifkin demonstrated the point in a recording of the B minor Mass made at the time of the 1981 American Musicological Society meeting (and rashly advertised as 'the first recording of the original version'). At the time, the most obvious recording to compare this with would still have been Nikolaus Harnoncourt's 1968 period-instrument recording which claimed to be based on 'Bach's choral and orchestral sound'.[44] Harnoncourt does observe the (conventional) shift

[42] Igor Stravinsky, *Autobiography* (New York, 1936; revised ed. 1962), p. 71.

[43] Rifkin, 'Bach's Chorus', p. 753.

[44] Telefunken Das Alte Werk SKH20/1–3 now available on CD as Teldec Das Alte Werk 4509–95517–2. The essay in the booklet accompanying the recording read, 'Bach's choral and orchestral sound . . . thus form the basis of this recording. It was never our intention, however, to transfer a performance from Bach's age into ours in a sterilized state, so to speak, as an enormous piece of musicological industry. On the contrary, working with

from soloists to choir. This is clearly not what Bach expected, yet it could be argued that the re-scoring does not work against the music in any serious way since it reflects a genuine change in musical register. And, in other ways (overall standard of intonation, the quality of the singers, and some less tangible aspects of the musicianship), Harnoncourt's recording seems more pleasurable as a listening experience than Rifkin's. (To be fair, Rifkin has since gone on to produce more persuasive performances of this repertory.) Clearly, historical legitimacy cannot override all other considerations in determining the success or otherwise of a performance.

But conforming as closely as our current state of knowledge permits to historical circumstance can offer a powerful way through to a wholly satisfying performance. Taruskin would not agree:

> We now think, for example, that we possess knowledge both of how Bach performed his concerted vocal music and of how he wished to have it performed. The two are not the same. Which one gets the privilege? The one represented by the surviving performance parts, of course, because (we think) they tell us what Bach did, not what he 'intended' to do. Bach's unrealized (and therefore unheard) wishes are treated by performance practitioners exactly the way musical text critics treat the conjectural products of classical text editing: they are despised as representing (in the words of the *New Grove*) 'nothing that existed at or soon after the period of the work itself'. Documents outrank people, no matter who.[45]

In fact, there is nothing that should lead us to believe that Bach would ever have wanted more than he asked for in the *Entwurff*. We cannot assume that there *is* a difference between what Bach did and what he 'intended' to do. Through his performances, Andrew Parrott manages to demonstrate that the focussed sound obtained from really well-tuned concertists and ripienists can hold its own against a baroque orchestra based on the kind of string numbers envisaged in the *Entwurff*. There are other musical advantages too (most obviously increased flexibility) that derive from a basically solo-voice situation.[46]

But we cannot assume, either, that in different circumstances Bach would not have adjusted. (In fact, the relationship between, say, the Brandenburg Concerti and their antecedants show him doing exactly that.) So, if I had the opportunity to do the B minor Mass I would have to think very carefully about the particular situation before committing to any particular disposition of vocal lines. Between 1990 and 1999 I conducted The Tudor Consort, a very good, but amateur, student-based choir with whom I was far more likely to get

Bach's music, with the instruments of that time and with modern instruments over many years has convinced us that we can reproduce this music truly better, more convincingly in this manner and with these instruments than with modern resources. It was the free decision of the performer to present the work in the best possible manner, not the dream of the historicist of reviving a sound-picture of the past.'

[45] Taruskin, *Text and Act*, p. 45.

[46] In August 2000 I had the pleasure of working with Andrew Parrott on a three-day workshop at Merton College, Oxford, on Bach cantatas and was delighted by the sheer musical pleasure of the experience.

satisfactory tuning with three or four singers per section ('current orthodoxy') than with one and occasionally two voices to a part. (In this situation, there is nothing like security of numbers to offset the damaging effects of performance nerves.)[47]

Does this mean I should abandon all attempts to perform Bach works with period instruments? Possibly. After all, madrigals are generally best left to single-voice ensembles and string quartets to string quartets (rather than, *pace* Mahler, string orchestras). But it might seem a pity to consign the Bach Passions, the B minor Mass, and the riches of the cantata cycles to the larger choral societies who are untroubled by the debates raging in the pages of *Early Music*. It seems to me that as a practical musician I am thrust into a situation where, like Bach, I am trying to get the best result from the resources available. That may well mean (as a compromise, if you like) making choices that are consciously different from Bach's own (such as performing Bach choral works with three or four voices per part) even though I could put my hand on my heart and claim that what I would most like to do in performance is to get as close as possible to what we can know of Bach's conception.

The Bach resources debate provides a classic instance of musicology producing results which are uncomfortable – which do not fit the structure of early 21st-century performing institutions (by which I mean principally the way established choirs tend to be constituted). It may have encouraged some 'decidedly shaky musicology' (to return to Andrew Parrott's phrase) though the most obvious cause of the shakes is a fear on the part of performers that they might have to implement the conclusions of their own or their colleagues' research. When performance practice research is seen as inescapably an applied science, it stands a very good chance of being distorted.

So, the first (of two) modest conclusions I would like to offer in this essay is to repeat that performance practice research should be driven first and foremost – like all good research – by intellectual curiosity. Peter Williams states a similar conclusion even more strongly:

> What performance practice studies expose are not simply a few little details of performance that need to be assimilated before one claims authenticity. Rather, they should lead performers to recognize the leap of conjecture their performance represents, bringing them to see that, create as many authentic conditions as they might, they cannot create them all; that their performance illuminates less or more, as the case may be, of the great mind of the composer concerned; that claiming authenticity in any respect is hasty, if not sometimes superficial or even fraudulent; and that it is in study, not in conclusions offered to a public, that understanding lies. The *studies* part of performance practice studies are their highest purpose.[48]

---

[47] This choir may be heard on *Peter Philips: Cantiones sacrae Quinis Vocibus*, Naxos 8.555056 (2001).

[48] Peter Williams, 'Performance Practice Studies: Some Current Approaches to the Early

The second and related conclusion is this: whether we like it or not, performers have the freedom to do whatever they choose. Performers (and even musicologist-performers) cannot be compelled to apply what musicologists find out. Even to hint otherwise sets up obstacles in the way of good scholarship, or at least runs the risk of creating a vested interest in reaching particular conclusions. If performers want to play Bach on a Steinway or a marimba, we cannot and we should not even try to stop them (though chapter 7 considers at more length how such practices might be regarded). But performers who accept the value of historical research need not feel guilty either about a reluctance to adopt practices which seem to run counter to 'good old-fashioned personal taste and individual musical instinct'. Such things probably will not work unless (or until) scholarship and musicianship converge.

While Andrew Parrott may lament, on the one hand, what he sees as a reluctance on the part of performers to adopt in practice the discoveries of Bach scholarship and, on the other hand, the complacency of musicologists prepared to accept and even enjoy performances which he sees as unhistorical, it is interesting to reflect that this particular debate has in fact had a huge impact on 'current orthodoxy'. Skirmishes about whether to use one or four singers per part in Bach choral works may still be going on – but at the time of that 'monumental' Harnoncourt/Leonhardt complete Bach Cantata series what accountants would call the materiality of the figures was entirely different. Harnoncourt's 1968 B minor Mass recording had a choir of forty-two singers. Nowadays a claim that such a performance was based on 'Bach's choral and orchestral sound' would be greeted with derision. In a sense, we do know better – and I have no doubt that Rifkin's 1981 paper has been a major factor in changing the basic arithmetic.[49]

So, like Little Bo-Peep's sheep, the discoveries of musicological research may well come home eventually even if in stages and incompletely. Consider the following questions: (1) Does a 16′ string instrument sound out of place in Purcell orchestral music? (2) Does the presence of a keyboard continuo in purely instrumental movements of late 17th-century French opera seem instrusive? (3) Would you prefer to hear a baritone, a counter-tenor, or a soprano singing the role of Nero in Monteverdi's *L'incoronazione di Poppea*? I cannot, of course, predict what readers' responses to those questions would be, but my own answers are different from those I would have given when I first became involved in period instrument performance in the 1970s. It has even seemed to me that one's reaction to the sound of a period instrument that has a modern counterpart may often be to notice what appears to be lacking in the earlier version. Appreciating the historical instrument's special qualities may

Music Phenomenon', in *Companion to Contemporary Musical Thought*, ed. J. Paynter et al. (London and New York, 1992), p. 946.

[49] I note, however, that the London Proms series for 2000 included a B minor Mass conducted by Sir Roger Norrington with very substantial vocal forces. Performing such works in venues as large as the Albert Hall involves at least a tacit acknowledgement that no serious attempt is being made to re-enter Bach's sound world.

come next. I am thinking particularly of the fortepiano here, which at first sounded to me like a rather deficient pianoforte. Now, as one who savours the timbre and expressive possibilities of that instrument, that initial response survives only as a puzzling memory. And having just defended the idea of departing from Bach's practice where there seems good reason for doing so, I must now confess that I am starting to feel bothered by hearing solo lines being treated chorally in Bach cantatas. I am at a loss to pinpoint exactly when an intellectual acceptance of a musicological argument has become metamorphosed into a way of listening but I assume that the process that has gone on here is one with which readers of this book will be familiar. My point is that performers' and audiences' musical instincts (i.e. what we like to hear) do tend eventually to be modified in response to musicological clarification of historical practice. The starting point in that process, of course, is a willingness on the part of performers to commit to testing musicological findings in the conviction that that will bring its own musical rewards.

To return to the question posed in my title: in my ideal world, performance practice research would be driven by curiosity about the past without regard to its possible application to modern performance. It would thus be freed from the worry that it might produce uncomfortable conclusions. If musicologists *were* supposed to be the thought police I promise you that we could (like the repressive and hypocritical Angelo of *Measure for Measure*) walk into the middle of any baroque orchestra currently performing and close it down for suspect historical practices.

Musicologists can, though, widen horizons for performers. So often research in performance practice does not produce firm conclusions – and, from a performer's point of view, this is not such bad thing. A host of contradictions can at least encourage re-thinking something we might otherwise take for granted and open up possibilities outside received tradition. What we want from musicians doing research is intelligence, freedom from prejudice, and a willingness to accept inconclusiveness where that seems best to reflect the truth. What we need from performers is something different: an openness to the possibilities thrown up by research, yes, but decisiveness, imagination, and a desire to communicate. We must not confuse the distinct roles of scholar and performer, otherwise we might find ourselves echoing the melancholy Jacques' line from *As You Like It*: 'I do not desire you to please me. I do desire you to sing.'[50]

---

[50] *As You Like It* ii. v. 15.

4. What's the score?

Like the actors learning Shakespeare's plays, the performers in 17th-century ensemble music had only their own lines in front of them; as far as we know, they got to know the piece as a whole only with their ears. At least that seems to have been the case with most forms of concerted music. But sonatas for violin and basso continuo (or sonatas for violin with a bass instrument) stand out as something of an exception in that, from quite early on, a score of some sort was more or less standard. In this essay, I ask why this was the case. What can the fact of there being a score tell us about the genre and about the way it was approached by performers? And (again) how many people actually read from each copy of the score at any one time?

Nowadays we take for granted that a score has at least a dual function. (I say 'at least' because a score of some sort must have been a normal part of the compositional process.) The score is, first, the most complete record of the composition. In this sense, the word is sometimes used as a synonym for 'work'. (Among the list of definitions of the word in *The New Grove II* we find, 'by extension, a piece of music customarily written "in score"'.) But just as Lydia Goehr and others have forced us to confront the fact that the concept of 'the work' is itself historical, the examples I am about to present illustrate clearly that our modern sense of 'score' and 'work' as (nearly) synonyms is one which might have puzzled musicians in earlier periods.[1]

Second, the score is a tool for performance. Orchestral conductors and pianists performing chamber music, for example, expect to have a score on their stands and even groups such as string quartets who do not actually play from a score will regularly use one as a rehearsal aid.

Some years ago, in an article on Geminiani, I noted that the justification for publishing instrumental music in score in early 18th-century England was always a quasi-educational one. Even in the 1770s the catalogues of the publisher John Johnson grouped scores, not in music 'for Concerts', but under a separate heading: 'Books on Composition, Scores for the Improvement of Composers, and Rules for Thorough Bass'.[2] Performance was never men-

---

[1] L. Goehr, *The Imaginary Museum of Musical Works: An Essay in the Philosophy of Music* (Oxford, 1992).

[2] See Peter Walls '"Ill-compliments and arbitrary taste"? Geminiani's Directions for Performers', *Early Music* 14 (1986), 222.

tioned. Yet what makes the score format of Corelli Op. 5 and its analogues, imitations, and antecedants interesting is that it clearly did have a performing purpose. Op. 5 itself might be seen as spearheading a quite modern – but historically untypical – duality between the score as record of the composition and the score as a performing tool.[3] But this duality emerges at the end of a long period in which the score seemed first and foremost related to performance.

Examining the performance implications of this format means trying to work out how musicians in the 17th century regarded this very special kind of printed book. To pick up on Taruskin's binaries, this is a matter of examining a shifting equilibrium in the score's allegiance to text (the 'work') on the one hand and act ('performance') on the other.

It is interesting to consider the development of the convention of publishing this repertory in score. From one point of view, it goes back to Frescobaldi's *Primo libro delle canzoni* of 1628. This was published as a score in the same year that another publisher issued a set of parts.[4] The score 'brought it into the light' (as the title page puts it) on the initiative of Frescobaldi's pupil Bartolomeo Grassi 'for the convenience of performers on all sorts of instruments so that they will be able to see at the same time all of the parts', something which he says is 'very necessary for those who wish to play well'.[5] This is a remarkable statement: an acknowledgement at the outset of the benefits a score could bring to performance. Such a point of view seems to have been forgotten for almost the next century. Since Grassi's score covers the entire volume (and not just the canzoni à 1 or à 2), it is for my present purposes less directly relevant than publications which, in one way or another, are more genre-specific.

G. B. Fontana's *Sonate* of 1641 is one such publication.[6] The first six of the eighteen sonatas in this collection are for 'Violino solo' and the violin part is found, not just in the 'canto primo' part but in the 'partitura' – the score.[7] (The 'partitura' volume reverts to just a figured bass line for the sonatas involving more than one violin.) Here we see something that is effectively like the

---

[3] In *Playing with History* (Cambridge, 2002), John Butt explores the multiple perspectives on notation adopted at various points in history in a chapter entitled 'Negotiating between Work, Composer and Performer: Rewriting the Story of Notational Progress'.

[4] (1) *In Partitura Il Primo Libro delle Canzoni a una, due, tre e quattro voci. Per sonare con ogni sorte di Stromenti. Con dui Toccate in fine, una per sonare con spinettina sola, overo Liuto, l'altra Spinettina è Violino, overo Liuto, è Violino* (Rome: Masotti, 1628); and (2) *Il Primo Libro delle Canzoni, Ad una, due, trè e quattro voci. Accomodate, per sonare ogni sorte de stromenti* (Rome: Robletti, 1628).

[5] 'Hò posto questo volume in partitura accio sia comodo à i professori d'ogni sorte di strumenti, & che nell'istesso tempo possino vedere tutte le parti cosa necessarissima à chi desidera sonar bene.' Preface 'Alli studiosi dell'opera'. This volume also contains the Toccata for 'Spinettina è Violino', the first example of a genre that leads on the one hand to the Bach Sonatas for Harpsichord and Violin and, on the other, to Mondonville, the accompanied sonata, and eventual development of the duo sonata.

[6] *Sonate a 1. 2. 3. per il violino, o cornetto, fagotto, chitarone, violoncino o simile altro istromento* (Venice: Magni, 1641)

[7] In this part book the designation 'basso continuo' is also found at the head of Sonata 1.

standard modern format for violin and keyboard sonatas with a (single-line) part for the violinist and a part in score for the 'accompanist'. A similar arrangement can be seen in Agostino Guerrieri's *Sonate di violino*, Op. 1 (Venice: Gardano, 1673) where the sonatas for solo violin at the beginning of the collection are presented in score in the basso continuo part book (which reverts to a single figured-bass line thereafter).

Giovanni Leoni's *Sonate di violino a voce sola* (Rome: Mascardi, 1652) was the first publication to be devoted exclusively to sonatas for solo violin and basso continuo. The thirty-one sonatas are presented in score with a separate violin part. Pietro Degli Antonii's *Sonate a violino solo con il basso continuo per l'organo*, Op. 4 (Bologna, 1686) similarly has two part books – one for violin and one in score (with a figured bass).[8]

Uccellini's *Sonate over canzoni da farsi a violino solo*, Op. 5 (Venice: Vincenti, 1649) has a fascinating variant of the violin part plus score format. It contains one ingenious sonata 'à duoi violini'. Here, the single line in the violin part book is headed up 'Violino Pr[imo] e Sec[ondo]' with an instruction to the second violinist to read the part backwards from the end (Illus. 4.1 and Ex. 4.1). The partitura (or score) makes no attempt to decode the piece as I have done here; instead it simply carries a similar rubric to that which appears in the violin part (with the one amusing addition that, in the score, this instruction is printed upside down at the end of the piece).[9] Such an example seems to presuppose that the score is exclusively a performance tool – not a record of the composition.

One of the most interesting uses of a score format for the continuo line in conjunction with a single-stave violin part occurs in Antonio Veracini's *Sonate da camera a violino solo*, Op. 2. (Modena: Rosati, [*c.*1695]). Here Veracini presents all the slow movements in score but has just a figured bass line for the fast movements. Illus. 4.2 shows (at the top) the opening (Grave) of Sonata 5 in the 'violino' and beneath it, this same movement as it appears in the 'cimbalo o violone' part. It can also be seen that the concluding Allegro of the previous sonata is presented in this part book simply as a figured bass line. This mixed format conveys a very strong sense that continuo players needed to be ready to accommodate considerable flexibility from the solo violinist in Adagio movements (while rhythmically stable Allegros were, in that sense at least, less problematic). A presumption of improvised ornamentation would also make it particularly valuable for bass line players to be able to keep their eye on the basic outline of what the violinist was doing. In other words, it is the particularly soloistic features of the performance that seem to have prompted the presentation in score.

---

[8] A unique example of a score survives for his Op. 5 set which appeared in the same year as Op. 4 (and with a virtually identical title). We can't be sure, but my guess is that a separate violin part has been lost.

[9] The rubric at the head of the score reads 'The second violin begins at the end and is played backwards throughout.' ['Violino per il second Violino si prencipia al fine, & si sonna sempre all roversa.']

Illus. 4.1 Marco Uccellini, *Sonate over canzoni da farsi a violino solo*, Op. 5 (Venice: Vincenti, 1649), Sonata 13 'a duoi violini'; The Bodleian Library, University of Oxford, Mus. Sch. 157a–c

(a) canto

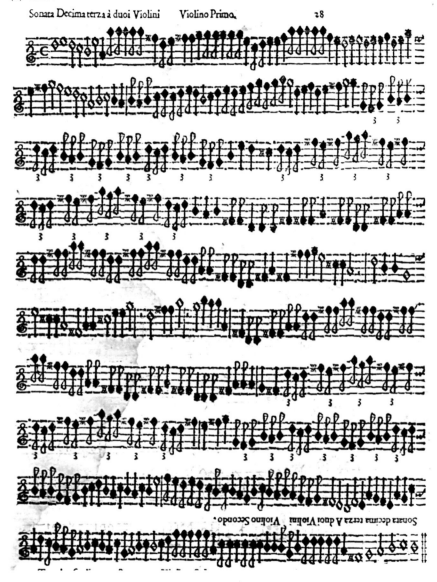

Veracini follows a similar procedure in his *Sonate da camera a due, violino, e violone, ò arcileuto, col basso per il cimbalo*, Op. 3 (Modena: Rosati, 1696). This, though, has separate partiture/bass line combinations in two part books designated respectively 'violone, ò arcileuto' and 'cimbalo'. Mostly the two parts are identical and it is clear that often exactly the same type has been used

Illus. 4.1 (*cont.*)

(b) partitura

for both versions of the partitura – and for the solo violin line (illus. 4.3). This, in fact, must have been one of the relatively few advantages of moveable type. Rather than re-engraving an additional part, the type could be moved into a different form for printing as a separate violin part (or, in the case of the 'violone ò arcileuto' part, the running title at the top could simply be changed). There are a few instances where the 'violone ò arcileuto' part has an independent, or at least an elaborated line. The last movement of Sonata III, for example, ends with a few bars in which more virtuoso writing is assigned to the string player an octave above an outline version of the same thing in the harpsichord part (ex. 4.2).[10] The second movement of Sonata 6 provides the most striking

---

[10] Note the use of tenor clef at this point in the violone etc. part. Other instances where the 'violone ò arcileuto' departs from the 'cimbalo' part are Sonata 4, ii (Vivace), Sonata V, ii (Vivace), and Sonata VI, ii (Vivace).

Ex. 4.1 Marco Uccellini, *Sonate over canzoni da farsi a violino solo*, Op. 5 (Venice, 1649): Sonata No. 13 'a duoi violini'

instance of divergence in the two bass-line parts. Here, the violone is withheld until bar 4 where it enters with an answer on the dominant. Eight notes into this answer the harpsichord part retreats to a skeletal version of the line, but it never establishes a separate bass-line identity. In other words, all the harmonic information about chord positions etc. is already there in the violone line (ex. 4.3).

These points of difference account for the provision of an additional (bass line) part for these sonatas 'a due' (rather than the part book/partitura arrangement of Op. 2). Here (anticipating an issue that I shall return to consider more fully shortly) it is worth noting that for most of the time the two bass-line parts are identical and, where they are not, the violone part is essentially an elaboration of the cimbalo part. Particularly when we allow for the fact that this kind of elaboration may be regarded as written-out examples of the kind of a practice envisaged (if not recommended) by figured bass treatises, it would seem foolhardy to conclude that Veracini necessarily intended a different line-up of bass-line instruments for Opus 2 and Opus 3.[11] In other words, a separate part is

---

[11] Borgir writes about instances where two bass parts are included in a publication: 'The inclusion of two bass parts is unusual and most often unnecessary. Continuo manuals recommend that the fast figuration be left to the bass-line instrument and that the chordal instrument play a simplified line of the kind written out by Gasparini. His reason for including two parts is that in some cases the continuo bass contains progressions that would not have been immediately clear if the player of the chordal instrument had used the florid part.' Borgir, *Performance of the Basso Continuo*, p. 43 (in chapter 5 on secular vocal music). Gasparini, in fact, writes 'I do not approve of the diminution of the bass itself, because it is very easy to miss or depart from the intention of the composer and from the proper spirit of the composition – and to offend the singer. But we say 'to accompany' advisedly: he who accompanies must take pride in the title of a good, solid accompanist, not of a spirited and agile performer. He may suit his fancy and unleash his brilliance when he plays alone, not when he accompanies; I, at least, intend to suggest how to play with

Illus. 4.2 Antonio Veracini, *Sonate da camera a violino solo*, Op. 2 (Modena: Rosati, [*c.*1695]), Sonata 5; The Bodleian Library, University of Oxford, Mus. Sch. e.552a–b

(a) violino

(b) cimbalo, o violone (also showing the end of Sonata 4)

Illus. 4.3 Antonio Veracini, *Sonate da camera a due, violino, e violone, ò arcileuto, col basso per il cimbalo*, Op. 3 (Modena: Rosati, 1696), Sonata 1; The Bodleian Library, University of Oxford, Mus. Sch. c.197a–c

(a) violino

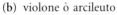

(b) violone ò arcileuto

Illus. 4.3 (*cont.*)
(c) cimbalo

Sonata I.

provided for Op. 3 only because for some of the time it would not be possible for the melodic bass-line player to read from the harpsichordist's score.

G. B. Degli Antonii used score format for two sets of pieces for solo violin and bass: his Op. 3 *Balletti . . . a' violino, e clavicembalo; ò violoncello* published in 1688 and for a similar collection published as Op. 6 in 1690.[12] On the other hand, his 1689 *Ricercate a' violino, e violoncello o' clavicembalo* has two part books, one for 'violino' and the other – with just the bass line – for 'violoncello ò clavicembalo'.[13]

grace and not with confusion.' Francesco Gasparini, *The Practical Harmonist at the Harpsichord*, trans. F. S. Stillings and ed. D. L. Burrows (New Haven and London: Yale University Press, 1963), p. 90. And see Lorenzo Penna: 'When accompanying the instruments that are playing it is not good to introduce movement, otherwise the listeners will not be able to hear the *concerto*, imitations, calls and ripostes between them', quoted by Allsop *The 'Trio' Sonata*, pp. 41–2.

[12] *Balletti a violino, e violoncello, o' clavicembalo*, Op. 6 (Bologna: Micheletti, 1690).

[13] Interestingly, the Bodleian copy of these part books has a slightly different description of the set as 'Duo di Munino à Violino, e Violone' written in ink in a hand which (from the signature-like inscription 'Gio Batt degl' Antonij') may be the composer's own. And, regardless of the printed title, the character of the bass part suggests that these works were conceived as string duos: violin and bass lines are equally active and the latter (which has no figures) changes frequently between tenor and bass clefs (something that, despite the insistence in figured bass manuals on keyboard players being fluent in all clefs, tends to indicate violone or violoncello writing).

Ex. 4.2 Antonio Veracini, *Sonate da camera a due, violino, e violone, ò arcileuto, col basso per il cimbalo*, Op. 3: Sonata No. 3, fifth movement, 'Aria vivace', last 6 bars

The publication of Arcangelo Corelli's Opus 5 *Sonate a violino e violone o cimbalo* seems suitably epoch-making to justify the composer's dating his dedication 1 January 1700. One of the many reasons for the volume's importance is that it utilised the technique of engraving. This, of course, was not new. Music engraving had first been used in Italy *c.* 1536 and it had been experimented with (but then abandoned, for the time being) in France and England early in the late 16th and early 17th centuries.[14] It was widely used in Germany and Austria from the 1660s on. But Italian presses had stuck with moveable type which placed quite severe restrictions on what composers were able to communicate in these publications.[15]

[14] See, for example, the *Intabolatura da leuto del divino Francesco da Milano* (before 1536) and *Parthenia* (London, 1613).

[15] See Peter Allsop, 'Violinistic Virtuosity in the 17th Century: Italian Supremacy or Austro-German Hegemony?' *Il saggiatore musicale* 3 (1996), 233–58.

Ex. 4.3 Antonio Veracini, *Sonate da camera a due, violino, e violone, ò arcileuto, col basso per il cimbalo,* Op. 3: Sonata No. 6, second movement, Vivace

There are, then, quite a variety of formats used before 1700 for solo violin and basso continuo sonatas (even within the output of a single composer): (1) separate single-line parts, (2) single-line parts with the bass part in score for slow movements, (3) scores with a single line part for the violin, and (4) a few instances of scores without (apparently) a separate violin part. But the prevalence of scores with separate violin parts is striking.

In a way, the most interesting thing about the score plus violin part publications (all of which may be regarded as antecedents of Corelli Op. 5) is that they may solve (or rather do not raise) the problem of how soloist and accompanist managed with only one copy of the music. Moreover, they suggest very strongly that the reason the score format became associated with this genre is an inbuilt expectation of soloistic flexibility. In this sense, the solo violin sonata parallels accompanied solo song (even more standardly presented in score format throughout the 17th and 18th centuries). Here iconography suggests that supplementary parts often were made for the singer. At least, there are numerous instances of singers (particularly women) holding music while their instrumental associates read off their own copies.[16] (The difficulty of making it clear that the subject of the painting is, in fact, singing may account for the artist's interest in having the singer hold some music.)

Having raised the question of part sharing, I wish to return to the question posed in my title and reformulate it as a query about the total number of musicians who would use one of these books simultaneously in performance. In other words, how did performers use these published editions?

My interest in this question was initially part of a more general attempt to make some progress with the vexed 'violone ò cimbalo' issue (examined in the previous chapter). Here I want to focus on the question of how several players got by with, apparently, just a single copy of the music

The likelihood (or otherwise) of part-sharing has emerged as an issue in various debates about the numbers of performers originally envisaged for particular repertories. The lack of evidence for singers' sharing music in Bach's choral works has been one strand in the case put by Joshua Rifkin and Andrew Parrott for the use in that repertory of solo singers (with occasional reinforcement from single-voice-per-part ripienists).[17] Of more direct relevance here, Peter Holman and Richard Maunder have used numbers of surviving parts to support their argument that musicians in 18th-century England thought of the concerto as a one-to-a part genre.[18] Moreover, Maunder has a larger study in preparation which will argue this kind of performance was the norm in most European centres, at least until the 1740s.[19]

With sonatas for solo violin, the question of instrumental doubling does not, of course, arise except as a possibility for the bass line. But starting to think about the way printed music was actually used has implications which go beyond the bass line. Even if we accept (or assume) that only one player – a harpsichordist or cellist – played the basso continuo line it is still something of a puzzle as to how that person and the violinist managed with (apparently) only one score.

Perhaps we need to bear in mind two broad categories of users of these publications. First, there are the amateurs – the dozens of well-bred enthusiasts who first 'dispeopled Italy of violins' and then used sonatas as study material. And then there are the professionals – the virtuosos who, apart from performing their own works, clearly felt that including a sonata by Corelli in a concert programme established their credibility as violinists in some way.[20]

[16] See, for instance, Antonio Domenico Gabbiani (1652–1762), 'Florentine Musicians', reproduced in *Early Music* 18 (1990), 429.

[17] See Parrott, *The Essential Bach Choir*, especially chapter 5 (pp. 43–57).

[18] Peter Holman and Richard Maunder, 'The Accompaniment of Concertos in 18th-Century England', *Early Music* 28 (2000), 637–50.

[19] *ibid.*, p. 637. Richard Maunder has kindly sent me a draft of his wider study.

[20] Le Blanc's judgement on Geminiani was that 'his playing was admired as much as the

It is just possible that some players acquired more than one copy of such scores. But there is no firm evidence for this. As far as I am aware, two copies of the same score looking obviously as if they have formed a cognate pair do not survive. Nicola Cosimi is an interesting figure here since his meticulous keeping of an income diary gives a uniquely complete picture of the economics of producing an edition of this kind. In this diary he recorded exactly how he disposed of the copies of his 1702 *Sonate da camera a violino e violone o cembalo*. He did present two to his patron, the Duke of Bedford, but these were ornately bound and so were unlikely to have been intended for practical use. And that seems to have been the end of paired copies. Cosimi had eleven other presentation copies bound and another twenty-five stitched between blue paper covers. James Sherrard sold nine copies for him and someone called P. Graham another three.[21] The persistent odd (rather than even) numbers here suggest that these were all disposed of (sold or given away) singly.

It is also possible that violinists routinely expected to copy parts from editions they had bought. If so, all such parts have sunk without trace – though I might mention here that in many places in the Bodleian Library's extensive collection of 17th-century Italian music one finds the instruction 'copiare' written in ink (usually, I might add, mid-sonata and sometimes even mid-movement).

There are a few instances where music sharing becomes an issue acknowledged within the edition. But this, as we shall see, tends to complicate rather than resolve the questions.

Michele Mascitti's *Sonate*, Op. 1 (1704) has a mixture of nine solo sonatas and *sonate à tre* (see above, p. 36). The score format is maintained throughout – but in a rather extraordinary way. For the solo violin sonatas the score is complete – just as we would expect. But the three *sonate à tre* occupy a three-stave system showing violin 1, violoncello, and basso continuo lines. The second violin line is not included in the score but was printed separately. What makes this arrangement so interesting is that the cello part is almost identical to the bass line apart from occasional elaborations. In other words, if the purpose of the score were to give a more-or-less complete picture of the composition, then Mascitti might have done better to print the occasionally more active cello part separately rather than the entirely-independent second violin part. Hence, this score is decidedly not a complete picture of the work; it is only a performance tool. Moreover, it seems to presuppose that cellist, keyboard player, and first violinist would play from the same part.

Mascitti did the same thing with his Op. 4 of 1707. Here he has a note preceding Sonata XI: 'The six sonatas which follow are the trios that the second

---

sonatas of Corelli which he performed'. Locatelli's rendering of the opening Adagio of Corelli Op. 5, No. 4, was, according to one account, enough to make a canary fall from its perch in a swoon of pleasure. And see Owain Edwards, 'The Response to Corelli's Music in Eighteenth-Century England', *Studia musicologica norvegica* 2 (1976), 77.

[21] These figures are taken from Lindgren, 'Nicola Cosimi in London', 239–41.

Illus. 4.4 Jean-Féry Rebel, *Sonates à violon seul mellées de plusieurs récits pour la Viole* (Paris: l'Auteur & Foucaut, 1713), Sonata 2, 'Viste'; Cliché Bibliothèque nationale de France, Paris

violinist will play from the separate part.'[22] The use of verb 'jouera' – rather than something like 'trouvera' – again points us directly towards the *use* of the edition. But what did the *first* violinist play from or alternatively, what did the bass line player(s) use? The second violin part, incidentally, has disappeared entirely (so we should not rule out the possibility that other separately copied – or separately printed – violin parts have also been lost).

Jean-Féry Rebel in his *Sonates à violon seul* of 1713 presents us with a different kind of conundrum. In the second sonata, the final movement marked 'Viste' departs from the score format and is instead set out on one opening with the Dessus (violin) part on p. 10 and the Basse facing it on p. 11. Rebel has a note at the beginning of the violin part reading 'It has been necessary to present this piece in separate parts in order to avoid page turns' (illus. 4.4).[23] Single-line parts do allow for greater compression, of course, since longer note values do not have to be aligned with groups of shorter notes in the other line. It is interesting to see not just an awareness of such practical concerns in the production of this edition but an underlying assumption that the players will be sharing a single printed volume.

The sonata volumes by the brothers Francoeur make it clear that several bass-line players read off the score. Both have numerous passages in which the *basse continue* utilises two voices, presumably through the use of two instruments. Ex. 4.4 is from the Louis Francoeur's *Premier Livre de sonates à violon seul et la basse* (Paris, 1715), while ex. 4.5, with its specification of 'viole' and 'b[asse] c[ontinue]', is from his younger brother's *deuxième livre* (1720).

Finally, it is interesting to come back to consider what kind of score the 1700 edition of Corelli Op. 5 is. It is an exquisitely-produced edition, one that would accord well with Corelli's acknowledged status as a 'classical' author. Hence, it might justifiably be regarded as an example of the score as picture of the work. But it is also a practically-minded edition. Except for the Folia variations, every page turn comes at the end of a movement – and is indicated by the instruction 'Volti'! Sometimes a blank stave is left at the end of a page to facilitate this; Sonata VII ends on p. 45 and a blank stave is left so that Sonata VIII can begin on a new page.

---

[22] 'Les Six Sonnates qui Suivent Sont les Trios que le Second Violon jouera dans la partie Separée.'

[23] 'On a eté obligé de mettre cette piece en parties separées pour ne pas tourner.'

Ex. 4.4 Louis Francoeur, *Premier Livre de sonates à violon seul et la basse* (Paris, 1715): Sonata III, iii 'Gavota', bars 27ff

Ex. 4.5 François Francoeur (le cadet), *Sonates a Violon seul avec la Basse Continue . . . II Livre* (Paris: author, 1720): Sonate III, ii Allemande

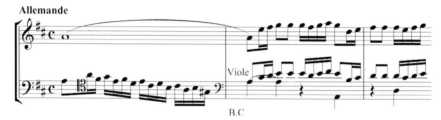

In the Folia variations, the page turns always come at the end of a variation (a nicety which is not preserved in all subsequent editions). As we might expect in a work this long, the turns are not always in very manageable places; pp. 63–4 divide across a pair of clearly-related variations. In practice this score was used by *at least* a violinist and a bass-line player. But, some of the examples alluded to earlier show that it is not impossible that scores that, on the face of it, are intended for similar resources may have been used by a violinist and *several* bass line players.

There are two dimensions to this question. First it is interesting to be confronted with situations which make it clear that the multivalent concept of the score that we take for granted is one that only gradually evolved. Second (and I am thinking again here of the 'violone ò cimbalo' issue), we can see that it makes drawing any conclusions about part-sharing in relation to the bass line a hazardous business if we cannot answer the more basic question of how a single booklet provided for the performance of both violin and basso continuo lines.

Of the two groups of users identified earlier, it is of course possible (even

Illus. 4.5 The Somis family trio, drawn by Lorenzo Somis (Current owner unknown but, if traced, will be acknowledged in any subsequent reprint. This image is reproduced from *Early Music* 12 (1984), 401)

likely) that professional violinists routinely memorised their parts. Such a practice would fit well with the expectation that the violinist would 'improvise' graces for the adagios. But our amateur users exploring this repertory would certainly have had to see the music somehow.

Paintings (surprisingly, perhaps) don't offer much help here. Although there are lots of pictures of single violinists (many of them with music open on a

Table 4.1 Sonatas for violin and basso continuo by members of the Somis family

Giovanni Battista Somis (1686–1763), *Sonate da camera a violino solo, e violoncello o cimbalo* (Amsterdam: Roger, *c.* 1617)

G. B. Somis, *Sonate da camera a violino solo, e violoncello o cimbalo*, Op. 2 (Turin: author, 1723)

G. B. Somis, *Sonate da camera a violino solo, e violoncello o cimbalo*, Op. 4 (Paris: Boivin, 1726)

G. B. Somis, *Sonate da camera a violino solo, e violoncello o cimbalo*, Op. 6 (Paris, 1734)

Giovanni [Francesco] Lorenzo Somis (1662–1736), *Opera prima di sonate a violino e violoncello o cimbalo* (Rome, 1722)

F. L. Somis, *Sonate da camera a violino solo e violoncello ò cimbalo*, Op. 2 (Paris, *c.* 1740)

table in front of them), there are very few from the late 17th or early 18th century that could conceivably depict the performance of a sonata for solo violin and basso continuo. It is one thing to imagine a cellist reading from music placed on the harpsichordist's music desk and being used by its player (a practice for which it is relatively easy to produce iconographic support) but quite another to envisage a violinist looking over the harpsichordist's shoulder. One interesting example, however, is the drawing of the Somis family trio (which must date from before 1736 – the year in which Francesco Lorenzo Somis, here seen playing the cello, died). All three are playing from a single score – and (for all that Cristina is gazing at the 'audience') the two men actually seem to be trying to read from it (illus. 4.5).

If the Somis family were playing their own music then there is quite a long list of possibilities – four sets of twelve sonatas by Giovanni Battista, who studied for a time with Corelli, and two (twenty sonatas altogether) by his younger brother Lorenzo, who was a pupil of Laurenti in Bologna (see table 4.1). All of these collections (and for that matter, Lorenzo's *Sonate à tre*, Op. 5 (Paris, 1734)) describe their basso continuo lines as being for 'violoncello o cembalo'.

I might leave the last word to Michel Corrette who in his double bass treatise recommends players to get themselves a good pair of spectacles. Although the treatise was published late in the 18th century, Corrette claims to be recalling an incident that had taken place some years earlier. His (presumably greatly embroidered) anecdote brings home the difficulties of having too many musicians clustered around a single score:

> I trust that it is pointless to warn those who wear spectacles and who play beside the harpsichord to have a pair for long distance. I remember having been at a concert in a little English town where I saw a trio of bespectacled musicians [grouped] at the harpsichord with each player jostling for a view of the music desk

with their heads. The result was that their heads were banging into each other. The singer, who was a castrato newly arrived from Italy, not finding it easy to see – despite having three pairs of spectacles on his nose – took it into his head to sit astride the hunchbacked harpsichordist. But this advantage lasted for hardly any time at all, because unfortunately the Archlute player at the side of this unwieldy group had a wooden leg, and as he played he wasn't able to see any better than the two others despite the telescope which he wore on the end of his beetroot-coloured nose, with the result that by dint of marking the beat, sometimes on the back of the castrato sometimes on that of the hunchback and in the process of trying to indicate to them in the Hebrew manner to turn the page for the da capo, his wooden leg happened to slide which caused them all to fall like Phaeton. A lover of novelty who witnessed it all began to call out 'Bravo, bravo!'[24]

---

[24] M. Corrette, *Méthodes pour apprendre à jouër de la contre-basse à 3, à 4. et à 5 cordes* (Paris: Chez Mlle Castagnery, 1773; 2nd ed. 1781; repr. Geneva: Minkoff, 1977), p. 4. 'Je crois qu'il est inutile d'avertir ceux qui portent des lunettes et qui jouent à coté du Clavecin, d'en avoir de longue vüe. Je me souviens d'avoir eté dans un Concert d'une petite Ville d'Angleterre ou je vis un Trio de Lunettes au Clavecin, dont chacun des concertants se disputoit la preseance du pupitre avec la teste: de sorte qu'après que les testes se furent heurtteés l'une contre l'autres, le chanteur qui etoit un Castra nouvellement arrivé d'italie ne se trouvant pas à son aise pour voir, quoi qu'avec trois paires de Lunettes sur le nez, savisa de se mettre à califourchon sur la Bosse du Clavessiniste; mais cette avantage ne luy dura gueres, parce que celuy qui jouoit de l'Archiluth à côté de ce groupe gigantesque avoit mal'heuresement pour lui une jambe de bois, et com[m]e il jouoit de bout et malgré le Teslescope qu'il portait sur son nez de beterave ne voioit pas mieux que les deux autres, de sorte qu'à force de battre la mesure, tantôt sur le dos du Castra et tantôt sur celui du Bossu et pour leur faire signe de tourner le feuillet au da Capo à la maniere Habraïque, sa jambe de bois vint à glisser ce qui leurs fit faire à tous la chûte de Phaeton. un Amateur de la nouveauté qui etoit là Spectateur se mit a crier, Bravo, bravo.'

5. The well intentioned musician

A few years ago Charles Rosen, in his disarmingly outrageous way, suggested that 'The antiquarian and the opera buff have stopped short of insisting on a return to the castrato . . . only because they think they have no chance of getting away with it.' This was by way of amplifying an assertion that 'There is often a lack of frankness about the special pleading for old performance practice and old instruments' that amounted to a failure to face up to the fact that 'an "authentic" performance of a Scarlatti opera . . . is not going to be approached in this life'.[1] Adolescent males of today hardly need the strong arm of the law or even the moral scruples of early music and opera buffs to protect them from the mutilation that for centuries was inflicted on so many of their counterparts (many more, so we are told, than subsequently enjoyed successful singing careers). But anyone who has listened to the plaintively melancholy voice of Alessandro Moreschi (apparently past his prime and singing quaintly unsuitable songs into primitive recording equipment) must surely have wondered what the great castrati of the 18th-century stage really sounded like. For all that basic human decency makes the recreation of the castrato voice repugnant, the fact remains that there is a vast repertory of brilliant arias created especially for these artists – in response, one assumes, to their particular sound and their technical abilities – that we can never hear as it was conceived. All of this must now be assigned to women (which was a normal practice, incidentally, when the right castrato was not on hand) or to counter-tenors (*not* an historical solution). (It has been interesting to note the ever-increasing virtuosity of counter-tenors singing operatic repertory since the 1970s. One of the ironies of the early music movement is that it has nurtured an unhistorical category of specialist performers.)

The use of castrati is far from being the only feature of historical performance that is destined to remain in the past. The most obvious example lies in orchestral and operatic direction. Nobody is ever likely to reinstate the French practice of keeping the ensemble together by the having the *maître de musique* audibly beat time. This, famously, proved fatal for Lully who, 'rapping forcefully' with his cane while directing his Te Deum in 1687, stabbed himself in the foot and thus inflicted a wound that turned gangrenous. Despite its

---

[1] From a review of the edition of *The Operas of Alessandro Scarlatti* (Cambridge, Mass., 1974–85) that appeared in *The New Yorker*. I noted the passage quoted when I read the review but, unfortunately, have been unable to retrace the original.

proven health risks, the practice of banging a cane on the floor continued through the 18th century. Baron Grimm complained in 1753 that the music director at the Paris Opéra made a noise as if he were splitting wood, adding that no matter how loudly the beat was rapped out the musicians were never together.[2] Fifteen years later in his *Dictionnaire de Musique*, Jean-Jacques Rousseau referred approvingly to Grimm's comments and noted (in the entry on 'bâton de mesure') that 'At the Opera in Paris it is not a question of a roll of paper but of a very large wooden staff which the music director beats with force so as to be heard a long way off.'[3] Complaints about this method of holding performances together continued into the early 19th century.[4]

Even something which seems so evidently undesirable had its defenders, however. When, in the 1760s, the celebrated violinist Pierre Gaviniès managed to put an end to the practice with the orchestra at the Concert Spirituel, the *Mercure de France* greeted the reform with scepticism, describing it as an advantage which 'undoubtedly has its price':

> They have done away with marking the beat with a cane in all the symphonies just as the Italians do . . . [This is] much less of a boon to true musicians than to those who dabble in this art, blindly idolising everything which is foreign to our national practice.[5]

It was not just French conductors who made more noise than we would nowadays find acceptable. Audience behaviour, too, was often of a kind that would not be tolerated today (except, perhaps, when musical groups are engaged to perform 'background music' at corporate receptions and the like). When Nicola Matteis first arrived in England in the 1670s good friends had to take him aside to explain that he was developing a reputation for arrogance by his insistence that his listeners should be quiet when he played. An anonymous

---

[2] Fridrich Melchior von Grimm, *Le petit prophète de Boehmischbroda* (Paris, 1753), pp. 10–11.

[3] J. J. Rousseau, *Dictionnaire de Musique* (Paris, 1768), pp. 48–9. The article in which Rousseau elaborates on Grimm's satire is 'Battre la mesure' (pp. 50–1).

[4] See D. J. Koury, *Orchestral Performance Practices in the 19th Century: Size, Proportions, and Seating* (Ann Arbor, 1986), pp. 76–7.

[5] *Mercure de France* (September 1762), p. 181; Quoted by Lionel de La Laurencie, *L'École Française de Violon de Lully à Viotti*, 3 vols. (Paris, 1922–4) ii, 285. 'On est dispensé de marquer la mesure avec le bâton dans toutes les symphonies, ainsi que cela se pratique en Italie . . . avantage qui, sans doute, a son prix.' This was 'beaucoup moins merveilleux pour les vrais musiciens que pour les demisavants dans cet art, aveuglément idolâtres de tout ce qui est étranger à la pratique nationale'. The practice has found an unlikely (albeit tongue-in-cheek) defender in Charles Rosen: 'On the other hand, no one as far as I know has revived the French eighteenth-century operatic practice of keeping orchestra and singers together by a loud banging on the floor with a big stick. Of course, the practice was deplored even at the time as distracting in soft passages, and it was not strictly part of the music, but surely it was a part of the auditory experience less incidental than the underground rumbling of the subway in Carnegie Hall, or the whine of an overhead plane at an open-air concert. A good thump at the beginning of every bar must have added definition and even induced a little rhythmic excitement.' ('The Benefits of Authenticity', pp. 214–15.)

account from 1785 of that 'army of generals', the Mannheim orchestra, makes one wonder how anyone ever realised that they played with the precision for which they became famous:

> That evening there was an academy, or what I would call a concert at court . . . Around and to the right of the windows card tables had been set up, and to the left was the space for the orchestra, raised somewhat off the floor and encircled with a railing. After six o'clock the court entered, the elector and electress, the dowager electress of Bavaria, and the ladies-in-waiting and cavaliers. Then the music began, and at the same time everyone began to play cards . . . There was such a crush of people that I at first gave up any hope of getting through to see their highnesses up close. But then I decided, together with some priests to endure and also mete out some elbows in the ribs – and in this manner we finally came close to the two princely tables.
>
> And what did I see there? Well, Carl Theodor in a new robe, just as in former times. But the electresses . . . were seated so that I was unable to see their faces. . . So I waited patiently, and in the meantime listened to the orchestra, which through the magical tones of one Mamselle Schäfer reconciled me to my fate. The elector stood up every now and then and went from table to table with a cheerful laugh. Finally, the two electresses had the honour to satisfy my curiosity by getting up from their seats and going up to the orchestra, giving me the opportunity to examine their faces to my heart's content . . .'[6]

When Charles Burney went to the opera in Naples in 1770 he complained that he could not hear the singers, even though 'on account of the King and the Queen being present, the people were much less noisy than on common nights'.[7]

At the first performance of his 'Paris' Symphony (K[6] 300a) in 1778, Mozart had an appreciative audience – but not a quiet one. He reported to his father that 'just in the middle of the first Allegro there was a passage which I felt sure must please. The audience were quite carried away – and there was a tremendous burst of applause. But as I knew, when I wrote it, what effect it would surely produce, I had introduced the passage again at the close – when there were shouts of "Da capo".'[8] Mozart's expectations of audience behaviour were very different from ours – he was as confident of applause mid-movement as a jazz player today finishing a solo break might be.

There are at least three types of defunct musical or concert practice that need to be distinguished here. First, there are those that are dependant on social conditions that no longer prevail and are incapable of revival. In the case of the use of castrati we confront a practice that does impinge on the original conception of the repertory in question. The second type of defunct practice

---

[6] Quoted from Neal Zaslaw, ed., *The Classical Era*, Man and Music (London, 1989), pp. 226–7.
[7] Charles Burney, *Music, Men and Manners in France and Italy 1700*, ed. E. H. Poole (London, 1974), p. 193.
[8] To Leopold Mozart, 3 July 1778. *The Letters of Mozart and his Family*, trans. Emily Anderson, 3rd ed. (London: Macmillan, 1985), p. 558.

also arises from a change in social conditions but (in the case of audience behaviour, anyway) seems rather more incidental to the character of what is being performed. The interest of such a change resides in the recognition that it may signify a different way of listening to music, or even a revised attitude to what music actually is. Third, there are those changes (like audible conducting) that have been abandoned because of a (usually tacit) agreement that better ways of doing things have been worked out.[9] Such a change involves the rejection of features of the original performances that are judged not to constitute an integral part of the musical intentions embodied in the score.

This third category is of special interest since it is subject to constant re-evaluation. Performers, some performers at least, might realise tomorrow or next year that reabsorbing an aspect of early technique or expressive vocabulary (not to mention reverting to elements of instrument technology currently considered obsolete) could bring musical rewards. And even seemingly incidental features sometimes turn out to have some musical value. From time to time early music groups are enjoined to don period costume. This can seem not just irrelevant, but distracting in its creation of associations that work against the character of the music itself. The semiotics of 18th-century costume, at least to the uninitiated, tend towards the communication of emotional restraint and pointless ornament. Yet it would be foolish to deny that the historically 'right' clothes could teach singers something about how to move and even (off the stage) instrumentalists something about the management of their instruments. Discussions about how to hold the baroque violin, for example, rarely factor in the impact of wearing musicians' livery. Quantz provided the following tip for flute players whose embouchure is made slippery by perspiration induced by performance nerves and warm weather: 'Quickly . . . let the flautist wipe his mouth and the flute clean, then touch his hair or wig and rub the fine powder clinging to his finger upon his mouth. In this way the pores are stopped and he can continue playing without great hindrance.'[10] Such advice does not by itself furnish a compelling reason for getting into a wig and tights – but it is nevertheless interesting to have an 18th-century informant suggesting a very

---

[9] 'Performers may want to know how Beethoven's concertos were done in his own day out of an honest desire to respect the composer's wishes. And they may do so without any intention of allowing historical verisimilitude to displace all other values, of single-mindedly pursuing that elusive and by now rather tarnished Holy Grail of "authentic" historical performance. The difficulties attendant to such a pursuit, of course, are legion. Should the test of historical accuracy extend to the external circumstances of the performance? If so, some of Beethoven's concertos would apparently require renting a cold hall and seeking out amateur string players who would be permitted only a single rehearsal. And if the goal is limited to replicating as closely as we can the *sound* of Beethoven's performances, those underrehearsed string players are surely still a factor, as are the weak-sounding pianos of which Beethoven perpetually complained, and above all, far-reaching uncertainty about the very notes the composer played in the free-flight of improvisation.' (Plantinga, *Beethoven's Concertos*, p. 280.)

[10] Quantz, *On Playing the Flute*, p. 199.

18th-century remedy for a problem that recurs as a factor in the success or otherwise of a musical performance.

Obviously the ultimate aim is not to clone musical performances from times past. If it were, then we would want to bang our canes on the floor. As I have already noted, the reason that certain historical practices are not thought worth reviving is that they are not perceived as enhancing any musical result. But this kind of selectivity takes us to the heart of the enterprise: the underlying ideals and motivation for period instrument performance. There is implicitly an acknowledgement that musical judgement – *subjective* judgement – is always going to be part of the equation. So, what, broadly speaking, is the purpose of the commitment to historical awareness in performance and how does this affect the particular historical features that are selected as desirable constituents of such a performance?

The answers to those questions might vary from one person to another. As I see it, though, the main reason for a performer to be interested in historical performance practice is that it holds out the possibility of finding the most satisfying way of performing good music. It may also help us to recognise what is 'good music' (thus contributing to the perpetual revision and extension of the canon). With such deliberately bald statements I betray (unashamedly) an allegiance to a clutch of very unfashionable concepts – not just the notion of a value-endowed canon itself but the idea that a performer's responsibility might consist in being faithful to the work being performed or, in fact, of adhering as closely as possible to the composer's intentions.

Before attempting any justification of such a position, I would like to summarise some of the relevant historical attitudes first to the work concept and then to the idea of honouring composer intention.

James Johnson tells us that audiences went quiet (at least in Paris) around 1800 and that that reflected a new reverential attitude to musical works as aesthetic objects.[11] He and others have argued that not until after a Kantian aesthetic perspective had been developed was it possible to regard musical works as artistic productions that could be detached from their social milieu. At any rate, for music before *c.* 1800 the very concept of a 'work' has been called in question. Robert Morgan, for example, writes:

> Early music was not intended to be performed in concert. Indeed, if we take the notion of context at all seriously, we are left with the painful realization that *any* concert performance of this music constitutes a basic perversion of its original intentions. The authentic function of the music – its *raison d'être* – is lost to us and cannot be reconstituted. As soon as we place these works in a museum, we wrench them out of their own frame and utterly transform their original meaning.[12]

The double metaphor here – of wrenching works 'out of their own frame' to

---

[11] J. Johnson, *Listening in Paris, a Cultural History* (Berkeley and Los Angeles, 1995).
[12] In Kenyon, ed., *Authenticity*, p. 71.

place them in an art gallery – is counter-intuitive (deliberately, I presume). And the broad sweep of the expression 'Early Music' is alarming. But clearly the accusation of de-contextualising places a question mark over the ultimate value of historical reconstruction. Performing music in a concert setting dislocated from its function (as an element in the liturgy, for example) is seen as virtually invalidating the historical verisimilitude of what is taking place.

This is a central theme of Lydia Goehr's book, *The Imaginary Museum of Musical Works*. Goehr's purpose is to examine the implications of what she sees as the profound change in sensibility that appears to have taken place at the end of the 18th century. She emphasises the way in which Kant's *Critique of Judgement* (the *Kritik der Urteilskraft*, 1790) provided a framework for the aesthetic appreciation of works of art – nothing less than the contemplation of art in a disinterested manner, freed from any considerations of external purpose. This has been taken to imply that it is an anachronism even to think about autonomous works of art before about 1800 – at least, not without acknowledging that this was an emerging, rather than a self-evident, concept. The apparently new aesthetic consciousness provided the *sine qua non* for the development of the *Werktreue* concept, first articulated by E. T. A. Hoffmann in his seminal essay on 'Beethoven's Instrumental Music' in 1813:

> The genuine artist lives only for the work, which he understands as the composer understood it and which he now performs. He does not make his personality count in any way. All his thoughts and actions are directed towards bringing into being all the wonderful, enchanting pictures and impressions the composer sealed in his work with magical power.[13]

Such a concept is clearly apposite to the idea of an authenticity motivated by the ideal of being faithful to the implicit intentions of the composer. Yet, according to Goehr, to place early music in a concert hall (the 'Imaginary Museum') and thus to apply to it a 'work' mentality with all the consequences that that has for approaching its performance is already to violate its original purpose. She writes, 'since about 1800, it has been the rule to speak of early music anachronistically; to retroactively impose upon this music concepts developed at a later point in the history of music. Implicit existence has become here essentially a matter of retroactive attribution.'[14]

Since the publication of her book Goehr has been at pains to clarify that she had not intended to deny the existence of recognisable musical artefacts (works) before 1800, but rather to stress that the concept of the musical work as it emerged at the end of the 18th century had a regulatory force, one which impacted on, for example, performer and audience behaviour.[15] Her identifica-

---

[13] Quoted by Goehr, *Imaginary Museum*, p. 1.

[14] ibid., p. 115.

[15] See Lydia Goehr, ' "On the Problems of Dating" or "Looking Backward and Forward with Strohm" ', in *The Musical Work: Reality or Invention?*, ed. M. Talbot (Liverpool, 2000), pp. 231–46. See also *The Imaginary Museum*, p. 113: 'Nor does it [the central claim of this book] imply that composers producing music in centuries prior to the nineteenth were not

tion of a major perceptual shift has, however, been taken up – exultantly – by others. Taruskin, for instance, felt it was grist to his mill in his efforts to demonstrate the wrong-headedness of a reverence for historical detail:

> The 'work concept,' as Lydia Goehr so excellently shows in her recent treatise on the philosophy of musical museum-culture, regulates not only our musical attitudes but also our social practices. It dictates the behavior of all members of the classical music community, whether composers, performers, or listeners. It imposes a strict etiquette, for instance, on audiences. On performers it inflicts a truly stifling regimen by radically hardening and patrolling what had formerly been a fluid, easily-crossed boundary between the performing and composing roles.[16]

Goehr's analysis of changing currents in aesthetic thinking carries conviction. But Taruskin's colonisation of her thesis as a philosophical objection to performers' goals approaches caricature. It is in the last sentence of the quoted paragraph that the supposedly coercive effect of the dominant aesthetic attitude is made to seem most threatening. Yet here Taruskin's evocation of a 'stifling regimen' rides rough shod over the obvious – that an ideal of respecting the integrity of an artistic work in certain repertories would necessarily involve striving to maintain at least the practised illusion of an informed confluence of composing and performing roles. It is one thing to treat every note as sacrosanct in a Bach two-part Invention and quite another to take such an attitude in a Corelli Adagio. I shall return to the question of how to read music later in this chapter. First (and without wishing to challenge the broad outline of Goehr's case) it is worth reviewing the pre-history of the concepts of the autonomous work, the canon, and fidelity to composers' intentions as a step on the way to defending the musical worth of attempting to discover the original intent of the scores we perform.

The concept of an artistic 'work' was alive and well long before Kant and Hoffmann. After all, the word 'opus' – work – was being applied to musical compositions as early as the 15th century (with Tinctoris's *Liber de Arte Contrapuncti*, according to Davd Fuller in *The New Grove II*) and by the mid-17th century it had become a standard way of asserting the importance of (usually) a collection of pieces by a single composer.[17] By then, the Italian form of this same word – opera – had shed all its qualifiers (*opera scenica* or *opera*

---

producing works. Thus, despite the story of its emergence into a regulative concept in the late-eighteenth century, the use of the work-concept is not confined to products only of this and later periods.'

[16] Taruskin, *Text and Act*, p. 10.

[17] Reinhard Strohm's 'Looking Back at Ourselves: The Problem with the Musical Work-Concept', in Talbot, ed., *The Musical Work*, gives an historiographical account of the reification of the work concept and makes the point that 'the historical narratives that diagnose a major watershed or categorical breakthrough in the development of the work-concept and related phenomena around 1800 evade the burden of proof that ought to be placed on them: to show that previous phenomena were essentially – philosophically – different' (pp. 150–1).

regia) to become the normal way of describing an entirely-sung and staged musical drama.

Ben Jonson was mocked for the presumption implicit in bringing out his collected *Works* in folio (1616). Earlier, in publishing his *Masques of Blackness and of Beauty*, Jonson's stated purpose had been to give a more enduring life to artistic works whose only existence otherwise would have been a single spectacular, but essentially unrepeatable, performance:

> The honor, and splendor of these *spectacles* was such in the performance, as could those houres have lasted, this of mine, now, had been a most vnprofitable worke. But (when it is the fate, euen of the greatest, and most absolute births, to need, and borrow a life of posteritie) . . . I adde this later hand, to redeeme them as well from Ignorance, as Enuie, two common euills, the one of *censure*, the other of *oblivion*.[18]

Here, publication extends into perpetuity the 'profit' to be derived from something that otherwise would have been ephemeral. The same impulse lies behind the publication of music for the *Balet comique de la royne* in 1581, the 1689 Florentine intermedii, or – for that matter – of Peri and Caccini's scores for *Euridice* or Monteverdi's for *Orfeo*. Monteverdi, in fact, begins his dedication to Francesco Gonzaga by writing 'The story of Orfeo, which has already been represented musically under Your Highness's auspices on the confined stage in the Academia of the Invaghiti, [ought] now to appear before all mankind in the grand theatre of the universe . . .'[19] In all of these cases, it is an assertion that these events deserve admiration as artistic conceptions that justifies publication, not the prospect of repeat performances in the future. (The list of instruments at the beginning of Monteverdi's score has a very different significance from the apparently similar listings found at the head of most modern orchestral scores.) It is interesting to watch publication as a blueprint for revival in performance emerging and then establishing an equilibrium with publication as a way of documenting an historical event.

Heinrich Schütz petitioned the Duke of Saxony in 1651 'to grant that I be graciously accorded a less onerous position, that I be exonerated from the regular service of the choir (in order that, for the honour of my name, I may dedicate myself to collecting, completing and printing the musical works begun in my youth)'.[20] Just three years earlier, in his preface to *Geistliche Chor-Music*, he had conveyed a strong sense of awareness of a canon (even employing the word 'Canonisirte', 'canonised'): 'for the example of all, I should like to point to those

[18] Ben Jonson, *The Characters of Two Royall Masques* (London, 1608), lines 1–14. Jonson masque texts provide other instances of his determination that his literary conception should outlive the vicissitudes of a particular performance; see my *Music in the English Courtly Masque 1604–1640* (Oxford, 1996), pp. 17–20.

[19] 'La favola d'Orfeo che già nell'Academia de gl'Invaghiti sotto gl'auspitii di V. A. fù sopra angusta Scena musicalmente rappresentata, dovendo hora comparire nel gran Teatro dell'universo à far mostra di se à tutti gl'huomini, . . .', *La Favola d'Orfeo* (Mantua, 1609).

[20] Quoted in Lorenzo Bianconi, *Music in the Seventeenth Century*, trans. David Bryant (Cambridge, 1982), p. 296.

Italian musicians whose names, so to speak, have been canonized by the opinion of the very best composers as also to the other *classici autores*, both ancient and modern, whom, with their excellent – not to say – incomparable – works, shine clearly forth as exponents of both styles of composition for whomever wishes to study and examine them with diligence and let himself be guided down the straight and narrow path of contrapuntal studies'.[21] Henry Peacham's extended discussion of the composers 'whom among other authors you should imitate and allow for the best' in *The Compleat Gentleman* (1623) is another attempt to summarize the canon (though, as with Schütz, the composers listed are presented as models for emulation rather than simply for admiration).[22]

John Barnard's *First Book of Selected Church Musick*, an anthology of 'master-peeces' written for the Anglican liturgy and published on the eve of the Civil War, conveys a strong sense of a canon that needs both faithful documentation and (especially given the part-book format of the publication) continued performance. In his dedication, Barnard wrote:

> [Queen Elizabeth's] reigne brought forth . . . Famous Composers in Church-Musick. Since which time . . . the choycest Master-peeces left us in Hymnes, Anthems, and Services, these my labours have averted from the danger of perishing, or corrupting in erronious and manuscript obscurity, and bound them up in a safe bundle of perpetuall memory . . .[23]

What this particular corner of print culture tells us is that many writers and composers thought their works should claim an allegiance to *ars longa* rather than *vita brevis*; that, in other words, they should be regarded as autonomous artistic works as we still understand that idea. Thus, the work-concept has an ancient lineage.[24]

So too does the contemplation of artefacts in specialised environments conveying (pre-Kant) an expectation of aesthetic interest and evaluation. As Peter Vergo has observed, 'The collections [which the princes and statesmen of Renaissance Europe] amassed . . . the *studiolos* and cabinets of curiosities . . . were museums *avant la lettre*.'[25] And the attitudes and modes of behaviour

---

[21] Quoted in Bianconi, *Music in the Seventeenth Century*, p. 299. The original German reads: '. . . besondern will ich vielmehr alle und iede an die von allen vornehmsten Componisten gleichsam Canonisirte Italianische und andere Alte und Newe Classicos Autores hiermit gewiesen haben als deren fürtreffliche und unvergleichliche Opera denen jenigen die soche absetzen und mit Fleiß sich darrinnen umbsehen werden; in einem und dem andern *Stylo* als ein helles Liecht fürleuchten und auff den rechten Weg zu dem *Studio Contrapuncti* aufführen können.' (*Geistliche Chormusik 1648*, Neue Ausgabe sämtlicher Werke 5 (Kassel and Basle, 1955), p. vii.)

[22] See O. Strunk, *Source Readings in Music History*, rev. L. Treitler (New York and London, 1998), p. 349.

[23] John Barnard, *The First Book of Selected Church Musick* (London, 1641).

[24] The (emergent) idea of the canon can be traced as far back as the late 13th century when Anonymous IV identified Leonin and Perotin as the greatest composers respectively of organum and discant.

[25] Peter Vergo, ed., *The New Museology* (London, 1989), p. 2.

Table 5.1 Structure of the Vespers service

Antiphon 1 (plainchant)
Psalm 1 (elaborately composed setting)
Repeat of Antiphon 1 (plainchant) [often substituted by an instrumental sonata or
    vocal concerto]

Antiphon 2 (plainchant)
Psalm 2 (elaborately composed setting)
Repeat of Antiphon 2 (plainchant) [often substituted by an instrumental sonata or
    vocal concerto]

Antiphon 3 (plainchant)
Psalm 3 (elaborately composed setting)
Repeat of Antiphon 3 (plainchant) [often substituted by an instrumental sonata or
    vocal concerto]

Antiphon 4 (plainchant)
Psalm 4 (elaborately composed setting)
Repeat of Antiphon 4 (plainchant) [often substituted by an instrumental sonata or
    vocal concerto]

Antiphon 5 (plainchant)
Psalm 5 (elaborately composed setting)
Repeat of Antiphon 5 (plainchant) [often substituted by an instrumental sonata or
    vocal concerto]

Hymn (plainchant)

Antiphon for the Magnificat (plainchant)
Magnificat
Repeat of Antiphon for the Magnificat (plainchant) [often substituted by an
    instrumental sonata or vocal concerto]

provided for by museums clearly pre-date Elias Ashmole's founding in Oxford
in 1683 of what is credited with being the first modern institution of this kind.
In *Twelfth Night*, Sebastian – having been shipwrecked in Illyria where
(naturally) he has no pressing business – suggests to his companion Antonio
that they fill in time looking at the equivalent of our museums and art galleries:

> . . . What's to do?
> Shall we go see the relics of this town?
> . . .
> I pray you let us satisfy our eyes
> With the memorials and the things of fame
> That do renown this city.   [III. iii. 18–24]

This is a recreational activity and we surely recognise a continuity between
Sebastian's interest in 'memorials' and 'relics' and our museum culture with its
commitment to detached aesthetic contemplation. Perhaps we should not
forget in all of this the etymology of the word museum as a temple dedicated
to the muses, which in its 3rd-century BC Alexandrian prototype housed a
community of literary people and scientists whose library was intended both to

preserve the literary heritage of centuries and to aid the regeneration of poetry in their own age.[26]

Compositions produced for quite particular functional and (ostensibly at least) non-musical contexts, were nevertheless regarded both by their creators and their 'audiences' as having an intrinsic value that complemented or even outstripped their usefulness as an element in a liturgy or state ceremonial. The pull between music as sensual experience (that is, music as music) and music as the vehicle for divine praise or edification has troubled religious figures from Augustine on – with Martin Luther, John Calvin, and Pope Gregory XIII (in the wake of the Council of Trent) as notable contributors to debate on the subject. Monteverdi, explaining his reasons for not wishing to return to a post in Mantua in 1620, wrote that not only did the Venetians pay him on time and defer to his judgement about the engagement of singers or organists, but that they actually seemed to like his music: 'when I am about to perform either chamber or church music,' he wrote, 'I swear . . . that the entire city comes running'.[27]

Much of the church music Monteverdi had in mind was written for the Vespers service which could fairly be described as a concert with a religious pretext (see table 5.1). It was almost continuously musical. Moreover, the Venetian practice of substituting instrumental pieces or vocal concerti for the repeated antiphon at the end of each psalm setting (a practice frowned upon by Rome) seems a good indication that their priorities were at least as much musical as devotional. The enraptured accounts written by foreign visitors to Venice are further testimony to the fact that this was being enjoyed *as music* (especially since some of these accounts originate with Protestants whom we might expect to have been alienated by the specifics of the liturgical context). In 1611 Thomas Coryat described the music for the feast of St Roch as 'so good, so delectable, so rare, so super excellent that it did ravish and stupefy all those strangers that never heard the like'.[28] André Maugars was similarly impressed with the performances of music in the *stile recitativo* that he heard when he visited Rome in 1639:

> The best I have heard was in the Saint Marcel Chapel where there is a congregation of the Brothers of the Holy Crucifix, composed of the greatest nobles of Rome, who as a consequence have the power to bring together every rarest thing in Italy and indeed, the most excellent musicians are proud of being there and the most excellent composers seek the honour of having their compositions performed there, and try to present what is best in their studios.[29]

[26] See R. Pfeiffer, *History of Classical Scholarship from the Beginnings to the End of the Hellenistic Age* (Oxford, 1968), pp. 96ff.

[27] Denis Stevens, ed., *The Letters of Claudio Monteverdi* (Oxford, 1995), p. 191.

[28] In *Coryat's Crudities* excerpted in Carol MacClintock, ed., *Readings in the History of Music in Performance* (Bloomington and London, 1979), p. 115.

[29] From Maugars, *Response faite à un curieux sur le sentiment de la musique d'Italie*, excerpted in MacClintock, *Readings*, p. 119. Later in the same 'letter', Maugars refers to 'the great Monteverdi, master composer of the church of St. Mark' and undertakes to procure 'some new work of his'.

Here, it seems, the religious order, performers, composers, and audience were all complicit in ignoring the functionality of church music and enjoyed it as what we would now characterise as an aesthetic experience.

Those who wish to stress a change in the way we apprehend musical performance tend to exaggerate the difference between the conditions under which composers worked in an age of aristocratic patronage and the circumstances surrounding the production of new works today. Goehr, for example, writes 'The very idea of having to enquire about the conditions for which one is to compose one's music, what sort and how many instruments one is writing for, and how long one's composition should last, is not met with full comprehension today. But once it was quite normal and, furthermore, it made sense.'[30] Goehr's implication that these conditions would now be regarded as overly restrictive is not, in fact, sustainable. A huge number of commissions for new pieces now are at least as prescriptive as anything envisaged here (with instrumentation, duration, date due, date of first performance, and subsequent performing rights all specified).

For all that the specific notion of fidelity to the composer's concept, or *Werktreue*, was not clearly articulated until the early 19th century, it does not follow that it is completely anachronistic to apply it to music of earlier periods. The promulgation of the philosophical concepts in the late 18th century should not be mistaken for actual historical change. There is, as I have endeavoured to show, ample evidence to suggest that composers, performers, and listeners have long had a sense of musical compositions as works of art that elicit appreciation as such. The justification for period-instrument performance (if it needs one) may, accordingly, reside after all in striving for fidelity to the work or fidelity to the composer's aims.

At this point, before embarking on a discussion of what such fidelity might involve, a brief excursion on the subject of concerts (or CD recordings) presented as 'liturgical reconstructions' might be apposite, given that these embody a recognition that the 'works' performed originated as part of a larger structure with a non-musical justification. This, however, is not a way of side-stepping what we might call the 'imaginary museum' problem. The audience attending a 'liturgical reconstruction' is in essentially the same relationship to the material being presented as in any other concert. For all that Coryat, Maugars, and their fellow tourists seem to have derived a purely musical enjoyment from what they heard in Venetian and Roman services, their pleasure probably needs to be regarded almost as an incidental by-product of the occasion. (Those officiating, presuming that they took seriously their role of presiding over a religious observance carried out for the greater glory of God, might well have put the question, 'Who cares if you listen?'[31]) The presentation

[30] Goehr, *Imaginary Museum*, p. 179.

[31] The title given by the magazine *High Fidelity* to a famous article written in 1958 by Milton Babbitt about the predicament of composers in the mid-20th century. This article is reproduced in *Music in the Western World: A History in Documents*, ed. P. Weiss and R. Taruskin (New York: Schirmer, 1984), pp. 529–34.

of liturgical reconstructions, far from avoiding the problem of detaching music from its context, might be viewed (even more than conventional programmes) as the aural equivalent of museum exhibits. Not, I hasten to add, that such exhibits necessarily imply a detached perspective (about which more in chapter 8). Personally, I find the liturgical reconstruction capable of simultaneously catering to a natural historical curiosity and offering rich musical satisfaction.

It is interesting, too, to consider the amount of artistic planning that goes into the presentation of a liturgical reconstruction. Since the 'slots' in the programme are more-or-less predetermined and since the particular musical compositions assigned to each of these slots must be drawn from sometimes quite a restricted range of options sorted by category it might seem that an abdication of musical judgement is involved. But selection, nevertheless, is an unavoidable part of the process. It can be very satisfying in designing a programme to feel that the sequence of works is not simply arbitrary. The particular liturgy chosen (artistic choice No. 1) provides a matrix for the programme, a process that is no different from the adoption of any other organising principle in planning a concert. In other words, both in respect of the relationship between material presented and the audience and in overall design concepts, concerts presented as liturgical reconstructions do not essentially move closer to a pre-Kantian apprehension of musical experience.

If we are to assert the relevance of thinking in terms of aesthetically-autonomous musical 'works' for the Baroque and Classical eras, and therefore of trying to do justice to them by respecting the composer's intentions as embodied in the score, we need to be clear headed about exactly what all of that implies. To begin with, setting out to realize a composer's intentions presents many difficulties – and not just because for early music the composers are no longer there to tell us exactly what they wanted. For reasons given in Wimsatt and Beardsley's famous 1946 article, 'The Intentional Fallacy', the whole enterprise is recognized as philosophically perilous.[32]

Before attempting to disentangle the theoretical issues, it is worth noting that the idea of fidelity to composers' intentions has always seemed a goal so obvious that many composers have referred to it without fear of their readers accusing them of naivety. Composers themselves have always tended to assume or assert that realising their intentions should be central in performance. Such a notion is implicit in Monteverdi's (or, for that matter, Verdi's) pronouncements on the kind of singers they wanted for specific roles.[33] These reflect an expectation that their views should shape the eventual performance. On the face of it, having the composer as performer or director (virtually the norm in the 17th and 18th centuries) ensured an identity of intention between

[32] W. K. Wimsatt and M. C. Beardsley, 'The Intentional Fallacy', *Sewanee Review* (1946), 466–88.

[33] See Stevens, ed., *Letters of Claudio Monteverdi*, pp. 319f (letter, 7 May, 1627) on the casting of *La finta pazza Licori*; and *Letters of Giuseppe Verdi*, trans. C. Osborne (London, 1971), p. 59 (letter, 23 November 1848) on the casting of *Macbetto*.

score and performance.[34] So much was this taken for granted in the 18th century that Johann Matheson felt that performances that did not have the benefit of the composer's guiding hand required very special care:

> The greatest difficulty associated with the performance of someone else's work is probably the fact that keen discernment is necessary in order to understand the real sense and meaning of unfamiliar thoughts. For those who have never discovered how the composer himself wished to have the work performed will hardly be able to play it well. Indeed, he will often rob the thing of its true vigour and grace, so much so, in fact, that the composer should he himself be among the listeners, would find it difficult to recognize his own work.[35]

Gluck was even more adamant that the composer's presence was essential to correct performance. In the preface to *Paride ed Elena* he used his celebrated 'Che farò senza Euridice' (admittedly an aria with a rather tenuous hold on pathos as an affect) as an instance where parental guidance seemed essential:

> Let us take as an example my aria from *Orfeo*, 'Che farò senza Euridice': the slightest change exaggerating or falsifying the expression turns it into a marionette dance. A note sustained a little too much or too little, a misplaced or careless crescendo, an ill-proportioned appoggiatura, trill, or roulade can ruin the effect of an entire scene in a work of this character, even though in another conventional work it would scarcely make any difference. Thus, when it comes to performance, the presence of the composer is as necessary to the work, so to speak, as the presence of the sun is to the works of nature; he is the soul, the life. Without the composer all is confusion and chaos.[36]

One of the most interesting manifestations of composer involvement in establishing the true character of a work was the practice of having the composer direct opera performances for the first few nights before handing over to someone else once things were well in place musically. When, in 1782, the opera *Die Entführung aus dem Serail* was presented in Vienna before members of the Russian royal family, Mozart wrote to his father that for this particular performance 'I thought it advisable to resume my place at the clavier and conduct it. I did so partly in order to rouse the orchestra who had gone to sleep a little, partly (since I happen to be in Vienna) in order to appear before the royal guests as the father of my child.'[37]

The assumption that performers would see it as their responsibility to respect composers' intentions is very often explicit. Mersenne, advocating the use of a pitch standard, wrote that 'All the musicians of the world will be able to sing a

---

[34]   I write 'on the face of it' here because composers as performers of their own works – most famously, Stravinsky – have frequently been found guilty of departing from their stated 'intentions'.

[35]   *Der vollkommene Capellmeister* (1739); translation from Robin Stowell, *The Early Violin and Viola* (Cambridge, 2001), p. xiii.

[36]   Dedication to the Duc de Bragance; *Christoph Willibald Gluck: Sämtliche Werke* vol. 4, ed. R. Gerber (Kassel, 1954), p. 4.

[37]   Mozart, *Letters*, p. 285.

single piece of music according to the intentions of the composer, that is to say, at the pitch he wishes it to be sung.'[38] In prefaces to published sets of concerti grossi, various composers give instructions about the number and disposition of players needed for performances to conform to 'la mia intentione'.[39] Gasparini advised continuo players against bass-line diminutions 'because it is very easy to miss or depart from the intention of the composer and from the proper spirit of the composition'.[40] Geminiani saw playing in good taste as a matter of 'expressing with Strength and Delicacy the Intention of the Composer'.[41] And Quantz was very clear that 'In all pieces, but especially in slow ones, the performers must always assume the sentiment of the composer, and seek to express it.'[42]

In the 19th and 20th centuries, composers have been equally emphatic about the performer's role. Wagner, living in Switzerland and unable to direct performances of his own works, wrote in frustration to Ferdinand Heine, 'I care *absolutely nothing* about my things *being given*: I am anxious that they should be *so given* as I intended; he who will not or cannot do that, let him leave them alone.'[43] In a similar vein, Marguerite Long reports an exchange between Ravel and Toscanini about the speed of Bolero: (Ravel) 'That's not my tempo'; (Toscanini) 'When I play your tempo the piece is ineffective'; (Ravel) 'Then don't play it.'[44] According to Ernest Newman, Elgar complained that 'all his music required was to be left alone to say what it had to say in its own way: the expression was *in* the music, and it was not only unnecessary but harmful for the conductor to add to it an expression of his own'.[45] Stravinsky, for his part, praised Ernest Ansermet for his ability to 'transmit my musical thought to the public, without ever falsifying it by personal or arbitrary interpretation'. He continued,

> Music should be transmitted and not interpreted, because interpretation reveals the personality of the interpreter rather than that of the author, and who can

---

[38] Marin Mersenne, *Harmonie Universelle* (Paris, 1636–37); Eng. trans. of the book on instruments by R. E. Chapman (The Hague, 1957), p. 199.

[39] See, for example, Torelli's prefaces to his Op. 5 (1692), Op. 6 (1698), Op. 8 (1709); Valentini's preface to his Op. 7 (1710); and Avison's to his Op. 3 (1751).

[40] Gasparini, *Practical Harmonist*, p. 90. See above p. 58n.

[41] Francesco Geminiani, *The Art of Playing on the Violin* (London, 1751), p. 6.

[42] Quantz, *On Playing the Flute*, p. 231; see also pp. 216–17: 'It follows that in a ripieno part neither the violinist nor any other performer upon a bowed instrument has the freedom to slur or detach the notes as he pleases; he is obliged to play them with the bowing the composer has indicated at those places which deviate from the customary manner.' Francesco Veracini's preface to his *Sonate Accademiche* (London and Florence, 1744) is headed up 'Intenzione dell' Autore'. (Far from being prescriptive, this preface makes it clear that Veracini was happy for performers to exercise their own judgement about how many movements of a particular sonata they should play in a particular context.)

[43] Letter of 30 December 1852. Richard Wagner, *Sämtliche Briefe*, ed. Gertrud Strobel and Werner Wolf (Leipzig, 1993), v, 150. '*Gar nichts* liegt mir daran, ob man meiner Sache *giebt*: mir liegt einzig daran, dass man sie *so* giebt, wie ich's mir gedacht habe; wer das nicht will und kann, der soll's bleiben lassen.'

[44] M. Long, *At the Piano with Maurice Ravel* (London, 1973), p. 18. Long (p. 16) also reports Ravel as saying, 'I do not ask for my music to be interpreted, but only for it to be played.'

[45] Quoted by Robert Philip, *Early Recordings and Musical Style* (Cambridge, 1992), p. 10.

guarantee that such an executant will reflect the author's vision without distortion.[46]

Anyone who has been involved in the first performance of a new work will almost certainly have had the experience of the composer being present at rehearsals trying to ensure that what comes out is what was meant.

On the other hand, it needs to be acknowledged that not all composers have adopted such a proprietorial view in relation to performance. The pithiest statement of the antithetical position comes from Brahms: 'Machen Sie es wie Sie wollen, machen Sie es nur schön' ('Do it how you like, but make it beautiful').[47]

But now we come to the crux of the matter: what, in practice, can it mean to be faithful to the composer's intentions? Thus far in this chapter, I have quoted from composers' letters, prefaces, and autobiographies, I have referred to anecdotes about their views, I have drawn on contemporary accounts that throw light on performing circumstances in the 17th and 18th centuries, and I have cited performance treatises. We need to ask how relevant any of this can be when the only document that can determine the identity and character of a musical composition (at least in Western music of the early modern age) is the score.

Despite what was said at the beginning of chapter 4 about the casual use of the two terms as synonyms, the score is not the same thing as the musical work (which arguably cannot exist until it is realised in sound) and no score is capable of prescribing every detail of performance. Jean-Jacques Nattiez, in considering where exactly the identity of a musical work resides cites Roman Ingarden for whom 'the work is a purely intentional object, immutable and permanent, whose heteronomous *existence* is no more than a reflection of its *being*: the existence of the work finds its source in the "creative act" of the performer, and its foundation in the score'.[48] Nattiez goes on to consider the idea that 'any "execution" that creates an acceptable correspondence between graphic source and performance may be considered an "authentic" execution' and moves from there to question the very possibility of fidelity to the work given the essential heteronomy of performance.[49]

Because it under-determines the sonic result, the score is inevitably an 'open' text capable of a range of realisations that are all identifiably the same work. It would be tempting at this point to abandon any hope of historical fidelity and to accept (as Nattiez, in fact, does) a relativist position. But I wish to argue that the score as an attempt to represent a composer's idea need not be so imprecise

---

[46] Igor Stravinsky, *Autobiography* (New York, 1936; repr. 1962), p. 75.

[47] Quoted by Fanny Davies, 'Some Personal Recollections of Brahms as Pianist and Interpreter', in *Cobbett's Cyclopedic Survey of Chamber Music* (London, 1929), p. 184. Marc Pincherle gives a list of composer-authorised freedoms: see 'On the Rights of the Interpreter in the Performance of 17th and 18th-Century Music', *The Musical Quarterly* 44 (1958), 147–53.

[48] Jean-Jacques Nattiez, *Music and Discourse: Towards a Semiology of Music*, trans. Carolyn Abbate (Princeton, 1990), p. 69.

[49] Ibid., p. 74.

as to legitimise whatever performers want to do with it. It is important to clarify how and to what extent we can know the original intention of a musical work. In particular, for those interested in historical performance practice, this involves considering how the kind of supplementary material (treatises, letters etc.) referred to above might be used to illuminate the significance of a score. Wimsatt and Beardsley give us a useful framework in which to consider this question. Many who invoke 'the intentional fallacy' as a concept seem to assume that composers' (authors') intentions cannot be known. Insofar as 'the intentional fallacy' has evolved into – or been displaced by – the idea of the death of the author, that might seem to be the case. But, as Peter Kivy has reminded us, Wimsatt and Beardsley themselves were not claiming that authorial intention is unknowable. Kivy explains: 'Far from denying that authors' intentions are accessible, for some deep reasons of epistemic debility, they are merely telling us . . . where the most reliable evidence for such intentions is to be found . . . namely, in the . . . work itself . . .'[50] It follows that for a performer, fidelity to the intentions of the author merges with fidelity to the musical work itself. In fact, I would go so far as to say that the idea of being faithful to the composer's intention is a kind of metaphor for the goal of attempting to a reach a proper understanding of the work. And, of course, we have no way of considering the work outside its written record – the score.

One way of looking at the whole enterprise of performance practice is to see it as a matter of literacy. How do we read this score (the composer's way of communicating intentions)? On one level, this amounts to no more or less than a thorough understanding of the implications of the notation, an ability to read it with a proper sense of the idiom. We are used to taking account of shifts of meaning in language, and thus understanding, for example, that in the line from *Dido and Aeneas* 'take a boosey short leave of your nymphs on the shore', 'boosey' means amorous, not (as 21st-century listeners are inclined to think) drunken. In the same way, we need to understand that the same 'spellings' – that is to say, apparently identical groups of notes – can imply rather different things for different repertories. The differences extend from the rhythmic conventions attaching to a particular style (whether it be early 18th-century French dances or 19th-century Viennese waltzes), to the degree of prescriptiveness assumed (punctilious and strict or a framework for free embellishment), and, of course, to the particular implications (in terms of numbers, strength, and timbre) of instrumental or voice-type specifications. As Nattiez observes, 'a given notation is only possible within the context of specific acquired practical skills, and the moment a given practice falls out of use, the notation falls silent'.[51] Performance practice research might be justified as aiming to halt or reverse that process.

Even apparently more remote aspects of context, such as performing milieu or programming rationale, might be regarded as implicit in notation – the sub-text, so to speak. (It is nonsense to blame the *Werktreue* concept for the 'truly

---

[50] Kivy, *Authenticities*, p. 15.
[51] Nattiez, *Music and Discourse*, p. 78.

stifling regimen' Taruskin refers to; in the final analysis, such inflexibility is just the consequence of performers not understanding the implications of the scores they utilise.)

Wimsatt and Beardsley distinguished between internal and external evidence for the meaning of a literary work. They pointed out that, paradoxically, internal evidence (that found in the work itself) is public whereas external evidence (revelations from letters, for example, about why a poem was written) 'is private or idiosyncratic; not a part of the work as a linguistic [or we might say 'notational'] fact'.[52] But they then talk about evidence of an intermediate kind – evidence that explains the particular significance of words or phrases for the author:

> The meaning of words is the history of words, and the biography of an author, his use of a word, and the association which the word had for *him*, are part of the word's history and meaning . . . The use of biographical evidence need not involve intentionalism, because while it may be evidence of what the author intended, it may also be evidence of the meaning of his words and the dramatic character of his utterance.[53]

This analysis suggests how context may be valued as a key to the interpretation of notation. It suggests a framework in which treatises, letters, prefaces, iconography, archival records and the like may legitimately be brought to bear on the task of reaching a sufficiently complex and rich understanding of the notation itself. As Stanley Boorman put it:

> Each notation, and each source using it, assumes a series of understandings on the part of the reader. The most obvious examples are again the performance conventions that actually change the aural effect of the notation – double dotting, portamenti in late nineteenth-century string playing, or canonic composition that is not written out. These were all implicit in the notation at the time of composition: thus they did not need to be written down.[54]

Semiotics provides another model which allows us to see knowledge of historical performance practice as a matter of musical literacy rather than simply a rather arbitrary selection of one amongst many possible approaches to the realisation of a musical work. Charles Sanders Peirce, refining Saussure, described the function of signs and interpretants in a way that might suggest how musical notation provides a link between composer and performer, albeit a somewhat equivocal link:

---

[52] Wimsatt and Beardsley, 'Intentional Fallacy', p. 477.
[53] Ibid., p. 478.
[54] Stanley Boorman, 'The Musical Text', in Cook and Everist, eds., *Rethinking Music*, p. 408. Boorman points out (p. 420) that there may be agendas other than the composer's reflected in a musical source. His cogent article takes a rather more pessimistic view than I would of the possibility (and therefore the value) of reading scores in a richly-contextualised fashion. He is thus readier to dismiss 'authenticity' as an achievable goal in performance.

A sign or *representamen* is something which stands to somebody for something in some respect or capacity. It addresses somebody, that is, creates in the mind of that person an equivalent sign, or perhaps a more developed sign. That sign which it creates I call the *interpretant* of the first sign. The sign stands for something, its *object*.[55]

Peirce goes on to explore the triadic relationship between representamen, object, and interpretant.

Instead of the interpretant being a more developed sign, it might (where ambiguity exists) attach itself to a subtly (or even radically) different meaning. In music, notation is both the sign by which the composer communicates the content of the work and the interpretant (the equivalent sign) used by the performer to understand it. Performance practice studies can be seen and justified as a way of getting as close an identity as possible between sign and interpretant. This is a matter of properly defining the extent to which a notation is determinative (rather than accepting, as many seem to do, that it can indicate little beyond a profile for relative pitch and rhythm). In other words, the performer may need the notation to be richly contextualized for it not to be misleading. Depending on where and when it originated, a group of four stepwise quavers assigned to an instrument called 'violin', for example, might imply *notes inégales*, or some form of over-dotting, or be seen as a framework for free gracing. It might have been written assuming that the violinist would choose fingerings allowing for portamenti (as in illus. 6.3 on p. 94). And the composer may have taken for granted in specifying 'violin' that that would mean an instrument strung in gut, held without the aid of a chin rest, and played with an outcurving bow, or that it would be played on an instrument with a more modern set-up and with Tourte-style bow. Indeed, the designation may have been meant to indicate not a single violin but a section of sixteen players. Viewing the study of performance practice in this way, as a matter ultimately of musical literacy involves recognizing that much of what is conventionally considered 'interpretation' is implicit in the score itself. In other words, features which are normally thought of as traits (arbitrary traits, even) of a particular performance may be viewed as an intrinsic part of the score. Or, to appropriate Taruskin's terminology, the boundary between text and act shifts a little as a larger number of features are subsumed into the 'text' category. This is in no way to deny the extent to which any performance whatsoever will involve innumerable 'decisions' that fit within the latitude of even the most prescriptive notation.

---

[55] *Collected Papers of Charles Sanders Peirce*, ed. C. Hartshorne, P. Weiss and A. W. Burks, 8 vols. (Cambridge, Mass., 1931–66), ii, 135; quoted by Kofi Agawu, 'The Challenge of Semiotics', in *Rethinking Music*, pp. 138–9.

6. The compromised composer

The previous chapter embraced the idea that fidelity in performance to the essence of a musical composition might be reducible to a question of musical literacy, where the full understanding of a notation presupposes a richly explored sense of its context. To those interested in historical performance practice, it is axiomatic that reading a score with a proper sense of its implications will often involve taking account of performance conventions that have fallen into disuse.

Sound recordings reveal just how recently certain mannerisms have been discarded. Or, to put this another way, they demonstrate that so many features of mainstream orthodox performance have become established only within the last fifty years or so. For late 19th- and early 20th-century repertory, recordings offer the opportunity of actually hearing performances that arise from the composer's own milieu. Thus, for this repertory, they add a particularly interesting dimension to the discussion about intentions and outcomes.

In the first section of this chapter, I wish to explore two performance features of the early-recording era that had all but disappeared by the mid-20th century – the string portamento and a particularly extravagant kind of rubato. The neglect of these in contemporary performance of romantic repertory is all the more interesting in view of the fact that it is so widely known that both were prominent in performance a century ago.[1]

The portamento – an audible slide when changing positions on the violin – was already part of musical vocabulary in the second half of the 18th century. Its use, though, seems to have increased markedly in the early years of the 19th century. Salieri mocked violinists who used it, claiming that what had started as a joke – the imitation of cats miaowing – had become a fashion.[2] In 1808 Spohr attracted critical contempt for his use of the device.[3] Clearly, however, the mannerism increased its currency until portamenti had become a standard part of the string player's armoury.

A charmingly naive example of its expressive function may be found in

---

[1] '. . . the greatest change in orchestral string practice in the early twentieth century was in the use of portamento'. Philip, *Early Recordings*, p. 180.
[2] See Neal Zaslaw, 'In Vino Veritas', *Early Music* 25 (1997), 569.
[3] For the Salieri and Spohr references (and much else) see Clive Brown, 'Bowing Styles, Vibrato and Portamento in Nineteenth-Century Violin Playing', *Journal of the Royal Musical Association* 113 (1988), 123.

Illus. 6.1 G. M. Cambini, *Nouvelle Méthode Théorique Et Pratique Pour Le Violon* (Paris, 1803), Melody by Haydn, p. 22

Pénétrez vous, d'abord, du sentiment naïf et tendre, qu'une jolie vil-
-lageoise, encore vierge, éprouve, en reprochant à son amoureux l'infidelité
qu'elle méritoit si peu. Supposez lui un caractère encore plus naïf que
celui de Colette, dans le Devin du Village; elle ne connoit pas le dépit elle
n'écoute que sa tendresse elle ne dit que les paroles suivantes.

Quoi! tu peux m'être infidèle!
Qui t'aimera plus que moi!
Si je te parois moins belle,
Mon cœur n'est il rien pour toi!

Ou quelque chose de semblable, mais mieux exprimé. Alors électrisez
vôtre bras d'un feu plus doux, plus bienfaisant que celui dont vous vous
êtes servi pour la phrase de Boccherini, et récitez avec intérêt ce troisième
exemple. Avec le doigté et les signes que j'ai indiqué. (Ce que je dis là, vous
ne pourrez pas l'exécuter de si-tôt, mais du moins, d'après mon indication
vôtre maître pourra vous en donner une juste idée.)

Cambini's *Nouvelle Méthode pour le violon*, published in Paris in 1803. Cambini cites a single phrase by Haydn which he fancifully describes as expressing the naivety and innocence of a shepherdess reproaching her love for his infidelity. He then adds a few bowings and articulation marks and pronounces that 'you should already feel that the beginning of this air has gained a certain nobility . . . It should make the girls smile.'[4] Finally fingerings to indicate portamenti and a few dynamic marks are said to transform the phrase so that it now conveys something like the emotions expressed by the pretty and innocent village girl, Colette, feeling the first pangs of a lover's betrayal in Rousseau's *Devin du Village* (illus. 6.1).[5]

Charles de Bériot discriminates in his *Méthode de violon* (1858) between portamenti of different speeds and intensity.[6] In the early years of the 20th

---

[4] G. G. Cambini, *Nouvelle Méthode théorique et pratique pour le violon* (Paris, 1803; repr. 1972), p. 21.

[5] See Roger Parker, 'Verdi through the Looking Glass', in A. Groos and R. Parker, eds., *Reading Opera* (Princeton, 1988) for another instance (discussed) of an early 19th-century French writer using a text to explicate the 'meaning' of a piece of instrumental music.

[6] See Brown, 'Bowing Styles', p. 126.

Illus. 6.2 Felix Mendelssohn, *Concerto for Violin and Piano, Op. 64, Newly Revised and Provided with Numerous Explanatory Remarks for Concert Performance with Special Reference to the Artistic Conception of Joseph Joachim*, ed. Heinrich Dessauer, Carl Fischer's Music Library Edition No. 321 (New York and Boston: Carl Fischer, 1903), bars 139–176

E) In playing this wonderfully expressive melody, it is permissible to employ the vibrato or tremolo effect upon a few and appropriate notes, but without the least exaggeration; above all the tremolo upon every note, a fault which brings about a style of playing both affected and full of mannerism, must be positively avoided.

F) In the fourth bar before letter F the liberty of introducing a very slight Ritardando may be taken, but following the hold, the first tempo must be resumed at once. The brilliant and piquant figure commencing shortly after "F," must be played very brightly and with exceedingly accurate finish of technical detail; the latter being particularly difficult in bars fourteen and fifteen. To facilitate the study of this part, various fingerings have been added all of which can be recommended. It is for the player to choose the one most suitable to his individual liking.

century Heinrich Dessauer (1863–1917) produced an edition of the Mendelssohn violin concerto 'carefully marked and with explanatory hints for concert performances'. Dessauer claimed that he had 'endeavoured to embody the interpretation of those artists, who like Joseph Joachim were fortunate enough to enjoy the personal and artistic intercourse with the master and his contemporaries. The object of these explanatory remarks, derived from the above traditional sources is to aid and simplify the student's task of acquiring the correct and artistic interpretation of Mendelssohn's master-work.'[7] As we can see from Dessauer's note at the top of the page (illus. 6.2), vibrato was reserved as a special colouring for particular notes – but many of the fingerings specified (in, for example, bars 19 and 22) involve portamenti. Dessauer was far from being the last to think of portamento as a very normal expressive element. Leopold Auer, Carl Flesch and others discussed its uses and abuses and it survived well into the 20th century.

Gustav Mahler regarded the portamento as an important and expressive feature of string playing. In the 1960s some aged musicians who had played

[7] Felix Mendelssohn, *Concerto for Violin and Piano, Op. 64, Newly Revised and Provided with Numerous Explanatory Remarks for Concert Performance with Special Reference to the Artistic Conception of Joseph Joachim*, ed. Heinrich Dessauer, Carl Fischer's Music Library Edition No. 321 (New York and Boston: Carl Fischer, 1903), p. [1].

under Mahler in the New York Philharmonic Orchestra recorded their impressions of him as a conductor. What they had to say on the subject is interesting:

> He sang more. He made us sing the music instead of just playing it mechanically, which doesn't happen very often today. He'd tell us what he wanted and if we didn't play the way he wanted, he'd sing it for us – he'd phrase it for us with his voice. He used a lot more vibrato than most conductors do today; he insisted on it . . .
>
> Well that brings me to something that I could never understand. But, you know, he's a Viennese and, you know, Strauss and all that and they used a lot of that in their music. His Fourth Symphony, his theme is [sings]; my God, he asks all the first violins to [sings with portamento] He insisted on certain slides in his music. Sometimes in a slow movement in other composers he would do that too. For instance he said you couldn't go [sings a wide, if rather indeterminate, interval]. Nobody sings like that. So you'd have to slide to get there. [sings with portamento]. He would sing that for you that way. Well, how else would you play it?[8]

The opening of Mahler's Fourth Symphony mentioned in those reminiscences is, as it happens, a particularly interesting example. Mahler's score is quite specific about the way in which that melody is to be played. The violin part is very precisely fingered (illus. 6.3). It would be easy (logical, even) to play this beginning with the first finger in third position. A uniform A-string tone would still be achieved without any shifts until the descent to B'. The fingering Mahler gives together with the oblique stroke marked before the new finger 2 on G" (and the explanatory note at the foot of the page) is an explicit direction to use the very portamento that that New York violinist was remembering.[9]

But most conductors ignore that specification. This is not a matter of musicians disregarding features that are merely implicit in the notation. In this case, Mahler has been quite explicit. The apparent incredulity that surrounds the composer's stated instructions here undoubtedly follows from a more general rejection of this device. Table 6.1 lists a selection of recordings of Mahler's Fourth Symphony. All the recordings above the line dispense with the portamento. It is worth noting that these include performances conducted by Bruno Walter (an ardent admirer and personal friend of Mahler) and Leonard Bernstein (who also claimed a special affinity with Mahler and saw many

[8] Herman Martonne (violinist for the Philharmonic Society of New York) and Herbert Borodkin (viola player) were interviewed by William Malloch in the early 1960s. The interviews were originally released as 'Remembering Mahler' on side 4 of Leonard Bernstein's lp recording for Columbia of the Mahler Sixth Symphony with the New York Philharmonic Orchestra. These interviews have been re-released on the 'Mahler Plays Mahler' cd GLRS 101 (1993).

[9] Mahler regarded his New York performance of the Fourth Symphony as definitive, referring in a letter to Emil Freund to 'der IV. Symphonie nach erfolgter Aufführung unter meiner Leitung in der dann endgültig festgestellten Version'. See the Revisionsbericht, *Symphonie Nr. 4 Fassung 1911* Gustav Malher: sämtliche Werke, vol. 4 (Vienna, 1995).

Illus. 6.3 Gustav Mahler, Symphony No. 4, 1st movement, bars 1–4 (Copyright 1963 by Universal Edition (London) Ltd, London)

parallels between their lives).[10] Only Lorin Maazel with the Vienna Philharmonic observes the portamento. It is a very discrete gesture on this recording, but it is certainly there – and it *is* expressive. The most surprising recording to find above the line in table 6.1 is that conducted by Willem Mengelberg (1871–

---

[10] Robert Philip comments about Walter's recording of the third movement of Mahler 4, 'Mahler's Symphony No. 4 includes passages where portamentos are indicated by Mahler in the score (for example at bar 221 of the slow movement). Even these specified portamentos are treated with discretion in Walter's performance, and the slow movement as a whole is as "clean" as it would be in a modern performance.' (Philip, *Early Recordings*, p. 201.)

Table 6.1 Selection of recorded performances of Mahler, Symphony No. 4

(a) **without portamento at bars 3–4**

Willem Mengelberg, Concertgebouw Orchestra, Amsterdam (1939); reissued AB 78 844–MONO ADD (1998)

Bruno Walter, Philharmonic Symphony Orchestra of New York (1946) LX949–54

Georg Solti, Concertgebouw Orchestra (1961) 415 745

Leonard Bernstein, New York Philharmonic (*c.*1967) SBR 475068

Bernard Haitink, Concertgebouw Orchestra (1967) 420350

Claudio Abbado, Wiener Philharmoniker (1978) 413 454–2

Herbert von Karajan, Berlin Philharmonic (1979) CD 415 323–2

Sir Georg Solti, Chicago Symphony Orchestra (1984) 410 188

Seiji Ozawa, Boston Symphony Orchestra (1987) 422–072–2

Leonard Bernstein, Concertgebouw Orchestra (1988) 435 162

Eduard van Beinum, Concertgebouw Orchestra (1988) 421 140

Michiyoshi Inoue, Royal Philharmonic Orchestra (1990) RPO 8017

Esa-Pekka Salonen, Los Angeles Philharmonic (1992) SK 48380

Sir Simon Rattle, City of Birmingham Symphony Orchestra (1998) EMI 5565632

Yeol Levi, Atlanta Symphony Orchestra (1999) Telarc CD–80499

Danielle Gatti, Royal Philharmonic Orchestra (1999) 75605 51345 2

(b) **with portamento at bars 3–4**

Lorin Maazel, Wiener Philharmoniker (1984) MK 39022

1951), though I should point out that he does insert the portamento when the same gesture returns at bars 17–18. (I shall return to Mengelberg's use of portamenti below.)

Having seen how Mahler's explicit request for a portamento – not to mention his expectation that this device would be a regular part of a performer's expressive vocabulary – is almost universally ignored (or rejected), we may move on to another neglected (though not forgotten) aspect of his approach to performance.

The welter of instructions on the first page of the Fourth Symphony is some indication of the importance Mahler placed on fine discrimination in matters of tempo and metre: 'Bedächtig' (slow, deliberate), 'Nicht eilen' (don't hurry), 'Etwas züruck haltend' (holding back somewhat), 'Recht gemächlich' (quite leisurely), and, most revealing of all, the concept of the basic tempo, the 'Haupttempo'. Mahler's attitude to tempo came up in the reminiscences of those ageing New York musicians.

Interviewer: *How could you characterise his sense of tempo? Were there wide tempo variations? Was it unyielding?*
Musician: That is very important. Flexibility – that's what Mahler had. You know, that's a study in itself. He practises what Wagner preached. The tempo – He followed according to understanding, after you take note of the initial marking, then you must do your part.

Interviewer: *Would you say the tempo variations were wide that Mahler indulged in?*
Musician: Just a shade – but it's the difference between freedom and slavery. A shade.
Interviewer: *They say that no two bars were the same tempo?*
Musician: And there you are, and yet it was the same.[11]

This emphasis on Mahler's fluid (and yet paradoxically stable) tempi is interesting. Mahler himself was reported as saying

All the most important things – the tempo, the total conception and structuring of a work – are almost impossible to pin down. For here we are concerned with something living and flowing that can never be the same even twice in succession. That is why metronome markings are inadequate and almost worthless; for unless the work is vulgarly ground out in barrel-organ style, the tempo will already have changed by the end of the second bar.[12]

But Mahler was not alone in approaching performance in this way. The person most famous for his advocacy of metrical flexibility was Richard Wagner. In his essay 'On Conducting' (1869) he described what he regarded as a basic principle, the 'modification of tempo':

What lies between these two extremes [of Adagio and Allegro] must be governed by a principle rooted in a sense of their *inter-relationship*, a principle which must be grasped in all its subtlety and manifold variety, since at bottom it is the same as that which governs the infinite variety of inflected tone. When I now turn to consider more closely this principle, summed up in the phrase, *modification of tempo* – a thing our conductors are so ignorant of that they stupidly denounce it as a heresy – the reader who has followed me thus far will realise that what we are dealing with is the principle conditioning the very life of music.[13]

Wagner goes on to examine the application of the principle to a number of works, including the prelude to *Die Meistersinger*. Of this he writes, 'Never have I heard those sensitive modifications necessary to an intelligible performance which I regard as no less crucially important than the playing of the right notes . . .'[14] And he goes through the piece in some detail describing where and why the tempo needs to be flexible.

[11] 'Remembering Mahler'; see note 8 above.
[12] Quoted by Philip, *Early Recordings*, p. 8.
[13] R. Wagner, 'On Conducting', in *Three Wagner Essays*, trans. R. L. Jacobs (London, 1979), p. 66.
[14] Ibid., p. 88. José Bowen discusses Wagner's theories of tempo modification in 'The Conductor and the Score: The Relationship between Interpreter and Text in the Generation of Mendelssohn, Berlioz and Wagner' (PhD thesis: Stanford University, 1994), chapter 8. See also his 'Can a Symphony Change? Establishing Methodology for the Historical Study of Performance Styles', *Musik als Text: Bericht über den internationalen Kongress der Gesellschaft für Musikforschung* ii (Kassel, 1998), 160–72; and 'Mendelssohn, Berlioz and Wagner as Conductors: The Origins of the Ideal of "Fidelity to the Composer"', *Performance Practice Review* 6 (1993), 77–88.

Ex. 6.1 Tchaikovsky, *Romeo and Juliet Fantasy Overture*, bars 386–440

When we compare early recordings of romantic works with those made in the last fifty years or so it is clear that the tolerated limits of tempo modifications have narrowed sharply. The kind of thing that Mahler and Wagner practised is just not heard today – at least, not if they were anything like what is preserved in Mengelberg's recordings. His Tchaikovsky *Romeo and Juliet* Overture (recorded with the Concertgebouw Orchestra in 1930) provides an outstanding and fascinating example of tempo flexibility.[15] Comparing this with virtually any currently-available recording produces interesting results. Take, for example, Charles Dutoit with the Montreal Symphony Orchestra. Dutoit's basic tempo as he approaches the climactic statement of the love theme at bar 410 is minim = 76 (see ex. 6.1).[16] On the first appearance of the theme at bar 388 he broadens out to minim = 74, and then finally at bar 410 to minim = 71. The tempo moves back up to minim = 76–78 at bar 445. All of this seems musical and very much in line with current taste.

Ex. 6.2 Tchaikovsky, *Romeo and Juliet Fantasy Overture*, bars 366–7

Mengelberg's orchestra plays with the kind of metrical freedom that might be expected from the most indulgent of romantic pianists. As a sheer achievement in ensemble this seems remarkable. Mengelberg does not simply broaden out towards the climax. In the first part of ex. 6.1 he seems scarcely to deviate from his principal tempo (again, minim = 76). Yet almost every bar has subtle metric inflections which give the whole a sense of spontaneity and freedom that seems truly romantic. In the repeated two-bar motif at bar 366ff (ex. 6.2), the first of each pair of bars is played in time while the second has a tenuto of varying length at its beginning (with the rising 7th in the uppermost voice). In bar 379 (marked 'poco a poco crescendo') he abandons these tenutos and surges forward in time into the love theme. At bar 393, there is a *Luftpause* (a 'breath pause' or aspiration) before the second half of the bar and he begins pulling back. By bar 417 the tempo has dropped to minim = 59 from where he begins an overall accelerando which proceeds by ebbs and flows back up to minim = 82 at the 'swordfight' music after bar 440. The effect of this very malleable tempo is intensified by the use of obvious portamenti (particularly in the progress back up to tempo). All of this I find quite compelling. The portamenti seem exactly

[15] LX 55–6.
[16] 430 507 (recorded in 1992).

right and the fluidity of the tempo comes across as a genuine response to the changing character of the music.

This was all part of an ethos that affected a large number of musicians and thus represents an important strand in late-Romantic music making. A year after Wagner's essay 'On Conducting', Liszt wrote 'the rubato may be left to the taste and momentary feeling of gifted players. A metronomical performance is certainly tiresome and nonsensical; time and rhythm must be adapted to and identified with the melody, the harmony, the accent and the poetry.' According to Joachim, Mendelssohn 'who so perfectly understood the elastic management of time as a subtle means of expression, always liked to see the uniform tempo of a movement preserved as a whole'.[17]

Brahms's position on this issue is particularly interesting. He also saw the metronome as, potentially anyway, an impediment to expressiveness:

> In my view, the metronome isn't worth that much; at least, so far as I know, many a composer has withdrawn his metronome markings sooner or later. Those which are found in the Requiem are there because good friends talked me into them. For I myself have never believed that my blood and a mechanical instrument go well together. The so-called elastic tempo is not a new discovery, after all, and to it, as to many another, one should attach a 'con dicrezione'.[18]

Morevoer, as Fanny Davies recalled, 'Brahms would lengthen infinitesimally a whole bar, or even a whole phrase, rather than spoil its quietude by making it up into a strictly metronomic bar. This expansive elasticity . . . was one of the chief characteristics of Brahms's interpretation.'[19]

Robert Pascall has drawn attention to the fact that Brahms actually wrote tempo modifications into his autograph scores of the Second Piano Concerto and the Fourth Symphony only to excise them before publication. He wrote to Joseph Joachim about those in the Fourth Symphony, suggesting that they had decreasing relevance as performers became more familiar with the work:

> I have pencilled in a few modifications of tempo into the score. They seem desirable, useful, even perhaps necessary, when dealing with a first performance. Unfortunately they then creep into print (with me and with others), where in the main they do not belong. Such exaggerations are only really necessary as long as a work is unfamiliar to an orchestra (or virtuoso). In this case I can often not do enough with the pushing on and holding back, so that the expression of passion or calm comes out as I want it. But when a work has got under the skin, my view is that there should be no more talk of such things, and the more one departs from

[17] Joseph Joachim, and Andreas Moser, *Violinschule/Violin School*, trans. Alfred Moffat, 3 vols. (Berlin, Leipzig, Cologne, London: Simrock, 1930), iii, 228–9; quoted by Stowell, *The Early Violin and Viola*, p. 154.

[18] Letter to George Henschel, written from Vienna, Feb. 1880: *Johannes Brahms: Life and Letters*, selected and annotated by S. Avins (Oxford and New York, 1997), p. 559. Brahms's other remarks on the metronome are worth noting; see Bernard D. Sherman, 'Tempos and Proportions in Brahms: Period Evidence', *Early Music* 25 (1997), 463–77.

[19] Davies, 'Some Personal Recollections', p. 184.

this, the more artificial I find the performance. My experience with my earlier works often shows how all this happens naturally and how superfluous many such markings of this type are! But how readily performers today seek to impress with this so-called free artistic interpretation – and how easy it all is, even with the worst possible orchestra and one rehearsal![20]

The implication of what Brahms writes here is that really thorough knowledge of a score will allow its performers to communicate its feeling in more subtle ways than obvious adjustments of the tempo in accordance with the feeling of the moment. What is so fascinating about this in the present context, of course, is that Brahms envisages performances faithful to the inner meaning of the work changing over time. For Brahms, re-creating an ideal first performance would, it seems, not be the way of honouring his intentions in the longer term.

While the list of those composers advocating subtle tempo adjustments could be extended, it needs to said as well that extreme flexibility of tempo was never universally accepted. Hanslick (predictably) disapproved strongly:

Were Wagner's principles of conducting universally adopted, his tempo changes would open the door to intolerable arbitrariness . . . *Tempo rubato*, that musical seasickness which so afflicts the performances of many singers and instrumentalists, would soon infect our orchestras, and that would be the end of the last healthy element in our musical life.[21]

Felix Weingartner (whose own recordings now seem far from strict in this regard) denounced Hans von Bülow and his followers as 'tempo-rubato conductors', with their 'continual alterations and dislocations of the tempo . . . in no way justified by any marks of the composer'.[22] Mengelberg was perhaps the end of the line.

There is a Stravinsky anecdote which points, not just to the co-existence of different attitudes to tempi, but to a more radical change of sensibility – one that, in this case, is obviously related to compositional style:

Nor do I greatly cherish my memories of Mengelberg. At the first rehearsal of the *Capriccio* he began to conduct in an impossible tempo. I said I was unable to play at that speed . . . Greatly flustered, he embarked on a self-justifying oration: "Gentlemen, after fifty years as a conductor I think I may claim to be able to recognise the proper tempo of a piece of music. Monsieur Stravinsky, however, would like us to play like this: tick, tick, tick, tick." And he cocked his forefinger in mockery of Mälzel's very useful invention.[23]

Stravinsky's story brings out the point that what might work for full-blooded romantic repertory is going to be highly inappropriate for disciplined neo-

[20] Quoted by Robert Pascall, 'The Editor's Brahms', in *The Cambridge Companion to Brahms* ed. Michael Musgrave (Cambridge, 1999), p. 266.
[21] Quoted by Richard Hudson, *Stolen Time: The History of Tempo Rubato* (Oxford, 1994), p. 313.
[22] See Hudson, *Stolen Time*, p. 314.
[23] Igor Stravinsky, *Themes and Conclusions* (London, 1972), pp. 226–7.

classical writing. But conversely, it suggests that the approach to metre in so many contemporary performances of romantic repertory may not be the best way to engage with those works.

There are, of course, a number of period-instrument orchestras tackling romantic repertory these days. On the whole, though, they don't go much further than lining up the right instruments. None so far indulge in romantic mannerisms or explore the expressive potential of a very malleable tempo to anything like the extent that at least some 19th- and early 20th-century musicians thought appropriate. Some would obviously like to keep it that way. Richard Taruskin has declared: 'As soon as a consensus develops that we must restore Tchaikovsky to his scoops and slides simply because that is what the evidence decrees, I shall be the first to join in a chorus of lament for our Alexandrian age and the doom that it forebodes.'[24] I shall return to reflect on his unhappiness in the final chapter when considering the charge that much period-instrument performance is profoundly unmusical.

Perhaps the most surprising view encountered so far in this chapter is Brahms's sense that fidelity to his own composition might mean something slightly different as the work in question became more familiar. Such a view implies that the relationship between intention, ideal, and score is dynamic rather than fixed. With this in mind, I wish to return briefly to Mahler's attitudes to the notation and performance of his Fourth Symphony. In the lead-up to its first performance he wrote

> the fact that I have never heard this work, that I am anxious about the rehearsals because of the unusual orchestration, and that I am not sure if I have really succeeded in expressing what I intended, all make me wish to be on the podium for the first performance, for I am the only one who knows my score by heart . . . I am not used to listening from the hall and making "apoplectic" changes. Up to now, I have always been able to go over my scores at least once with my own orchestra, and this gave me a certain sense of security. I have almost always had to make essential changes (during rehearsal).[25]

Here, Mahler's main concern is that the performance should reflect his intentions. He echoes Matheson and Gluck's view that this is much easier to achieve if the composer is at the helm (see above, p. 84). What is most interesting, however, is his admission that the score itself might not convey perfectly what he meant. Of course, he implies that eventually it would be a completely reliable guide, but only after adjustments made in rehearsal have been incorporated. In a sense, we can see that for Mahler the *score* is a step on the way to completing the *work*. These two things – score and work – are not, as Nattiez and Ingarden have reminded us (see above, p. 86), the same thing. But the score is, in the end, the only unimpeachable record of the composer's

---

[24] Taruskin, *Text and Act*, p. 151.
[25] Quoted by Donald Mitchell in *Mahler: The Wunderhorn Years* (London, 1975), pp. 298–9.

intentions, hence Mahler's anxiety about getting it right. What Wimsatt and Beardsley perceived was that, ultimately, for a literary text at least the idea of 'authorial intention' is synonymous with artistic result. The fact that the artistic result in the case of a musical work is completed only in performance does not alter our dependence on the score in determining a work's identity.

Mahler's letter raises the possibility (likelihood, even) that for composers unable to make these sorts of revisions the score might not be an infallible guide to composer-intention. Mahler had been persuaded by Wagner that Beethoven's scores might suffer from this kind of inadequacy. Wagner, in his 1873 essay on performing the Ninth Symphony, wrote about his own interventions in Beethoven's score. These involved amending Beethoven's orchestration in order to compensate for what he saw as infelicities attributable on the one hand to Beethoven's deafness and, on the other, to the limitations of the instruments (particularly natural horns and trumpets) that Beethoven had at his disposal. Wagner wrote that he was driven to make these changes 'when I could no longer tolerate the impediments to a clear understanding of the composer's intentions . . .'[26] This enshrines the bold claim of knowing more about the composer's intentions than the score itself could indicate.

It was a claim that Mahler accepted, however. As a conductor, Mahler was well known for retouching Beethoven's orchestration. In 1899 in Vienna, he gave several performances of the Beethoven Ninth Symphony in which he adopted Wagner's suggestions. When this drew criticism, Mahler responded by having the following fascinating statement distributed to audience members:

> Because of his deafness, Beethoven had lost his essentially close contact with reality and the physical world of sound, just at that period of his creativity when an enormous heightening of conception had led to the discovery of new means of expression and to totally innovatory ways of handling an orchestra. This is well known, as is also the fact that the design of brass instruments at that time precluded their playing those melodies which were necessary to the texture of the music. With the passage of time, this defect has been made good; and not to use this improvement to achieve the most accomplished performance possible of Beethoven's works seems nothing short of sacrilege.
>
> Richard Wagner, who throughout his life, strove by every means in his power to save Beethoven's works from ever-increasing neglect, has outlined in his essay 'On the Performance of Beethoven's Ninth' (Collected Writings, Vol. IX) the way to perform this symphony, so that it expresses the composer's intentions in the best possible manner, and since then all conductors have followed this line. Tonight's conductor has done the same, out of the strongest conviction from his own experience of the work, and without in any way going beyond the limits indicated by Wagner.
>
> Re-orchestration, alteration or even improvement of Beethoven's works are naturally out of the question. The now traditional increase in the size of the string section – which has been accepted for some time – has led to an increase in the number of wind instruments, which is necessary for greater volume, but in no way

---

[26] 'On Performing Beethoven's Ninth Symphony', *Three Wagner Essays*, p. 99.

implies an additional orchestral role. On this, as on the former point, as far as the interpretation of the work is concerned, both as a whole and in its component parts, the authority of the score is absolute (and the more one studies it, the more compelling it becomes). All that any conductor should do, far from being arbitrary and wilful, and in no way diverging from any 'tradition', is feel for Beethoven's intentions even in the tiniest details, and, in performance, make certain that none of his ideas is sacrificed, or allowed to become submerged in a bewildering maze of sound.[27]

I shall return to consider the question of 'updating' scores as a way of honouring composers' intentions in the next chapter.

For all that honouring composer intention seems a worthwhile performance goal, there can be enormous practical difficulties in establishing exactly what that might mean in a particular instance. The kind of thing I have in mind here is illustrated most graphically in opera. Despite our habit of associating operas with their composers (Donizetti's *Lucia di Lammermour*, Verdi's *Otello* etc.), the diversely collaborative nature of opera composition and performance intro-duces new levels of complication in the already difficult issue of determining composer intention.

In February 1998 I conducted the premier season at the New Zealand International Festival of the Arts of Jack Body's *Alley*. The opera's title derives from its central figure, Rewi Alley (1897–1987), a New Zealander decorated for bravery in World War I who from 1926 until his death lived in China where he did much to establish industrial cooperatives associated with the Gung Ho movement and founded schools (at which he himself taught). He was designated a hero of the Chinese Republic and lived through the disillusioning period of the Cultural Revolution. Alley also wrote poetry, much of it expressing his own fascination with China and its people.

Body, who has a long-standing interest in Asian music, had made a number of trips to China recording music there with, primarily, creative stimulus rather than ethnomusicological research in mind (though the latter has been well served by his work). He approached Geoff Chapple, the author of a book on Alley, to write the libretto, which incorporated some of Alley's own poetry.[28]

The action is set as Alley is dying. The title role is shared by two singer/actors, one representing the old Alley and the other his younger self. The old Alley's characteristic mode of communication is melodrama – measured speech over music – while the young Alley is a role for a baritone who is frequently required to sing falsetto. The old Alley, reflects on his life (at the front of the stage) while (behind him) the young Alley exposes a gap between memory and reality, sometimes conveying very strongly the lyricism or excitement behind

---

[27] Quoted by Mitchell, *Mahler: The Wunderhorn Years*, pp. 404–5.
[28] Geoff Chapple, *Rewi Alley of China* (Auckland, 1980). Chapple was also involved in a Phase Three Films/New Zealand National Film Unit documentary made in 1980 about Alley.

remembered events and sometimes accusing his alter-ego of various kinds of vanity and self-deception. The only other major figure in the drama is Yen Wang, a god of death who vocalises in Mandarin in a traditionally Chinese theatrical style. Two folk singers evoke the peasantry of ancient China while a chorus of young men represent the voice of revolutionary China.

The overall dramatic structure is that of an Everyman story: an old man weighs up achievement and failure as he approaches death. But it is an Everyman story developed from an historical figure. The librettist had envisaged communicating key biographical information about Alley through creative use of voice-over techniques, cinematic sequences and surtitles.

The director, New York-based Chen Shi-Zheng, arrived in Wellington at the end of January 1998 (a month before opening night). Shi-Zheng (who also choreographed and played the role of Yen Wang) had a very clear vision of what kind of dramatic impact he wanted *Alley* to make. He was unhappy with the sheer quantity of biographical information that audiences would have to cope with and insisted that all but a tiny percentage of this material should be cut. He complained that the opera was stuck half way between docudrama and psychodrama (and he was clearly more interested in the latter). He vetoed altogether the use of surtitles, with the result that all the material in Chinese (about half the opera) was left untranslated for the audience. Shi-Zheng was convinced that none of this was crucial in advancing the action of the drama and he trusted the clarity of the dramatic presentation (*l'evidenza della situatione* as Puccini would have called it) to convey all that was needed.

He was also worried about the length of some of the music provided for transitions between scenes and pleaded with the composer to abbreviate these sections. There was considerable discussion, but more often than not Jack Body complied with these requests, and for the first two weeks or so of rehearsal I was receiving replacement pages for my score on virtually a daily basis. At one point I intervened in this process when what I considered a particularly beautiful section of music (setting an Alley poem) was under threat of deletion on the grounds that dramatically it seemed to duplicate the events of an earlier scene. I suggested to Body that he integrate the threatened passage into the earlier scene.

There was another factor that came into play that would change the shape of the score. The two folk singers, who had travelled from Gansu province for the production, were extraordinary musicians. No one who heard them could remain unmoved by their plaintive singing (in which they reached very high notes with a raised larynx). Their scenes were constructed from genuine folksongs (transcribed by Body on his various visits to China) around which the instrumental components of the score were 'wrapped'. Typically, this involved unmeasured singing over a low instrumental pedal with more active instrumental interjections at appropriate points (no easy matter, since the transcriptions of traditional melodies in the score never corresponded exactly with what these particular singers produced). Since in their original context such songs would be unaccompanied, the two singers had to cope with an alien concept in attempting to relate their pitch to notes sounded in the orchestra.

After a considerable amount of time had been spent trying to get this right (with the help of our musical advisor and interpreter, Professor Du Yaxiong), Jack Body eventually decided that in a couple of instances it would be simpler to transpose the scenes to match the singers' likely arrival points.

Opening night was a resounding success and the three-night season was sold out. The score is brilliant and Shi-Zheng's staging (assisted by a very talented designer and lighting designer) was riveting. But – and this is the point – the work presented to the public was in some respects very different from the one I had collected from the composer two and a half months earlier. Some of the changes were refinements initiated by the composer, but many others were carried out at the behest of the director (whose conception of the work was crucially different from that of either librettist or composer). Others still were necessitated by the circumstances of that particular production.

Such a history makes the *Werktreue* ideal rather complicated. In particular, retrieving the composer's intentions would be no easy matter. It seemed to me that the composer was persuaded of the case for many of the alterations but still regretted the loss of some aspects of the original conception. The score as it exists now does not, for example, record all of the cuts (since replacement pages were bound in) and it certainly provides no sure guide as to which of these cuts the composer would want restored given different production circumstances.

Perhaps none of this seems surprising, given that *Alley* has elements that lie outside normal operatic conventions. But the making of *Alley* is a story with many antecedents. Goerge Bizet's *Carmen* is just one of them.

Anyone trying to perform the *Carmen* that Bizet would most have wished to hear and see would face an impossible task. As with *Alley*, the transformation of the score between completion of a fair copy and the first performance is well documented. Bizet's future plans for the work are also part of the record. But none of this makes it an easy matter to determine how the wealth of primary material that remains relates to the composer's ideal. The problems begin with major differences in attitude to the source material between Bizet, his librettists, and the opera management.

'Quelle vérité, mais quel scandale!' ('What truth, but what scandal!') was how one Parisian publication described *Carmen* when it opened at the Opéra Comique in March 1875.[29] The opera was an extraordinary departure for this theatre whose management were so worried about its impact that on the morning of the first performance they had published warnings in the local press that the show would not be suitable for betrothal parties (the Opéra Comique being a regular venue for the families of a future bride and groom to meet).

It had been Bizet's own suggestion to base the new opera requested in 1872 by the Opéra Comique on Prosper Mérimée's *Carmen* – a decidedly X-rated story. Both Mérimée's smugglers, El Remendado and El Dancaïro, meet bloody ends.

[29] The *Annales du Théâtre et de la Musique*; quoted by Winton Dean, *Bizet*, The Master Musicians (London, 1948), p. 89. Dean's book remains the best account of the composition, preparation, and reception of *Carmen*.

Don José (likened by Mérimée to Milton's Satan) is a murderer several times over when he is introduced at the beginning of the novel. After his desertion from the army, José leads a brutal and ruthless life, killing (among others) his commanding officer (Zuniga, in the opera) and Carmen's *rom* ('husband'), Garcia. Carmen herself takes numerous lovers for gain, is happy to use her seductiveness as a decoy for her smuggling comrades, steals, and, as a person, is entirely lacking in sentimentality. The Toreador is not much more than a passing infatuation in the novel (though, as in the opera, he arouses Don José's jealousy). Nor is he a particularly heroic figure.

Understandably, the subject caused considerable anxiety and the project was stalled until the resignation in 1873 of one of the Opéra Comique directors, Adolphe de Leuven. Bizet, however, appears to have had comparatively little interest in placating the theatre's bourgeois audience. He seemed, in fact, to be looking beyond the circumstances of his opera's genesis. In 1873 when he first began working on *Carmen* he promised his friend Ernest Guiraud, 'I shall shine at the Opéra Comique; I shall enlarge and transform the genre.'[30]

The librettists, Henri Meilhac and Ludovic Halévy (who were known for their collaborations in libretti for Offenbach), did not quite have Bizet's courage. Their libretto is a superb achievement in the way it reduces the number of characters to a manageable level for a stage drama and skilfully conflates a range of incidents in the novel.[31] But the libretto tones down the violence and immorality of the original considerably. The smugglers (unscrupulous men who are without the slightest vestige of compassion in Mérimée's story) and Carmen's (invented) friends, Frascita and Mercedes, are made to fit the imaginative world of the Opéra Comique. They become comic figures. Bizet responded to this new emphasis in numbers like the brilliant Act II Quintet and the A section of the card trio in Act III. The character of Micaela (the innocent, dutiful, and pious country girl) is introduced as a foil to Carmen (the amoral *femme fatale*). Dramatically, Micaela becomes one of the principal ways in which we can measure Don José's moral decline.

Bizet's own willingness to embrace the unremitting cynicism of Mérimée's story obviously did not sit comfortably with the anxieties of the librettists and Opéra Comique management. The rehearsals, which ran from the beginning September 1874 (intensively, from 12 November) until the opening of the season on 3 March 1875, were fraught. Bizet was forced to accommodate an uncooperative orchestra and a recalcitrant and incompetent chorus who insisted that his music was too hard. His Carmen, however, was Célestine Galli-Marié who was ready to give everything to the character she had been asked to play. Bizet greatly admired her – but her acting was altogether too strong for his associates. The librettists disowned her performance: 'Mme Galli-

---

[30] Dean, *Bizet*, p. 83.

[31] There are, for example, two scenes in the novel in which men ogle young women outside their work place – one of leather workers bathing naked in the dusk and the other of the cigar factory girls emerging from the factory.

Marié may have played Mérimée's Carmen, she did not play ours!'[32] (It should hardly surprise us that they also stopped Escamillo patting the cheeks of a couple of the gipsy girls in the chorus as he came on stage.) Even eight years later when the Opéra Comique finally plucked up courage to revive *Carmen* (which was by then internationally acclaimed) they cast a less flamboyant mezzo in the title role. The early reviews were shocked by Galli-Marié's explicit sensuality. One wrote that 'it would be difficult to go much farther without provoking the intervention of the police' while another claimed that Galli-Marié's gestures were the 'very incarnation of vice, and there is something licentious even in the tones of her voice'.[33] This, it seems, was exactly what Bizet was after even if it did not please his librettists.

When Bizet finished composing Act I he wrote to his friend Paul Lacombe that he was well pleased with it.[34] We can only assume that he felt similarly satisfied with the rest of the score. But during the more than five months of rehearsal the score and libretto underwent numerous cuts and changes. Not all of these alterations were driven by conflicting views about what it was proper for the Opéra Comique audience to see. Bizet's autograph and the conducting score copied for the premier and used through until *c.*1890 tell a fascinating story of the evolution of the opera in its final rehearsal stages.[35] While some of these changes may have been made at Bizet's instigation – and others with his approval – many look as if they have been prompted by practical, dramatic considerations. It is interesting to see how often (as with *Alley*) transitions between one event and the next are shortened.

An interesting case in point is the sequence that begins with the changing of the guard and the entrance of the urchins who mimic the soldiers. 'Piston en la (dans la coulisse)' ('cornet in A in the wings') appears at the top of the page in Bizet's autograph. After eight bars, the off-stage cornet part has been deleted and its fanfare written into the stave for the cornet still left in the pit. At some point in the rehearsal process, a decision was taken to have the bugle of the incoming guard answered by that of the guard that is about to stand down. At the end of this bugle call a pause has been deleted. Someone (Bizet or possibly the conductor, Deloffre) must have wanted to move more quickly into the piccolo ('fife') tune that follows. In the middle of the number, an extended section of melodrama was cut and replaced by spoken dialogue (and, eventually by one of Guiraud's recitatives). The reprise of the number (after the melodrama that became dialogue that became recitative) has also been cut to less than half its original length. The deleted passages include one entire stanza in which the semiquaver triplet movement, now found only in the playout at

---

[32] Dean, *Bizet*, p. 99.

[33] Ibid., p. 89.

[34] 'J'ai fini le premier acte de *Carmen*; j'en suis assez content.' The letter is undated but clearly written sometime before 8 June 1874. See Georges Bizet, *Lettres*, ed. Claude Glayman (Paris, 1989), p. 274.

[35] Bizet's autograph score is Paris, Bibliothèque Nationale, Mss 436–439; the conducting score is in the library of the Paris Opéra, Ms. Rés 2222.

Illus. 6.4 Georges Bizet, *Carmen*, No. 3 'Avec la garde montante'; Bizet autograph manuscript, Paris: Bibliothèque Nationale de France, Ms. 436, p. 43

the end of the number, was introduced (illus. 6.4). The orchestral introduction to the next number – the chorus of cigarette girls – has also been severely cut.

There is no way of knowing for certain, but it seems likely that these transitional passages were simply too long for the dramatic business which had to take place on stage. And for all that we may regret the loss of individual felicities (the attractively suave legato string writing in the original introduction to the cigarette girls' chorus, for example) the score seems all the stronger for the mid-stream editing. Who knows whether what we are witnessing here is the refining of Bizet's aims? It is said that Galli-Marié herself persuaded Bizet to re-compose her first aria in Act I. According to Guiraud, Bizet revised this aria thirteen times during the rehearsal period before coming up with the Habanera that was to become one of opera's greatest hits. It is equally likely that some, at least, of these changes were driven by the demands of the production.

Some alterations were made pretty much at the last minute. The libretto submitted to the censors for approval three weeks before opening night differs in a number of respects from the version published about the time of the first performance.[36] Many of the changes made in the final phases of rehearsal almost certainly indicate circumstance (hard reality) winning over vision.

One small example will suffice to illustrate this. Castanets are important in Mérimée's novel as a way of evoking Carmen's wild, defiant, and unruly gypsy nature. Carmen expresses irritation by clacking them together; she uses them to warn the smugglers of the approach of the guard. Don José relates that at the end of a day eating, drinking, and lovemaking, 'I told her that I would like to see her dance; but where were castanets to be found? Immediately she took the old woman's only plate, broke it in pieces and there she was dancing the gypsy dance while making the earthenware pieces clack as if she had had castanets made of ebony or ivory.'[37]

Bizet, and his librettists, liked this incident – and it is clear from the libretto submitted to the censors that in her Act II duo (where she dances for Don José at Lilias Pastia's) Galli-Marié was still struggling with broken pieces of pottery instead of the real castanets that were eventually adopted.[38] Even this came to be seen as achievement enough. The Choudens scores (both the vocal score of 1875 and the full score published in 1877) have a note saying that the castanets can be played either in the orchestra or on stage – and that if the singer does play them herself the part can be adjusted to suit her abilities.

The first vocal score published by Choudens in 1875 is generally agreed to give the best indication of what the first-night audience heard and saw. According to Winton Dean, it 'represents the most important evidence we have as to the definitive form that Bizet wished his opera to assume'.[39] It might

---

[36] See L. A. Wright, 'A New Source for *Carmen*', *19th-Century Music* 2 (1978), 61–71.

[37] 'Je lui dis que je voudrais la voir danser; mais où trouver des castagnettes? Aussitôt elle prend la seule assiette de la vieille, la casse en morceaux, et la voilà qui danse la romalis en faisant claquer les morceaux de faïence aussi bien que si elle avait eu des castagnettes d'ébène ou d'ivroie.' Prosper Mérimée, *Carmen, Suivi de Les Âmes du Purgatoire* (Paris, 1999), p. 41.

[38] See Wright, 'A New Source for *Carmen*', 62.

[39] Winton Dean, 'The True *Carmen*', *Musical Times* 106 (1965), 847. Dean revisited this topic in 'The Corruption of *Carmen* and the Perils of Pseudo-Musicology', *Musical Newsletter* 3/4 (Oct., 1973), 7–12, 20. The 1875 vocal score is rather more rare than library catalogues would lead us to believe. The British Library copy with the callmark F. 119.c is a first edition whereas the copy with the callmark R. M. 9.b.19 is (despite the catalogue entry) later and contains the Guiraud recitatives. The vocal score in the Cambridge University Library catalogued as the 1875 edition is also a later copy.

be more accurate to say that it represents the best evidence of what actually happened. Whether anyone (Bizet included) was capable of describing an ideal or definitive performance by then is a moot point.

But that is not the end of the story. The score did not stabilise with the first performance nor even with Bizet's death four months later. A new production was mounted in Vienna the following October for which Guiraud composed the recitatives that for many years standardly replaced the spoken dialogue and melodrama of the original.

For all that they patently do not form part of the composer's intentions as expressed in the score, it is not so easy simply to dismiss Guiraud's recitatives. The fact that Bizet did not write recitatives in the first place is a simple product of circumstance. Spoken dialogue was the norm at the Opéra Comique – it was a defining feature of the genre (a vital element, in other words, of what audiences expected to hear). Bizet had, in fact, undertaken to provide recitatives for the Vienna season of *Carmen*. Hence, Guiraud was attempting to carry out the composer's intentions. And it is obvious that, despite their sometimes rather flaccid character, Guiraud used as his model the genuine Bizet recitatives in the score. The problem for performers wanting to be true to Bizet's intentions in *Carmen* is not as straightforward in this regard as is sometimes thought. It is arguable, at least, that substituting the spoken dialogue for the recitatives may not bring us closer to Bizet's ideal performance. One might argue that the real task might be one of finding a completion with recitatives more in line with Bizet's own genius. That, as we know from the Mozart Requiem, the Bruckner Symphony No. 9, and Mahler Symphony No. 10 is unlikely to be a straightforward or uncontroversial matter.[40]

Significant aspects of the orchestration may have been determined by circumstance. For instance, cornets (rather than trumpets) were standard at the Opéra Comique. At the beginning of the boy's chorus (discussed above) the autograph has (crossed out) beneath the reference to the off-stage cornet a direction 'Clairon [bugle], derrière la scène – Les soldats du poste vont prendre leurs lances, et se rangent devant le corps de garde.'[41] There is no prevarication about the instrument involved here – the cornet is what was heard. But the longer note in the score is about dramatic action (and, of course, the cornet is imitating a military bugle). In the *Livret de la mise en scène* (the set of production notes sent out with the musical materials by Choudens to any company undertaking a production of the opera) and in the 1875 vocal score the same instrument is referred to as a trumpet. What this might suggest is the cornets in the orchestra were being thought of as trumpet (or bugle) substitutes. The substitution of trumpets for cornets in the only full scores so far published may have a sliver of justification.[42]

---

[40] I should add that the spoken dialogue enriches the characterisation of, especially, Don José and Carmen by incorporating considerably more detail from Mérimée's story.

[41] 'Bugle backstage—the sentry soldiers go to take up their lances [swords?] and line up in front of the guard corps'.

[42] The other interesting aspect of the Opéra Comique orchestra as revealed by Bizet's score is

The *Carmen* story is an instructive one. Trying to do justice to the composer's conception might remain a guiding principle, though establishing exactly what that was is a complicated business of trying to disentangle vision and circumstance. And that, to a greater or lesser extent, must always be the case. Above all, it must be clear that even such a well-documented performance history cannot be used as a substitute for musical judgement.

Statements from composers expressing frustration at the performance not being a true representation of the work are, of course, legion. Mozart wrote to his father on 29 July 1782 after the second performance of *Die Entführung aus dem Serail* complaining that the mistakes of his cast were playing right into the hands of those who did not wish him well:

> Can you really believe it, but yesterday there was an even stronger cabal against it than on the first evening! The whole of the first act was accompanied by hissing. But indeed they could not prevent the loud shouts of 'bravo' during the arias. I was relying on the closing trio, but as ill-luck would have it, Fischer went wrong, which made Dauer (Pedrillo) go wrong too; and Adamberger alone could not sustain the trio, with the result that the whole effect was lost and that this time *it was not repeated.* I was in such a rage (and so was Adamberger) that I was simply beside myself and said at once that I would not let the opera be given again without having a short rehearsal for the singers.[43]

Gluck, writing with a sense of mission, was even more aggrieved at the way in which it seemed that his (and Calzabigi's) reforms of *opera seria* were being dismissed on the basis of an inadequately-rehearsed and ill-conceived production of *Alceste*:

> I decided to publish the music for *Alceste* only because I hoped that I would find others who would imitate the style. I thought that, continuing my effort and encouraged by an informed public, these disciples would strive more actively to destroy the abuses from which Italian opera suffers and to raise the art towards an ideal state. My idea was foolish; I regret it. The arbiters of taste, the sham experts, infinitely numerous and against all progress, have ganged up against a method which, in being worked out, would ruin for all time their pretension and the despotism of their feelings and actions.
>
> It has been seen fit to pronounce judgement on *Alceste*, after insufficient rehearsals, bad preparation, and even worse performances; the effect that this drama would produce on stage has been decided in a chamber. It makes the same sort of sense as it would have in ancient times, in a town in Greece, to judge from a few feet away, statues before they were mounted on top of high columns. One of those amateurs with a too delicate ear would, in the right ambience, be offended by the vehemence of a cantilena, by an unexpected harshness without realizing

that they were still using natural horns in 1875. Not only is the autograph score full of directions to change the key of the instrument (see illus. 6.4, for example), but in places the importance of doing this quickly is indicated ('changer vite en La'!).
[43] Mozart, *Letters*, p. 807f.

that the right acoustic magnifies the expression and provides helpful contrast for this vehemence and harshness. Another amateur, with peevish pedantry, would notice an intentional negligence or perhaps a printing error, and would hurry to draw attention to an inexcusable transgression of the rules of harmony. Thus opinion labels and condemns this music as barbaric and extravagant.[44]

Monteverdi may be hinting that the original performance of *Orfeo* fell short of his conception in his reference to its being presented 'on a confined stage'.[45] In the course of five months rehearsal for *Arianna* in 1608, Monteverdi had had to cope with the illness and death of the principal singer and with an extended hunt for an adequate replacement. More to the point, it seems that the various stakeholders in this production intervened to modify the original conception during the rehearsal phase. Carlo Rossi reported to the Duke of Mantua on 27 February 1608 that 'Rinuccini, Monteverdi, the prefect and Don Federico met yesterday morning, and as regards *Arianna* they were in agreement. Here the [need for] haste was noted; of the rest I know nothing else. Madame has agreed with Signor Ottavio to enrich it with some action, since it is very dry.'[46]

The stories of the making of *Alley* and of *Carmen* clearly have parallels going back to the origins of the genre. Such histories discourage a clear-cut view of honouring the composer's intentions since they suggest that, particularly in a collaborative venture like opera, it can be quite hard to disentangle the relationship between original conception and final result.

---

[44] *Paride ed Elena*, dedication to the Duc de Bragance (see above, p. 84n)
[45] See above, p. 78; see also Paolo Fabbri, *Monteverdi*, trans. Tim Carter (Cambridge, 1994), p. 65.
[46] Fabri, *Monteverdi*, p. 82. I have changed 'conclusion' in Carter's translation to 'agreement'.

7. Loyal opposition: transcription and historical fidelity

The concept of 'early music' is problematic. It appears to indicate some temporal boundary separating early from (presumably) modern, yet it has become less and less obvious quite where that boundary lies. In his *Foundations of Music History* (originally published in 1977), Carl Dahlhaus conceptualised the distinction between 'early music' and the rest of Western composition in a way that made chronological distance subordinate to a different kind of separation from the sense of a current norm. For Dahlhaus, the distinction resided in whether the repertory in question was regarded as part of an unbroken tradition, or as susceptible to restoration:

> Tradition presupposes seamless continuity . . .; restoration, on the other hand, is an attempt to renew contact with a tradition that has been interrupted or has atrophied . . . And it is this element of restoration, not merely distance in time, that determines whether or not a work is to be considered 'early music': the inner, rather than the outward, merely chronological distance, is the deciding factor. In 1829, a century after its time of writing, Bach's St Matthew Passion already belonged to 'early music'; Beethoven's symphonies, after a century and a half, have yet to acquire this status.[1]

Two important aspects of this formulation need underlining. First, Dahlhaus argues that the classification of a repertory as early music presupposes a plan of action. Early music requires a special understanding (and consequently a particular approach to its performance). It needs restoration. Second, Dahlhaus argues that whether or not something qualifies as early music is entirely a matter of the way it is perceived. It does not, in other words, arise from its position in an historically-objective stylistic development. Such classification is, in other words, an aspect of reception. Dahlhaus's Bach and Beethoven examples make this clear by emphasising that viewing either composer's works as early music depends on the relationship between *two* historical moments – the date of the works in question and the historical position of those making the judgement. I should add the obvious, that this judgement will not be a matter of universal consensus at the time it is made (so, contemporaries will categorise the same works differently).

[1] Dahlhaus, *Foundations*, p. 67.

It is interesting to see the effect that the intense interest in historical performance practice has had on that relationship between composition date and contemporary perception since the publication of Dahlhaus's *Foundations*. In 1980 the 'Performing Practice' article in *The New Grove* declared that there was 'no "lost tradition" separating the modern performer from the music of Haydn, Mozart and their successors' (a statement that comes pretty close to Dahlhaus's own view of the situation as quoted above). That statement, however, drew such criticism that it was replaced in the revised version of the article that appeared four years later in *The New Grove Dictionary of Musical Instruments* by the following:

> (i) *Apparent continuity of tradition.* Superficially, there is a fundamental difference between the study of performing practice before 1750 and the study of it after that date. Unlike the music of Machaut or Monteverdi, the repertory from Haydn to Elliott Carter has been performed continuously since its creation. At this elementary level, the main difference between a string quartet by Haydn and one by Carter is the length of their unbroken performance histories . . . But on closer examination neither the assumption of an unbroken performing history nor the corollary of an unbroken performing tradition stands up.[2]

By the time this was published, those interested in historical performance practice had claimed Haydn and Mozart as core repertory and had turned their attention to Beethoven as a composer whose music would benefit from 'restoration'. Now, of course, period instrument ensembles have addressed the music of Berlioz, Brahms, and other 19th-century composers.

This progression into later and later composition confirms that what is at issue is not where a division between early and late might be positioned but rather how the music of even the very recent past should be regarded. In the interests of making the point that the performance of virtually any repertory might be enhanced by a stronger historical sense, the *New Grove Performance Practice Handbook* contained a chapter on music 'Since 1940'.[3]

To summarise: over the past twenty-five years or so there has been broad acceptance of the idea that what defines early music has less to do with chronology than with a mental outlook – that, in Dahlhaus's terms, it is the 'inner' rather than the 'outer' distance that matters. In other words, the concept relates to perceivers' attitudes rather than to objective stylistic criteria.

It is obvious that two distinct groups of musicians can view an identical repertory either as part of a continuous tradition or as music in need of restoration. Again, Dahlhaus provides us with a useful framework within which to consider this kind of divergence. He describes the attitude to performance of those who stand apart from the early music mentality as a brand of conservatism:

---

[2] This has been commented on by Nicholas Kenyon in his introduction to *Authenticity and Early Music*, pp. 11–12.

[3] Paul Griffiths, 'The Twentieth Century: Since 1940', in Brown and Sadie, eds., *Performance Practice: Music after 1600*, 483–91.

In aesthetic perception, conservative efforts to maintain tradition by altering the letter so as to preserve the spirit take the form of a tendency to see in the changing interpretations of musical works nothing more than contingent manifestations of an eternally unvarying substance, adapted to particular moments in history. Authentic conservatism is by no means as inflexible as its detractors claim; but it does reject the notion that music is 'historical through and through', insisting instead on distinguishing between central properties that are supposedly inviolable, and peripheral ones that are interchangeable.[4]

We can recognise Dahlhaus's traditionalists in those who have argued that in order to recapture the original *impact* (as distinct from merely the sound world) of works like the *St Matthew Passion* we should present them with the enhanced forces of our own time. The conservative traditionalists presuppose a transcendental vision of music, one in which a work's 'essence' resides in something other than the sum total of performance instructions represented by the score. Such a view normally involves an assumption that the music of whatever period (though, in practice, this tends to mean any music after *c.* 1680) is best served by the range of expressive devices that have been accepted as standard over the past fifty years or so.

The historicist, on the other hand, is someone for whom (according to Dahlhaus) 'The historical faculty that analyses works of music in the context of their time of origin should be taken virtually intact into the aesthetic experience.' The historicist believes that historical interest and artistic enjoyment

> should not be kept apart by a rigid compartmentalisation of art into its aesthetic and documentary aspects. Awareness of the past is not incompatible with aesthetic presence; on the contrary, it can be a component part of that presence. The historicist firmly believes that what a work has to say about the age in which it was written belongs at one and the same time to the past and the present, not because works are "timeless" but because past and present form an indissoluble alloy . . .[5]

While Dahlhaus is not concerned exclusively with performers, his model of the historicist fits those who strive to incorporate historical awareness in performance. I might add that it is a model with which I am personally happy to identify.

For the historicist, the starting point in approaching musical performance is what Dahlhaus calls a 'controlled estrangement', a recognition that one cannot simply assume an understanding of this music – that we all know how it goes. What follows on from 'controlled estrangement' is the attempt to create a bridge between what seems to be the historical meaning of the score and our own musical instincts (which are almost inevitably going to be modified along the way). The final goal is expressed in the conviction that assimilating what has been (re)discovered is likely to be the most expressive way of bringing a

---

[4] Dahlhaus, *Foundations*, p. 70.
[5] Ibid., p. 70.

particular work or repertory to contemporary audiences. Performers, more obviously than anyone else, have to mediate between an historic past documented in the score of a work and its correlative aesthetic present.

In practical terms, this means more than just recognising that musicians in the past did things differently (a matter of re-learning aspects of technique and style which have fallen out of use). It also – and perhaps more importantly – means breaking the association between musical feeling and current ways of demonstrating musical feeling. Hence, not only may players find that they need to acquire a different set of instincts relating to, say, the use of vibrato, but they (and, crucially, their audiences) may also need to dissociate vibrato from such concepts as 'warmth' or at least to open themselves up to other ways in which warmth might be communicated.

Communication (which we might see as the whole point of performance) depends on a relationship between performer and audience. And that, needless to say, immensely complicates the issues being discussed here since little is gained if performers arrive at a fresh understanding of a musical dialect if their audiences are not in a position to de-code what they are hearing, if in other words they are unable to relate to the music in the same way as the performers. The accusation that period-instrument performance all too often lacks *gravitas* where that is needed may be at least partly a failure to attune to a different expressive vocabulary – one that might convey seriousness without smothering clarity of texture or intended instrumental colour. A shared understanding between performer and audience must be built. Awareness of this kind of problem, however, helps to explain the tendency of early music concerts and recordings to provide audiences with so much in the way of explanation and documentation (about instruments etc.). It may also explain the time lag that is often evident between innovation and appreciation. (I well remember one critic's description of Emma Kirkby's voice following her Purcell Room debut in the early 1970s as 'a light, folksy soprano'.)

In chapter 5 I used a semiotic model that presented historical awareness of as a prerequisite for accurate interpretation of notation. There I suggested that a proper understanding of such things as rhythmic conventions, expectations relating to ornamentation, and instrumental specifications becomes a vital part of establishing what the notation means and therefore of finding one's way through to the communication and enjoyment of a work's aesthetic presence. Such a view involves an acceptance that we are not in a position easily to distinguish, as the conservative traditionalists assume they can do, between a work's central and peripheral properties. For example, a decision not to perform a work on the instrument(s) for which it was conceived often amounts to an assertion that the work's essence does not reside in its instrumentation. When performers depart in this way from the specifics of a score, they have embarked on a process of transcription.

The rest of this chapter examines the motivation for various kinds of transcription. This is a way of exploring the implications of two ideas that have been promoted by those who do not greatly value historical reconstruction as an approach to musical performance: first, that a quite radical reworking of a composition might be inspired by respect rather than disregard for its character; and second, that the many instances of works transcribed by their own composers suggest that these composers had a relatively relaxed attitude to specific instrumental timbre. Both claims may be seen as related to a conservative traditionalist (or anti-historicist) stance.

Adorno, militantly embracing the conservative traditionalist position, vaunted creative transcription as the most effective way of keeping faith with the past:

> Justice is done to Bach not through musicological usurpation but solely through the most advanced composition which in turn converges with the level of Bach's continually unfolding work. The few instrumentations contributed by Schoenberg and Anton von Webern, especially those of the great triple fugue in E flat major and of the six-part *Ricercata*, in which every facet of the composition is transposed into a correlative timbre and in which the surface interweaving of lines is dissolved into the most minute motivic interrelations and then reunited through the overall constructive disposition of the orchestra – such instrumentations are models of an attitude to Bach which corresponds to the stage of his truth. Perhaps the traditional Bach can indeed no longer be interpreted. If this is true, his heritage has passed on to composition, which is loyal to him in being disloyal; it calls his music by name in producing it anew.[6]

What Adorno's commentary on the Schoenberg and Webern transcriptions remind us is the way in which Bach's music appeared to relate so seamlessly to the interests of the Second Viennese School. In fact, these transcriptions may be seen as part of a concern on Schoenberg and Webern's part to legitimise their compositional procedures by demonstrating their continuity with earlier developments and in particular with the Germanic mainstream of the Western canon. And while their orchestrations are at the same time instructive and consciously creative, it is interesting that Webern, at least, appeared to regard instrumental timbre (or indeed any other specifically performance-related feature) in Bach's music as irrelevant – or even a kind of impurity. Thus, in *The Path to the New Music* we find the following epiphany:

> *For everything happens in Bach*: the development of cyclic forms, the conquest of the tonal field, and, with it all, staggering polyphonic thought! Horizontally and vertically. And here we must return to something earlier! It's important that Bach's last work was the *Art of Fugue*, a work that goes wholly into the abstract,

---

[6] Adorno, 'Bach Defended', p. 146. A similar concept of loyal disloyalty was attributed to the Shakespearean critic and director Jan Kott in *The New York Times*, 2 January 2002: ' "Jan Kott used to say that in order to do Shakespeare well you have to betray him and bring out those elements that resonate with us today," said Andrea Liberovici, a composer and founder of the experimental theater company Teatrodelsuono . . . "Shakespeare's truth still speaks to us; it's not just some period drama. The same is true with the violin. When Paganini was alive he didn't play music from 200 years before. I am convinced that if he were alive today he would play jazz." ' (A. G. Basoli, 'Paganini's Violin Encounters Jazz'.)

music lacking all the things usually shown by notation – no sign whether it's for voices or instrument, no performing indications. It's almost an abstraction – or I prefer to say *the highest reality!*[7]

This belief – that Bach composed an ideal music that ignored such worldly features as instrumental colour – freed Webern to use instrumentation to highlight essential contrapuntal features.

It is striking that Webern's instrumentation for the Fuga (Ricercata) from *The Musical Offering* (completed in 1934) is almost identical to that for his next orchestral work, the Op. 30 Variations for Orchestra (completed 1940). Both essentially use single woodwind and brass plus harp and strings (but with the Bach arrangement adding cor anglais and bassoon while lacking the tuba and celeste of the Variations). Curiously, the only intervals in the row for Op. 30 are semitones and (minor) thirds – the very intervals that dominate the *Musical Offering* theme until the conspicuously tonal cadential gesture which make up its last six notes (see ex. 7.1).

Ex. 7.1 Anton Webern, Concerto Op. 30, note row

Webern wrote of the Bach orchestration, 'My orchestration attempts . . . to reveal the interrelation of *motifs*. This was not always easy. It seeks of course in addition to show how I see the character of the work.'[8] The desire to demonstrate the motivic structure of the theme is seen clearly in the opening statement (ex. 7.2) where (a) the trombone is given the first five notes, (b) muted horn and trumpet isolate one pair of semitones, each with a different articulation, (c) the trombone takes the next pair of semitones back into a slur (thus demonstrating that, together, they make up a minor third), and (d) the cadential gesture referred to above is broken up into two perfect fourths (horn) and a final semitone (trumpet and harp in unison). That leaves only one note to be explained: the E-flat harp harmonic in bar 5 (three bars before the same pitch is sounded again on the harp – not, this time, as a harmonic). This is exactly halfway through the theme (the 10th of 20 notes). The sounding of this tone at this point casts the (faster) continuation of the chromatic descent and the fourth motif as a kind of ornamental prolongation.

Webern adheres to this motivic division throughout the piece, until the very final entry of the theme (in bar 197) where it is stated complete by all the bass instruments (bass clarinet, bassoon, cello and double bass). Most of this seems

[7] Anton Webern, *The Path to the Mew Music*, ed. Willi Reich, trans. Leo Black (Bryn Mawr, 1963), p. 34.

[8] Letter to Herman Scherchen, quoted here from the preface to Johann Sebastian Bach/ Anton Webern *Fuga (Ricercata) a 6 voci* Philharmonia score No. 465 (Vienna and London: Universal Edition, 1963).

Ex. 7.2 J. S. Bach/Anton Webern, Fuga (Ricercata), Nr. 2 aus dem *Musikalischen Opfer*, bars 1–9

unforced – a 'natural' way of colouring in the motivic structure of Frederick the Great's theme. The one feature that seems counter-intuitive is the splitting of the final six notes. The last note, the return to the tonic (which, in a uniform-timbre performance, is heard as an 'end is my beginning' gesture), is rendered 'invisible' by the orchestration since it is assigned to the second violins (beginning a counter subject).

Kathryn Bailey comments that 'Webern provided a good introduction to this eccentric type of orchestration (though this was not his purpose) in the arrangement he made in 1934–5 of the six-part ricercare from Bach's

Musikalisches Opfer. Here, because the music itself is tonal and conjunct, and, indeed, familiar, the linear connections are easier to grasp.'[9] In other words, the Bach orchestration might well help us come to terms with Webern's own music. But does it change the way we hear Bach? This is not, *pace* Adorno, a question that is susceptible to a general answer for our times. For my own part, I am not sure that allowing Webern to take us through the Ricercare is essentially any more illuminating than reading a good (academic) analysis – which is not to say that I don't enjoy the Webern reworking *qua* stand-alone orchestral composition.

Schoenberg's lush orchestration of the E-flat Prelude and Fugue BWV 552 is very different in its impact from the Webern Ricercare. But it might equally be 'read' as an analysis of the original (especially since, in addition to using instrumental colour to highlight aspects of the motivic structure, Schoenberg actually labels various lines 'Hauptstimme' (main voice) and 'Nebenstimme' (subsidiary voice)).

Ex. 7.3 Brahms, *Studien für Pianoforte*, No. 4, bars 1–10

Webern and Schoenberg's orchestrations were, of course, far from being the first creative transcriptions of Bach's works. Three of Brahms's *Five Studies for the Piano* (1877) are arrangements of movements from the solo violin sonatas. Numbers 3 and 4 are both based on the Presto from the G minor Sonata (BWV 1001), one with the violin part confined to the left hand and a new contrapuntal line (also in semiquavers) given to the right hand (ex. 7.3) and the other reversing this process. Study No. 5 is a version of the Chaconne from the D minor Partita (BWV 1004) for left hand alone (about which, more below).

Twenty years later, the Chaconne was also to receive Busoni's attention (as part of a more wide-ranging project that reached fruition in the publication of the *Bach–Busoni gesammelte Ausgabe* (Leipzig, 1920)).[10] Predictably, it is the sense of grandeur of this piece which Busoni's transcription projects. Perceiving that Bach's original conveys a sense of absolutely filling the instrument, Busoni sets out to do the same – but with a late 19th-century grand piano in mind rather than the violin. In fact, in illus. 7.1 we see him reaching out beyond the colours of the piano to imagine trombones at the arrival of the D major section.

[9] Kathryn Bailey, 'Webern', *The New Grove Dictionary of Music and Musicians*, 2nd ed., ed. Stanley Sadie and John Tyrell, 29 vols. [*New Grove II*] (London, 2001), vol. 27.
[10] The Chaconne was also transcribed for piano by Alexander Silotti (1865–1945). This version has been recorded by Risto Lauriala on *Bach Transcriptions for Piano* (Naxos 8.553761).

Illus. 7.1 Bach/Busoni, Chaconne für Violine allein, from the *Bach–Busoni gesammelte Ausgabe* (Leipzig, 1920)

V. A. 2884.

For over 150 years, it has been Bach works above all that have been the subject of transcription. Since the Swingle Singers and Jethro Tull in the 1960s, many transcriptions have been permutations of the 'switched-on Bach' idea. A report in *The Independent on Sunday* in October 2000 of a concert in the converted Fiat factory in Turin described Uri Caine's presentation of *The Goldberg Variations*:

The bill announces a performance of Bach's Goldberg Variations, which were written for solo keyboard; sure enough, there is a piano centre-stage.

Arranged around it, however, is an ensemble which might have surprised Bach. There's a jazz quartet of clarinet, trumpet, double-bass and drums, with a violin thrown in for good measure. There are two vocalists, gospel singer Barbara Walker and vocal improviser David Moss. To one side, a viola da gamba quartet, which Bach would recognise; at the rear, a choir which the composer would certainly know what to do with. But what would he make of the twin-turntable console of DJ Olive, whose scratch'n'mix improvisations punctuate the performance?[11]

Leaving aside the question of whether in fact Bach would have been reassured by the sight of a piano centre stage, have recognised a viola da gamba quartet, or 'certainly known what to do with' this particular choir, it must be clear that this kind of arrangement is doing something more than attempting to preserve the essence of the original for modern ears – though it may be building on what Caine perceived as an important dimension in the host composition. Caine is in no sense a conservative traditionalist. He is totally up-front about his appropriation of Bach's music for his own ends.

All of these Bach treatments might be seen both as an act of homage and as an original creative contribution. The arranger is acknowledged in what would seem to be an equal partnership with the original composer: it is the Brahms *Five Studies*, the Bach-Busoni *Ausgabe*, the Bach-Schoenberg *Präludium und Fuge* and so on. Various composers have commented on the particular pleasure and rewards of such enterprises. No one does this more interestingly (or in a way so germane to the concerns of this essay) than Stravinsky in describing the genesis of *Pulcinella*:

I have always been enchanted by Pergolesi's Neapolitan music, so entirely of the people and yet so exotic in its Spanish character. The proposal that I should work with Picasso, who was to do the scenery and costumes and whose art was particularly near and dear to me . . . all this combined to overcome my reluctance. For it was a delicate task to breathe new life into scattered fragments and to create a whole from the isolated pages of a musician for whom I felt a special liking and tenderness.

Before attempting a task so arduous, I had to find an answer to a question of the greatest importance by which I found myself faced. Should my line of action with regard to Pergolesi be dominated by my love or by my respect for his music? Is it love or respect that urges us to possess a woman? Is it not by love alone that we succeed in penetrating to the very essence of a being? But, then, does love diminish respect? Respect alone remains barren, and can never serve as a productive or creative factor. In order to create there must be a dynamic force, and what force is more potent than love? To me it seems that to ask the question is to answer it.

I do not want the reader to think that in writing this I am trying to exonerate

[11] Nick Kimberley, 'Fusion: You ain't heard nothing like this', in *The Independent on Sunday*, 8 October 2000, p. 10.

myself from the absurd accusations of sacrilege levelled against me. I am only too familiar with the mentality of those curators and archivists of music who jealously guard the intangibility of relics at which they never so much as look, while resenting any attempt on the part of others to resuscitate these treasures which they themselves regard as dead and sacrosanct. Not only is my conscience clear of having committed sacrilege, but, as far as I can see, my attitude towards Pergolesi is the only one that can usefully be taken up with regard to the music of bygone times. . . .

During the following month I gave myself up entirely to *Pulcinella,* and the work filled me with joy. The material I had at my disposal . . . made me appreciate more and more the true nature of Pergolesi while discerning ever more clearly the closeness of my mental and, so to speak, sensory kinship with him.[12]

On the face of it, Stravinsky – in rebutting the charge of sacrilege with a stance that comes close to Adorno's position quoted above – is defending himself against the stereotypical 'Early Music' buff. He insists that his refashioning of Pergolesi (or whoever it was that in fact wrote the rather slight trio sonatas on which *Pulcinella* is based) is an act of homage (of love, in fact); and that for him – and, we might assume, for his audience – the result was one which drew attention to the distinctive character of the original.

Stravinsky's sense of kinship with (his contemporary) Picasso is in a sense attested to by that other great modernist's multiple re-workings of the Diego Velazquez *Les Meninas.*[13] Every one of Picasso's images implies near-boundless respect for his predecessor by encouraging the viewer to see how each of his paintings in its turn contributes to a multiplicity of insights all present simultaneously in the Velazquez original. In this way, Picasso both empowers a reading of the original that may always have been available while at the same time providing a new and distinct aesthetic pleasure.

A parallel claim could be made for the refashionings of Bach considered here.[14] Each results in a 'new' composition, but each also belongs to history, being born out of respect for Bach and offering insights about the character of the Bach original. What Busoni does is present the grandeur of Bach in a language that listeners of the late 19th century were ready to recognise *as* grandeur. What Webern does is to remind us that, like Bach, he and the other musicians in Schoenberg's circle were interested in linear writing and in motivic manipulation.

So, Adorno is right in pointing out the capacity of creative transcription to bring into relief aspects of the original composition that converge with the musical preoccupations of a later generation (thus illustrating the contemporary relevance for that generation of Bach's writing), but he is surely wrong in implying that the only way we are likely to notice these aspects of the writing is

[12] Stravinsky, *Autobiography,* pp. 81–3.

[13] Velazquez's *Les Meninas* is in the Prado in Madrid. Picasso's numerous paintings based on it are in the Picasso Museum in Barcelona. (Francisco de Goya also copied *Les Meninas;* see Richard Morphet et al., *Encounters: New Art from Old* (London, 2000), p. 8.)

[14] Though I hasten to add that I have no way of assessing the Uri Caine Goldberg Variations.

through the mediation of later composers. Schoenberg and Webern were Adorno's contemporaries. Now, however, they are as historical as Bach himself. The insights they offer are limited in comparison with the multivalent possibilities of the original. One is tempted to respond to Adorno's claims for other composers' presentations of Bach with the kind of frustration expressed by Harold Bloom towards the anti-canonists' receptions of Shakespeare:

> Here they ['the partisans of resentment'] confront insurmountable difficulty in Shakespeare's most idiosyncratic strength: he is always ahead of you, conceptually and imagistically, whoever and whenever you are. He renders you anachronistic because he *contains* you; you cannot subsume him. You cannot illuminate him with a new doctrine, be it Marxism or Freudianism or Demanian linguistic skepticks. Instead, he will illuminate the doctrine, not by prefiguration but by postfiguration as it were: all of Freud that matters most is there in Shakespeare already, with a persuasive critique of Freud besides. The Freudian map of the mind is Shakespeare's; Freud seems only to have prosified it. Or, to vary my point, a Shakespearian reading of Freud illuminates and overwhelms the text of Freud; a Freudian reading of Shakespeare reduces Shakespeare, or would if we could bear a reduction that crosses the line into absurdities of loss. *Coriolanus* is a far more powerful reading of Marx's *Eighteenth Brumaire of Louis Napoleon* than any Marxist reading of *Coriolanus* could hope to be.[15]

Or, one might recap (less severely), Webern's reading of Bach offers a partial illumination of Bach and a valuable insight into Webern's own methods. It could never be a substitute for the original.

So much for explicit transcription, where an intermediary's intention to re-present a musical work in a way that differs from the specifications of the original score is transparent and deliberate. The very fact that the arranger is identified alongside the original composer encourages audiences to assess the result as an aspect of reception ('this is how Busoni saw Bach') and thus neutralises the issue of whether or not this might be doing violence to the original conception. Such transcriptions can be appreciated on their own terms. Clearly, though, this kind of explicit transcription (particularly in the case of the piano versions of Bach works by Brahms, Saint-Saens, Busoni and others) almost merges with what we might call 'implicit' transcription – the performance of Bach (or Handel, or Scarlatti) keyboard works on the modern piano (to take the most obvious examples). Nowadays, when it would be difficult for an educated musician to remain unaware of the possibility of performing this repertory on period instruments, the act of playing Bach on the piano constitutes (1) a deliberate decision (albeit one that might be driven by eminently sensible practical considerations), and (2) probably a declaration of allegiance to the 'conservative traditionalist' stance.[16] In other words, in assuming that the indications of the

---

[15] Harold Bloom, *The Western Canon* (New York, San Diego, and London, 1994), p. 25.

[16] I say 'probably' because, as Brahms's comments on his own transcription of the D minor Chaconne (quoted below) indicate, it is not inconceivable that a pianist performing Bach may do so with a sense of the added value that the original instrumentation might confer.

score vis à vis instrumentation may be interpreted to mean what are seen as modern equivalents (piano instead of harpsichord), the performer is adopting a transcendental view of the work – one that implies that its essence (which is somehow independent of the instructions presented in the score) will be well served by this approach (and certainly not damaged by it).

To perform Bach keyboard works on the modern piano is to transfer them to a medium that the composer could not have known. But does that necessarily mean that they are therefore less true to the composer's intentions? The conservative traditionalist and historicist answers to that question are clearly quite different. To the historicist, not to observe what can be established about an envisaged instrumental timbre must seem a violation of the composer's intentions. But it is not impossible that 18th-century composers themselves would have found such an attitude puzzlingly restrictive. After all, it is generally accepted that possibly all of Bach's harpsichord concertos are transcriptions of concertos for other instruments. This, on the face of it, might suggest a relatively relaxed attitude on the composer's part to timbre. Charles Rosen makes this point by referring to one of Bach's more radical re-workings:

> To take a harpsichord concerto by Johann Sebastian Bach and arrange it for a four-part chorus, organ, and orchestra would not, for most music lovers today, be considered the proper way to realize the composer's intentions or even to show decent respect for the score. Yet this is what Bach himself did to his own harpsichord concerto in D minor – which was, incidentally, in its original version a violin concerto of a somewhat simpler cast. The ideal of performing a work as it would have been done during the composer's lifetime or even by the composer himself gives rise to unexpected considerations, of which this is an extreme case, but by no means a rare one.[17]

In order to assess the validity of this conservative traditionalist challenge to the historicist position we need to look at 18th-century transcriptions of 18th-century works, and, in particular, at same-composer transcriptions.

One might begin with Francesco Geminiani, who stands out as an inveterate transcriber of his own (and of Corelli's) compositions. Some of his transcription ventures seem to have been completely opportunistic, driven by commercial motives and dismissed by Burney as 'musical cookery, not to call it quackery'.[18] But, for my present purposes, the most interesting objects of transcription by Geminiani are his Op. 5 cello sonatas. These were first published in Paris in 1746.[19] In the same year he brought out a companion volume of the very same sonatas arranged for violin.[20] (It would be unclear, in fact, which version was the

[17] Rosen, 'The Benefits of Authenticity', p. 201.
[18] Burney was referring specifically to Geminiani's arrangements of the Corelli ensemble sonatas, Opp. 1–4. See my 'Geminiani and the Role of the Viola in the Concerto Grosso', pp. 394–5.
[19] *Sonate pour le violoncelle et basse continue* (Paris: Boivin, 1746).
[20] *Sonates pour le violon avec un violoncelle ou clavecin* (The Hague: author, 1646)

Table 7.1 Geminiani transcriptions of his own Op. 5 Cello Sonatas

Geminiani Op. 5
  (i)   *Sonate pour le violoncelle et basse continue* (Paris: Boivin, 1746)
  (iia) *Sonates pour le violon avec un violoncelle ou clavecin* (The Hague: author, 1646)
  (iib) *Le VI Sonate di violoncello e basso continuo composte da F. Geminiani Opera VI Sono
        dallo stesso trasposte per il violino con cambiamenti proprij e necessarij allo stromento*
        (London: [author], 1747)
  (iii) *The Second Collection of Pieces for the Harpsichord* (London: author, 1762)

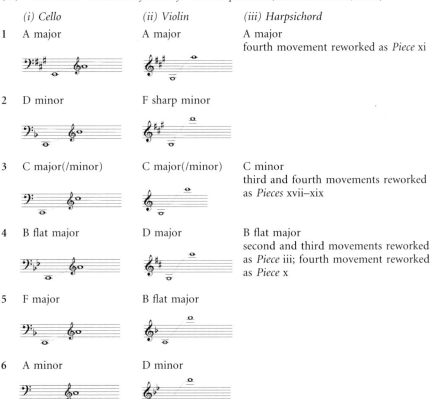

	(i) Cello	(ii) Violin	(iii) Harpsichord
1	A major	A major	A major fourth movement reworked as *Piece* xi
2	D minor	F sharp minor	
3	C major(/minor)	C major(/minor)	C minor third and fourth movements reworked as *Pieces* xvii–xix
4	B flat major	D major	B flat major second and third movements reworked as *Piece* iii; fourth movement reworked as *Piece* x
5	F major	B flat major	
6	A minor	D minor	

original were it not for a note on the title page of a new 1747 edition of the violin
versions saying that they had been 'transposed for the violin with such changes as
are appropriate and necessary for that instrument'.)

Enrico Careri, in his book on the composer, has assumed (like Rosen above)
that the implications of such piggy-backing are that Geminiani was not
particularly concerned with the specific sonority or idiom of the violin (or
even perhaps of the cello). Careri writes,

> The purpose of the transcription is only too clear; however, it raises a doubt whether
> Geminiani was genuinely inspired by the individual sound of the cello – or whether

any kind of instrument might not have been equally good. This observation is strengthened by the subsequent transcription for harpsichord of seven movements of Op. V, which appeared in the second collection of *Pièces de Clavecin* (1762).[21]

But was this really the case? The most straightforward way of transferring cello compositions to the violin is to transpose them up by a perfect 12th (the interval that separates the equivalent open strings on each instrument). Table 7.1 shows that no pair of sonatas has this relationship. For two he retains the key of the original in the violin version – but never simply by writing out the sonata at a different pitch. In two cases, he transposes the key of the original up by a major 3rd and in the remaining two by a perfect 4th. The choice of key in the transcriptions seems to be determined by the sonority of the violin.

Ex. 7.4 Francesco Geminiani, *Sonate pour le violoncelle et basse continue, Op. 5 (Paris, 1746) and Sonates pour le violon avec un violoncelle ou clavecin* (The Hague, 1746): Sonata No. 1, first movement; violin and cello versions compared, bars 1–5

A comparison of any pair of sonatas, far from suggesting an indifference to instrumental sonority, illustrates Geminiani's acute sense of the distinctive character of each instrument. The opening movement of the first sonata, despite being in the same key, contains numerous differences between each version (see ex. 7.4). The cello begins in unison with the basso continuo. Geminiani places a rest in the violin part, rather than opt for the octave which would have resulted from a straight transfer of the cello line. In bar 4, the cello drops a 10th from G sharp to a low E where the violin has the two pitches played as a double-stopped third. The cello version of the second sonata opens with chords whose richness

---

[21] Careri, *Francesco Geminiani*, p. 105.

the violin is not asked to emulate. In their place, the violin part has florid quasi-improvised passage work. Nothing could convey more clearly, Geminiani's sense of the distinct capacities of each instrument (ex. 7.5).

Ex. 7.5 Francesco Geminiani, *Sonate pour le violoncelle et basse continue*, Op. 5 (Paris, 1746) and *Sonates pour le violon avec un violoncelle ou clavecin* (The Hague, 1746): Sonata No. 2, first movement; violin and cello versions compared, bars 1–2

Careri further claims that the additional transcription of several of these movements for harpsichord proves the point that Geminiani was very little concerned with specific instrumental sonority or idiom. But this is not the case. The title pages of both collections of *Pièces de clavecin* state that their contents are 'taken from different works of F. Geminiani, and *adapted* by himself *to that instrument*' (my emphases).[22] Generally speaking, the extent to which Geminiani has transformed compositions written for other instruments into convincingly idiomatic harpsichord music is impressive. Both volumes – but particularly the first – manage to look like harpsichord music.[23] In *The Second Collection* the pieces are arranged in groupings that have more affinity with French suites than the slow-fast-slow-fast organisation of the Opus 5 sonatas. As table 7.1 illustrates, Geminiani retains the key of the cello originals in all the movements borrowed for the harpsichord volume and sometimes, it is true, very little change has been made. But there is scarcely a movement that does not reflect Geminiani's sense of what each instrument might do. He finishes the final movement of Sonata III, for example, differently for each instrument. This

[22] I quote here from the title page of *The Second Collection of Pieces for the Harpsichord* (1762) which is, in fact, an exact translation of the title page of the first volume of *Pièces de clavecin* (1743).

[23] See my 'Violin Fingering in the 18th Century', *Early Music* 12 (1984), 313. A few of pieces are designated 'per l'organo'.

Ex. 7.6 Francesco Geminiani, *The Second Collection of Pièces for the Harpsichord Taken from different Works of F. Geminiani and adapted by Himself to that Instrument* (London, 1762): piece [19] compared with *Sonate pour le violoncelle et basse continue*, Op. 5 (Paris, 1746): Sonata No. 3, fourth movement

is constructed as a C major/C minor gavotte pair (though the dance title is not used). At the end of the C minor gavotte, the cello is given a 'Da Capo al Segno' instruction while the violin has a written-out chordally-enriched reprise of the opening twelve bars. The harpsichord, however, does not return at all to the C major gavotte, but is given instead a variation on the B section of the C minor gavotte. The figuration here is clearly prompted by the character of the harpsichord. Ex. 7.6 shows this variation with, above it, the original melody as it appears at the opening of the harpsichord version and in the violin version (which, in this case, is identical to the cello version but an octave higher). While the two upper lines in ex. 7.6 are the same in respect of pitch and durations,

Geminiani does at least indicate bowings in the one and keyboard embellishments and articulations in the other.

In fact, any examination of alternative versions of Geminiani works would suggest that he had a very clear sense of what belonged to each instrument.

It is, however, to Bach that we must now turn since it is his transcriptions that supposedly exhibit a disregard for instrumental sonority as an integral part of the transcribed works' character.

Transcription played a major part in Bach's musical development. He copied out works by many of his contemporaries and immediate predecessors. His transcriptions of Vivaldi concertos, however, are of particular interest. Johann Nikolaus Forkel, relying on information from Carl Philip Emmanuel Bach, gave an account of Bach's reasons for transcribing these works:

> John Sebastian Bach's first attempts at composition were, like all first attempts, defective. Without any instruction to lead him into the way which might gradually have conducted him from step to step, he was obliged, like all those who enter on such a career without a guide, to do at first as well as he could. To run or leap up and down the instrument, to take both hands as full as all the five fingers will allow, and to proceed in this wild manner till they by chance find a resting place are the acts which all beginners have in common with each other. They can therefore by only 'finger composers' (or 'clavier hussars', as Bach, in his riper years, used to call them); that is, they must let their fingers first play for them what they are to write, instead of writing for the fingers what they shall play. But Bach did not long follow this course. He soon began to feel that the eternal running and leaping led to nothing; that there must be order, connection, and proportion in the thoughts, and that, to attain such objects, some kind of guide was necessary. Vivaldi's Concertos for the violin, which were then just published, served him for such a guide. He so often heard them praised as admirable compositions that he conceived the happy idea of arranging them all for his clavier. He studied the chain of the ideas, their relation to each other, the variations of the modulations, and many other particulars. The change necessary to be made in the ideas and passages composed for the violin, but not suitable to the clavier, taught him to think musically; so that after his labor was completed, he no longer needed to expect his ideas from his fingers, but could derive them from his own fancy.[24]

Forkel's assertion that 'The change necessary to be made in the ideas and passages composed for the violin, but not suitable to the clavier, taught him to think musically' bears repeating. It might be reasonable to draw from Forkel's claims the corollary that, while the act of transcription undoubtedly does indicate a willingness on Bach's part to set aside Vivaldi's specified instrumentation, this departure from the original nevertheless does not provide any encouragement for thinking that Bach was indifferent to questions of instrumental idiom and sonority. But this needs further examination.

[24] H. T. David. and A. Mendel, eds., revised and expanded by Christoph Wolff, *The New Bach Reader* (New York and London, 1998), pp. 441–2.

Table 7.2 Bach transcriptions of Vivaldi concertos

Original	Instrumentation	Transcription	Instrumentation
Vivaldi, Concerto in D from *L'Estro Armonico*, RV 230 [Op. 3, No. 9]	violin, strings and basso continuo	Bach, Concerto in D, BWV 972	harpsichord
Vivaldi, Concerto in G major, RV 299 [Op. 7, No. 2]	violin, strings and basso continuo	Bach, Concerto in G, BWV 973	harpsichord
Vivaldi, Concerto in G minor, RV 316 [Op. 4, No. 6]	violin, strings and basso continuo	Bach, Concerto in G minor, BWV 975	harpsichord
Vivaldi, Concerto in E major, RV 265 [Op. 3, No. 12]	violin, strings and basso continuo	Bach, Concerto in C major, BWV 976	harpsichord
Vivaldi, Concerto in G major, RV 310 [Op. 3, No. 3]	violin, strings and basso continuo	Bach, Concerto in F major, BWV 978	harpsichord
Vivaldi, Concerto in B flat, RV 381 [Op. 4, No. 1]	violin, strings and basso continuo	Bach, Concerto in G major, BWV 980	harpsichord
Vivaldi, Concerto in A minor, RV 522 [Op. 3, No. 8]	2 violins, strings and basso continuo	Bach, Concerto in A minor, BWV 593	organ
Vivaldi, Concerto in D major, 'Grosso Mogul', RV 208 [Op. 7, No. 5]	violin, strings and basso continuo	Bach, Concerto in C major, BWV 594	organ
Vivaldi, Concerto in D minor, RV 565 [Op. 3, No. 11]	2 violins, cello, strings and basso continuo	Bach, Concerto in D minor, BWV 596	organ
Vivaldi, Concerto in B minor, RV 580 [Op. 3, No. 10]	4 violins, strings and basso continuo	Bach, Concerto in A minor, BWV 1065	4 harpsichords, strings and basso continuo

Bach's Vivaldi transcriptions are shown in table 7.2. Of all Bach's transcriptions, those which take the form of harpsichord solos (BWV 972 to 980) approximate most closely to an important and enduring category of transcription that, paradoxically, rides rough-shod over the original instrumental colouring without implying the slightest disrespect for the very dimension it discards.[25] Forkel's claim is that Bach made these transcriptions in order to study the compositions. In doing this Bach was anticipating the countless keyboard reductions of orchestral scores that were to be such an important way

---

[25] This series also includes Bach's arrangements of concertos by Giuseppe Torelli (BWV 979), Benedetto Marcello (BWV 981), Prince Johann Ernst of Saxe-Weimar (BWV 982, 984, 987, and 592a), and Georg Philipp Telemann (BWV 985).

for musicians to become acquainted with works that – before the advent of the gramophone – could only occasionally be heard in their full glory. (Schumann wrote his celebrated analysis of the Berlioz *Symphonie Fantastique* using only Liszt's piano transcription of the work.) Few who made, studied, played, or listened to these transcriptions would have regarded them as a satisfactory substitute for the original composition (just as buying a CD is not a statement of preference for electronic reproductions over live performances).

Ex. 7.7 (a) Antonio Vivaldi, Concerto in E major, RV 265, third movement, bars 22–5

Ex. 7.7 (b) J. S. Bach, Concerto for Harpsichord, BWV 976, bars 19–33

Three features of the Vivaldi-Bach transcriptions for solo harpsichord stand out. First, as was the case with the Geminiani Op. 5 transcriptions, Bach does not unquestioningly take over the key of the parent work. Three of the Vivaldi harpsichord transcriptions are in their original key, but an equal number are not. In each case, the decision about where to relocate it seems to have been made on the basis of what tonality will sound best in the prevailing circular tuning systems for keyboards. The Concerto in C major, BWV 976, avoids many of the rather strained harmonies that would have resulted had the original key of E major been retained (see ex. 7.7). Even in BWV 978, where the change is from one key rich in pure thirds (G major) to another with quite similar characteristics (F major), it is clear that Bach's transposition achieves an increased sense of consonance. Examples like this provide further evidence in support of Carl Philip Emmanuel's contention that Bach's basic principles were 'anti-Rameau' (i.e. anti-equal temperament).

Ex. 7.8 (a) Antonio Vivaldi, Concerto in G major, RV 310, second movement, Largo, bars 1–4

Ex. 7.8 (b) J. S. Bach, Concerto for Harpsichord in F major, BWV 978, second movement, Largo, bars 1–4

The second notable feature is that any figuration that is specifically violinistic in the original is replaced by something that lies more easily under a harpsichordist's fingers. In the third movement of the Vivaldi E major concerto RV 265, for example, the first solo episode begins with a repeated-note figure based on string crossing. This is completely idiomatic on the violin but awkward on a keyboard. In BWV 976, Bach substitutes triadically-based figuration. An even more striking case of this kind of re-fashioning occurs later in the movement (ex. 7.7). And this is typical. The staccato tutti chords which punctuate the middle movement of the Vivaldi Concerto in G major RV 310 become an opportunity for the harpsichordist to fill the instrument in the Bach transcription (ex. 7.8).

The third aspect of these works that stands out is Bach's constitutional inability to resist the opportunity for introducing more contrapuntal interest. A further example from the RV 310/BWV 978 pairing will suffice. One of the solo episodes in the third movement is dominated by a repeated-note figure that suits the violin but would be uncomfortable on the harpsichord. It is accompanied by chords from the ripienists. Bach replaces the repeated-note idea with a more harpsi-chord-friendly figuration and introduces semiquaver movement in the left hand that begins in imitation of the upper part's downward scale (ex. 7.9).

Ex. 7.9 (a) Antonio Vivaldi, Concerto in G major, RV 310, third movement, bars 56–9

Ex. 7.9 (b) J. S. Bach, Concerto for Harpsichord in F major, BWV 978, third movement, bars 56–60

The Vivaldi concertos transcribed for organ are even more obviously adapted for the instrument than those for harpsichord. The opening of the D minor concerto BWV 596 (an arrangement of RV 565), for example, is an ingenious realisation of ideas that are implicit in the original. Vivaldi has the two solo violins moving in alternation through two octaves of D minor arpeggiation. Between each section of rising D minor arpeggio each violin marks time, so to speak, on the open D, thus implying a continuous tonic pedal. Bach realises the pedal – assigning it to the organ Pedale (Principal 8'). He then evokes the sense of two solo voices by dividing the lines between Oberwerk and Brustpositiv both marked Octava 4' to bring them into the right range (ex. 7.10).

In some ways, the Vivaldi transcription which exhibits least change is the B minor Four-Violin Concerto RV 580 which becomes the Concerto for Four Harpsichords, Strings and Basso Continuo in A minor BWV 1065. The change in tonality can once again be explained in terms of the consonance available on keyboards tuned to a circular temperament (since the F sharp major chord – as the dominant of B minor – is at the outer limits of acceptability). As the first movement nears its end, it becomes progressively more differentiated from the

Vivaldi original. First, at bars 72ff Bach turns what was a 'one violin at a time (plus basso continuo)' passage into a 'two harpsichord plus bass-line' passage; then at bar 89 Harpsichord I takes off with some virtuoso flourishes (see ex. 7.11).

Ex. 7.10 (a) Antonio Vivaldi, *L'estro armonico*, Op. 3 (Amsterdam, 1711): Concerto No. 11 in D minor, RV 565, first movement, bars 1–6

Ex. 7.10 (b) J. S. Bach, Concerto in D minor, BWV 596, first movement, Allegro, bars 1–6

The second movement is of most interest for anyone interested in the creative dimension to transcription. In the introductory dotted section, Bach utilises his four harpsichords to give enormous chords – with every player contributing eight notes (so thirty-two altogether across 10 pitches). But the minimalist second section of the slow movement, where Vivaldi explored different articulative and rhythmic patterns within virtually static harmonies, is less altered than might be expected. Given that his source was the Roger 1711 edition in which the first violin part is written as chords with the instruction 'Arpeggio battuto di Biscrome' ('Argpeggio divided into demisemiquavers') what Bach has done can be regarded as an unembellished straight transcription. Nevertheless, the whole idea is like an outlandish extension of Vivaldi's colouristic vision – as if Bach had been hit by the idea that the sparkle produced by these four violins doing slightly different things would be magnified if it were four harpsichords instead.

Unlike many keyboard transcriptions, this one could hardly have been made for practical reasons. Forkel ruefully remarked, 'I cannot judge the effect of this concerto as I have never been able to get together four instruments and four performers for the purpose.'[26] Its very impracticality argues against the idea that Bach in the harpsichord concertos was not placing a high priority on creating a specific sound world.

As noted above, Bach's own concertos for solo harpsichord and strings are all assumed to be transcriptions of existing works. In two cases the identities of the parent works are known: the Concerto in D major BWV 1054 is a re-working of the Violin Concerto in E major BWV 1042 while the G minor harpsichord concerto BWV 1056 is based on the A minor Violin Concerto BWV 1041. Despite their more complex harmonic language, the overall shape and character of these works seem to bear out Forkel's contention that Bach learned from transcribing Vivaldi (just as the Italian Concerto BWV 971 seems a direct descendant of the Vivaldi transcriptions for harpsichord BWV 972–980 discussed above).

As with the Vivaldi-derived works, the transcription process has involved the replacement of the most idiomatically violinistic passages with keyboard figuration, together with the recognition – everywhere – that the harpsichord is a naturally contrapuntal instrument. In the D major concerto BWV 1054 the harpsichord enters with a solo flourish that binds right- and left-hand voices together and then moves into left-hand/right-hand imitation based on a semiquaver elaboration of the opening motif (ex. 7.12). Two decades ago, Peter Williams convincingly advanced the hypothesis that the organ D Minor Toccata and Fugue BWV 565 must originally have been a violin piece by someone other than Bach.[27] So consistently does Bach re-think the most conspicuously violinistic features of his own and Vivaldi's concertos when transcribing them for harpsichord, that it seems unlikely that Bach was responsible for the transcription that has become so famous as his D Minor Toccata and Fugue. Had Bach made the arrangement, he would surely have replaced the most obviously violinistic passages with something more idiomatic for the keyboard.

---

[26] David and Mendel, rev. Wolff, *The New Bach Reader*, p. 470.
[27] See Williams, 'BWV 565', 330–7.

Ex. 7.11 (a) Antonio Vivaldi, *L'estro armonico,* Op. 3 (Amsterdam, 1711): Concerto No. 10 in B minor, RV 580, first movement, Allegro, bars 72–4

2

Ex. 7.11 (b) J. S. Bach, Concerto for Four Harpsichords in A minor, BWV 1065, first movement, Allegro, bars 72–4

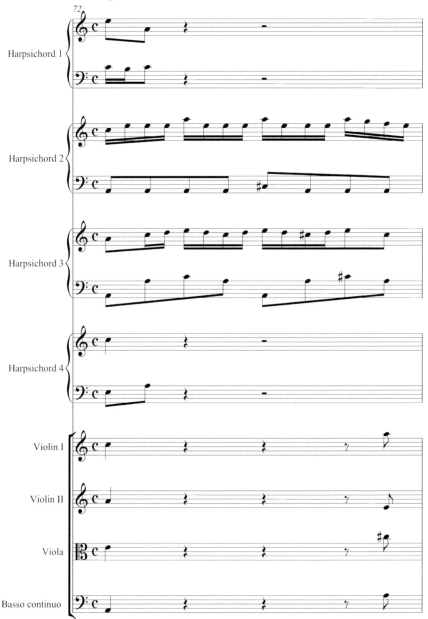

Ex. 7.11 (b) (*cont.*)

Ex. 7.12 (a) J. S. Bach, Concerto for Violin in E major, BWV 1042, first movement, Allegro, bars 11–13

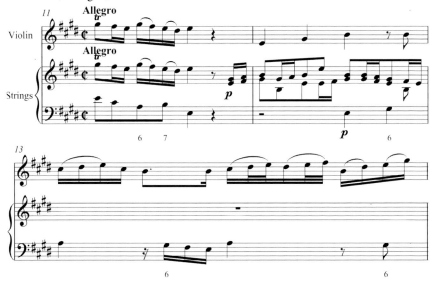

Ex. 7.12 (b) J. S. Bach, Concerto for Harpsichord in D major, BWV 1054, first movement, [Allegro], bars 11–13

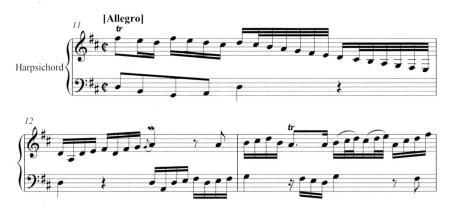

Thus it is not, I think, the case that transcription contemporaneous with the composition or transcription by the original composer necessarily implies a licence to ignore the specific instrumental designations of baroque and classical repertory. But, of course, to ignore these specifications by playing baroque works on instruments their composers could not have known but which audiences are expected to accept as modern equivalents is a form of unacknowledged transcription.

At this point I wish to return, briefly, to two of the creative transcribers discussed at the beginning of this essay, Brahms and Busoni. Brahms's attitude to his own Bach transcriptions (mentioned above) is particularly interesting for the way in which it stands apart from the conservative traditionalist values that Adorno was later to advocate so strenuously. As we have seen, Brahms's treatment of the G minor Presto – in adding an equally vigorous contrapuntal line to the original (twice) – is not unlike what Bach did to his own (and Vivaldi's) works in transcribing them for keyboard. The Chaconne, on the other hand, is (except for the occasional thickening of chords) quite a disciplined literal transcription apart (as we might expect) from the insertion of phrasing and dynamic markings in line with 19th-century notions of expressiveness. Brahms sent his Chaconne transcription to Clara Schumann with a fascinating covering letter:

> Pörtschach, June 1877
>
> Dear Clara,
>
> I do believe that it's been a long time since I sent you anything as diverting as today – if your fingers can stand the pleasure! The Chaconne is for me one of the most wonderful, incomprehensible pieces of music. On a single staff, for a small instrument, the man writes a whole world of the deepest thoughts and the most powerful feelings. If I were to imagine how *I* might have made, conceived the piece, I know for certain that the overwhelming excitement and awe would have driven me mad. Now if the greatest violinist is not around, then the best enjoyment is probably just to let it sound in one's mind . . .
>
> But the piece provokes one to become involved with it in all possible ways. After all, one doesn't always want to hear music merely ringing in thin air, Joachim is not often here, one tries it this way and that. But whatever I choose, orchestra or piano – my enjoyment is invariably spoilt.
>
> In one way only, I find, can I devise for myself a greatly diminished but comparable and absolutely pure enjoyment of the work – when I play it with the left hand alone! At times the story of the egg of Columbus even comes to my mind! The similar difficulties, the type of technique, the arpeggios, they all combine – to make me feel like a violinist!
>
> Do try it sometime, I wrote it out only for your sake! However: don't strain your hand unduly! It demands such a great deal of tone and power, so for the time being play it *mezza voce*. Also, make the fingerings practical and comfortable for yourself. If it's not too strenuous for you – which I believe to be the case, however – you are bound to have a lot of fun with it . . .[28]

This Chaconne for the piano is clearly an act of homage. Brahms also gives as its principal justification the difficulty of hearing the piece performed in the 'right' version. Interestingly, he acknowledges that the physical experience of playing the work is part of the total musical conception. What Brahms felt about the need to savour the work's virtuosity has been rediscovered by many period instrument performers in more recent times. One reason for returning to

---

[28] *Johannes Brahms: Life and Letters*, pp. 515–16. The editor provides the following note explaining the Columbus allusion: 'Columbus is said to have solved the thorny problem of how to stand an egg on end by setting it down so firmly he crushed the bottom, thereby creating a stable base.'

original instruments (apart from the sonority itself) is that so often they restore the sense of moving out to a technical frontier.

Busoni's attitude to transcription in general is equally interesting. In his *Entwurf einer neuen Ästhetik* (1907) he wrote,

> 'Notation' ('writing down') brings up the subject of Transcription, nowadays a term much misunderstood, almost discreditable. The frequent antagonism which I have excited with 'transcriptions,' and the opposition to which an ofttimes irrational criticism has provoked me, caused me to seek a clear understanding on this point. My final conclusion concerning it is this; Every notation is, in itself, the transcription of an abstract idea. The instant the pen seizes it, the idea loses its original form. The very intention to write down the idea, compels a choice of measure and key. The form, and the musical agency, which the composer must decide upon, still more closely define the way and the limits . . .
>
> The musical idea becomes a sonata or a concerto; the man, a soldier or a priest. That is an Arrangement of the original. From this first transcription to a second the step is comparatively short and unimportant. And yet it is only the second, in general, of which any notice is taken; overlooking the fact, that a transcription does not destroy the archetype, which is, therefore, not lost through transcription.
>
> Again, the performance of a work is also a transcription, and still, whatever liberties it may take, it can never annihilate the original.
>
> For the musical art-work exists, before its tones resound and after they die away, *complete and intact.* It exists both within and outside of time, and through its nature we can obtain a definite conception of the otherwise intangible notion of the Ideality of Time.[29]

In short, any written score should be viewed as a transcription of the composer's idea.[30] One implication here is, in fact, that any transcription might be seen as a glimpse of an enduring work at a particular moment in time. It thus constitutes a very documentable aspect of reception history. That is clear enough. But Busoni also argues (logically) that in this sense any performance (and not just those embracing what the historicist would see as anachronistic features) may be regarded as a transcription. He thus articulates a philosophical rationale for the conservative traditionalist position.

Luigi Pirandello went even further in his sense of performance as a transcription that allowed some aspects of a work to be resonated at the expense of others. Two years after the Busoni essay just quoted, Pirandello wrote, 'The theatre – not the work of art, of course – the theatre, for me, is the same as the vignette to the book it illustrates, or like a translation compared with the original: a reproduction which either spoils or diminishes the original.'[31]

[29] Ferruccio Busoni, 'Sketch of a New Esthetic of Music', in H. H. Stuckenschmidt, ed., *Three Classics in the Aesthetic of Music* (New York, 1974), pp. 85–6.

[30] This perspective anticipates the position adopted by the semiologist Jean-Jacques Nattiez who writes, for example, that 'Multifaceted analysis of a work – to which musical semiology aspires – cannot be realized without the intermediary of notation, or (expressed more precisely) of *transcription.*' (*Music and Discourse*, p. 72).

[31] From a letter written by Luigi to S. Munzone, December 1909; quoted in Gaspare Giudice, *Pirandello: A Biography*, trans. A. Hamilton (London, 1975), p. 105.

Among the Bach commemorations held in 2000 (the 250th anniversary of the composer's death) was a series of concerts in which Andras Schiff performed the Bach 'keyboard' concertos at the piano accompanied by the strings of the Philharmonia Orchestra. I expect that Schiff (a conservative traditionalist in Dahlhaus's terms) saw no contradiction in being, on the one hand, aware that these works were written for harpsichord and, on the other, sincerely convinced that his approach was true to Bach's conception. Here there is no question of musicians acting in bad faith. But, for all that, the concert was somewhat misleadingly presented as Bach the way Bach expected it to be. There were programme notes by an eminent Bach scholar and harpsichordist which did their best to avoid confronting the question of the specific instrumental colours Bach had in mind. At one point in these notes, for example, it was suggested that Bach may have been '. . . trying to prove a particular point, that the keyboard could be just as flamboyant as other solo instruments'.[32] (What sort of instrument, one might ask, is a keyboard?) I have some sympathy with the note writer since, obviously, the object of such discourse is not to undermine audience confidence in what they have come to hear. Many who have chosen to go to such a concert might well believe that Bach is best served by what might be regarded as creative transcription (and such a case has been argued often enough). But it seems unfortunate to gloss over the fact that that is what is happening.

James Urmson's observations on the question of ethics in performance seem apposite here:

> What is at least clear is that every performer must recognize some bounds of authenticity beyond which he should not go in representing to the audience that it is a performance of a certain work, though we know that not all performers will agree on where those bounds lie . . . In the end, the performer's duties to his audience seem not to differ widely from those of any purveyor of goods to his customer. There may be other and more important reasons for faithfulness of performance, but one reason is akin to that for obeying the Trade Descriptions Act; people should know what they are buying . . . I do not even try now to determine where the bounds of legitimacy or authenticity lie. I merely say that the performer has a duty to his audience not to overstep them, as he understands them.[33]

Urmson is right in stressing that there is ample room for discussion about where the bounds of authenticity might lie. And by extension, his perspective allows for the performer who wishes to present something which is knowingly a departure from the composer's intentions provided that the process is transparent. The danger with this stance, however, is that it can seem to provide a justification for the more outlandish re-inventions of musical works

---

[32] Programme notes by John Butt for a concert in the Sheldonian Theatre, Oxford, on 4 October 2000.

[33] J. O. Urmson, 'The Ethics of Musical Performance', in *The Interpretation of Music: Philosophical Essays* (Oxford, 1993), pp. 161–2.

(Uri Caine's Bach – or, for that matter, his Wagner and Mahler) while leaving no scope for the pianist who knowingly steps up to the 'wrong' instrument. Nevertheless, just as musicologists (like any scholars) have a responsibility to give as clear a picture as possible of historical performance practice, performers who wish to *claim* (or even to imply) fidelity to the composer's intentions surely have some responsibility to take account of the original instrumental specifications.

8. Legislating for inspiration

Adorno's principal complaint with what he called 'the early music crowd' was that their whole enterprise seemed profoundly unmusical:

> At times one can hardly avoid the suspicion that the sole concern of today's Bach devotees is to see that no inauthentic dynamics, modifications of tempo, oversize choirs and orchestras creep in; they seem to wait with potential fury lest any more humane impulse become audible in the rendition.[1]

The article in which that statement occurs, 'Bach defended against his Devotees', was written in 1951. Laurence Dreyfus's 'Early Music Defended against its Devotees' presents itself, in its revisionist allusion to Adorno's title, as a summation of attitudes in historically-oriented performance circles thirty years later. There Dreyfus made the claim that 'since the daily preoccupation of Early Music stresses the objective retrieval of historical practices, it fosters the attitude that subjectivity in interpretation (whether in performance or in criticism) is irrelevant or, at best, unknowable'. He added that 'The Early-Music fan . . . not only curbs his pleasurable response to the music, but brags about his command of authentic historical facts.'[2]

These accusations have been echoed on countless occasions. Richard Taruskin, in his contribution to *Early Music*'s 1984 'discussion' of 'the limits of authenticity' wrote (and notice that he begins here with a let-out clause – 'all too often'):

> All too often the sound of a modern "authentic" performance of old music presents the aural equivalent of an Urtext score: the notes and rests are presented with complete accuracy and an equally complete neutrality . . . Nothing is allowed to intrude into the performance that cannot be "authenticated." And this means nothing can be allowed that will give the performance . . . the authenticity of conviction.[3]

I find it astonishing that someone so intelligent could subscribe even in passing to the idea that a performance might 'present the aural equivalent of an Urtext score'. We all encounter bad performances, dull performances – but unless we are

---

[1] Adorno, 'Bach Defended', p. 143.
[2] Dreyfus, 'Early Music Defended', pp. 300 and 302.
[3] Taruskin, *Text and Act*, p. 72.

talking about the play-back facility on music-writing software, it is impossible to eliminate the performer's presence. Moreover, if we refused to perform anything that could not be historically authenticated, we would not get past bar 1.

Even Howard Mayer Brown wondered whether the quest for authenticity might, as he put it, be 'resulting in the dead hand of scholarship forcing performers into corners and quelling their creativity'? (He did, though, offer as an alternative, the prospect of its being 'an act of freedom, freeing the conservatory-trained student to think for himself about questions of style and history and helping him to present the music in the best light possible'.[4])

All of these writers – with the conspicuous exception of Adorno – profess at least an intelligent appreciation of the musical positives of period-instrument performance. You can imagine the results if I were to trawl through the writings of those who are openly out of sympathy with such activities.

What is even more fascinating than the spectacle of 'sympathetic' musico-logists fretting about unmusical outcomes, is the fear exhibited by historically-alert performers that they might be judged unmusical. Time and time again, they go out of their way to state their priorities: musicianship first, authenticity second. In so doing, they appear to be accepting an inherent contradiction between scholarship and musical expressiveness. It is this idea that I would most like to dismantle.

Nikolaus Harnoncourt produced an essay in 1954 that he was later to describe as the 'credo' of the Concentus Musicus (the baroque ensemble he founded just at that time). There, he warned against the perils of musicology as a stultifying influence:

> For us intensive study is required, an approach which can lead to serious error: a purely intellectual involvement with old music. The outcome is found in those familiar musical performances which are often historically impeccable, but which lack all vitality. Clearly, an interpretation that was historically uninformed but musically alive would be preferable. Musicology should never become an end in itself, but rather provide us with the means to make the best rendition, since a performance is only faithful to the original when a work is allowed to come most beautifully and most clearly to expression, something which happens only when knowledge and a sense of responsibility ally themselves with the deepest musical sensitivity.[5]

Note Harnoncourt's conviction (first) that expressiveness is to be achieved even at the cost of ignoring historical evidence and (second) that musicology is the servant of performance. There is certainly no realisation here that musicology which, as he puts it, has 'become an end in itself' has any intrinsic value or interest, let alone that it might ultimately be of more use to the performer than musicology pursued with its application directly in mind.

Once again, I find myself fascinated by the cluster of images that surround the

[4] H. M. Brown, 'Pedantry or Liberation?', in Kenyon, ed., *Authenticity*, p. 54.
[5] Reprinted in N. Harnoncourt, *Baroque Music Today: Music as Speech*, trans. M. O'Neill (London, 1988), p. 16.

topic of the historically-accurate but anti-musical performance. Harnoncourt, in introducing his 1968 recording of the Bach B Minor Mass (see above, p. 48ff.), spoke of avoiding 'sterilization':

> It was never our intention . . . to transfer a performance from Bach's age into ours in a sterilized state, so to speak, as an enormous piece of musicological industry . . . It was the free decision of the performer to present the work in the best possible manner, not the dream of the historicist of reviving a sound-picture of the past.

Predictably, Frederick Neumann provides us with a spectacular array of similar metaphors in the space of two sentences (and this after having just mentioned 'archeology'):

> the movement has had a certain stultifying effect through the dogmatic insistence of its practitioners on freezing old masterworks in the form of their alleged original sound, then hermetically sealing them as a protection against any harm from exposure to twentieth-century fresh air. In so doing, the authenticists behave like custodians of museum exhibits . . .[6]

Robert P. Morgan had also used the 'hermetically-sealed' image (though, thankfully, without mixing that with the concept of deep-freezing paintings). Morgan, sees the early music movement as part of the postmodern condition of dislocation from a past which is nevertheless yearned for as nostalgia and novelty. In advancing this idea, he characterises the approach of historicist musicians as analogous to trying to speak a dead language. From there he gets to palaeontology:

> Given the impossibility of finding any definitive means of interpreting early music on our own terms, one understands the appeal – or, in the view of some, the moral imperative – of treating this music as irrevocably cut off from the present, hermetically sealed from the contamination of anachronistic impurities. Thus the tendency to handle these [dead] musical languages as fixed and inviolable entities, impervious to time and historical process. Rather than trying to revive them to give them new life through an infusion of new ideas, lending them the sort of richness and flexibility characteristic of a living tradition, we bring them back as fossils, emblems from a lost world that we may greatly admire (indeed, perhaps infinitely prefer to our own) but in which we can never reside as natives.[7]

Taruskin joins those who condemn performers who seem interested in the past for its own sake. He describes it as 'antiquarian curiosity' which will produce, not a performance, but 'a documentation of the state of knowledge'.[8] Would that such a thing were possible – no substitute for performance, obviously, but fascinating nonetheless.

The museum returns as the central metaphor in this discourse. Many writers

---

[6] Neumann, *New Essays*, p. 30.
[7] R. P. Morgan, 'Tradition, Anxiety, and the Current Musical Scene', in Kenyon, ed., *Authenticity*, p. 70.
[8] Taruskin, *Text and Act*, p. 57.

have had recourse to it as an image of detached and un-involving antiquarianism. In the last chapter, I discussed the use of the same image for the concept of
a concert as a way of presenting musical works. The two notions, of stultified
antiquarianism and inappropriate aesthetic abstraction tend to overlap since
those who view the concert as inherently a-historical in relation to early music
have at least a tendency to see all historical reconstruction as misguided.[9]

Will Crutchfield criticises many early music performers for adhering to what
he calls 'the museum model, the precise reconstruction of sounds as near as
possible to those heard by the composer'.[10] Dreyfus, too (while putting forward
an alternative paradigm) asks the question 'Who today would freely admit the
wish to live as a fixture in an antique shop, a perhaps valuable but dead museum
piece?'[11] One recent final example makes all the others, Neumann included,
seem by comparison models of calm detached appraisal. Roger Scruton, in *The
Aesthetics of Music*, writes:

> a multitude of groups has sprung up, devoted to the task of historically 'authentic'
> performance . . . But the effect has frequently been to cocoon the past in a wad of
> phoney scholarship, to elevate musicology over music, and to confine Bach and
> his contemporaries to an acoustic time-warp. The tired feeling which so many
> 'authentic' performances induce can be compared to the atmosphere of a modern
> museum. A painting receives its final tribute from the scholar only in the form of
> a catalogue entry . . . Likewise, the works of the 'early' or 'ancient' composers have
> been confiscated by scholarship. They no longer have a place in our homes, played
> on our own familiar instruments [does he mean the CD player here?], but are
> arranged behind the glass of authenticity, staring bleakly from the other side of an
> impassable screen.[12]

There's not time here to disentangle the remarkable string of non-sequiturs
about authenticists depriving music-lovers of their birthright, but it is worth
noting that Scruton perceives the problem as one of musicology dominating
performance – the same old complaint.

We might wonder how museum and gallery professionals would regard this use
of their milieu as an image for the uninvolving, detached, display of scholarship
(and scholarship, moreover, which is more or less assumed to be boring). The new
museology (*sic*!) has been hosting a debate on the extent to which the museum
should be striving for a contemporaneous engagement with the past (or with
'other' cultures). One rather naïve response to the pressure to do exactly this has
been observable in the tendency for museums to mutate into 'theme parks' or
'time machines' – prompted, one suspects, by a lack of trust in the imaginative and

[9] Dahlhaus, discussing negative reactions to the preponderance of old music over new in
     concert programmes, notes that 'the word "museum", heard in aesthetic discussions,
     expresses weariness or even hatred of things cultural' (*Foundations*, p. 61).
[10] W. Crutchfield, 'Fashion, Conviction, and Performance Style in an Age of Revivals', in
     Kenyon, ed., *Authenticity*, p. 25.
[11] Dreyfus, 'Early Music Defended', p. 308.
[12] Scruton, *Aesthetics*, p. 448.

intellectual capacities of their audiences.[13] (We have a particularly sad example of this kind in New Zealand where our National Museum and Art Gallery has been re-invented as 'Our Place', Te Papa, with interactive themed zones whose closest affinities are with computer game arcades.)

What these developments fail to acknowledge is that the traditional gallery or museum always has been a time machine. For anyone of average intelligence and imagination, the contemplation of paintings by Titian or Rembrandt involves an engagement with their world – or, to put it another way, Titian and Rembrandt become our contemporaries.[14] Part of me wants to embrace the museum image by asserting that a thorough-going fascination with the past is in no way incompatible with the ambition of relating very directly to modern audiences.

But for the time being, the image of the museum (or the art gallery) has got stuck as a metaphor for the exhibition of an essentially alien past that is pushed beyond resuscitation by an historicist approach. It presupposes that approaching music of the past through a commitment to its history is to deny its aesthetic presence. What is at stake, here – the relationship between expressiveness and awareness of historical context – is crucial in any consideration of the musical value of the period-instrument approach to performance. It is, consequently, the central issue in this essay.

As we have seen, those who see imagination and respect for historical performance practice as being at odds assert (or assume) that the latter may consist in adhering (blindly) to sets of rules inferred from historical sources of one kind or another. Dreyfus complains that amongst some aficionados of early music there is a 'peculiar understanding of performance practice' as 'a set of rules which guarantees correct musical behaviour'. 'The typical Early Musician', he continues, '. . . reads the proper treatises, invests in expensive facsimiles, consults source-critical editions, and worries that he is deviating from the proper style.'[15] Daniel Leech-Wilkinson also warned against the resignation of artistic freedom implied in adherence to rules: 'the more we take to be authentic, the less choice we have about what we do, so it is clearly not in our interests to restrict our freedom of manoeuvre by considering as inviolable anything more of a performance style than has been convincingly established as such'.[16]

At this point, we need to consider how realistic it could ever be to abdicate musical judgement in favour of received 'rules'. I will argue first that the 'rules' (except in relation to small and very specific pockets of repertory) often turn out to be a sort of mirage; second, that many musicians in the 17th and 18th

---

[13] See Vergo, ed., *The New Museology*, especially the chapters by L. Jordanova ('Objects of Knowledge: A Historical Perspective on Museums', pp. 22–40) and C. Sorensen ('Theme Parks and Time Machines', pp. 60–73).

[14] My phrasing here is borrowed from the title of a book by Jan Kott: *Shakespeare Our Contemporary* trans. Bodeslaw Taborski (London: Methuen, 1964). For Kott's views on fidelity to Shakespeare's intentions see above, p. 117n.

[15] Dreyfus, 'Early Music Defended', pp. 318–19.

[16] Leech-Wilkinson, 'Limits of Authenticity', p. 15.

centuries were reluctant to provide definite guidelines in areas which they felt were not reducible to a list of dos and don'ts, and third, that, even where our informants did venture into prescription or proscription, consensus among the various sources is often hard to find. Historical evidence cannot, in the end, provide a convenient template which will guarantee stylish performance.

On the face of it, performance treatises give a lot of encouragement for thinking that historical fidelity might be a matter of establishing rules and adhering to them. A significant number of such treatises from Ganassi's *Regola rubertina* (1542) on even include the word 'rules' in their titles. Given that most of these publications are addressed to aspiring amateurs, it is an essential part of their discourse that they use language intended to give a sense of security about the advice given. (We are all familiar with parallel kinds of rhetoric – the music teachers who tell new pupils that they are going to have to take them right back to basics, for example.) The desire to inspire confidence in their authority is particularly evident in areas like ornamentation, tonguing for wind instruments, early keyboard fingering, and violin bowing.

The word 'rule' or 'rules' in association with bowing, for instance, occurs many more times than I could possibly enumerate here. Bow management from the late 16th century to at least the end of the classical era was dominated by the principle that in the 18th century was to be known as the 'rule of the down bow' – basically a matter of ensuring that rhythmically strong beats were taken on down bows. What follows is one fairly crude statement of this principle – from John Playford's 1667 'Instruction for the Treble Violin' (and notice all the imperatives):

Ex. 8.1 'John Come Kiss Me' (theme) from J. Playford, *An Introduction to the Skill of Musick* (**London, 1664**)

> In the moving your Bow up and down observe this Rule, when you see an even number of *Quavers* or *Semiquavers*, as 2, 4, 6, or 8, tyed together, your Bow must move up or forwards, though it was up at the Note immediately before; but if you have an odd number, as 3, 4 [*sic.*], or 7 (which happens very often by reason of a prickt Note or an odd *Quaver Rest*), there your Bow must draw down at the first Note.[17]

Playford's rule means that the last note (quaver no. 8) in the first bar of ex. 8.1 ('John Come Kiss Me', one of the 'Lessons' in the volume) should be taken on an up-bow even though the note before (quaver no. 7) will also be played up-bow.

---

[17] J. Playford, *An Introduction to the Skill of Musick* (London, 1664). The mistake was corrected in subsequent editions.

The most elaborate and systematic treatment of the subject comes in Georg Muffat's 1698 preface 'on the manner of playing *Airs de Ballets* in the French style' – these days, most often referred to simply as 'Muffat's *rules*'.[18] Obviously, Muffat had a limited and quite special repertory in mind and he alerts his readers to the fact that Italian music demanded a rather more fluid approach. But his rules make a conspicuous difference to the performance of works written in the French style.

Bach's B minor Orchestral Suite is provides a good example (ex. 8.2). The opening section of a French Overture is characterised by the prevalence of dotted rhythmic groups. In conventional modern string playing, the standard way of tackling such note groupings has been to use a single bow per beat, 'hooking' the short note into the same bow stroke as the longer note (though this 'orthodoxy' is becoming less and less common as conventional orchestral players assimilate some of the stylistic traits of their colleagues playing period instruments). This bow stroke suits the Tourte bow, with its ability to produce quite a strong sound at the point (and thus to make up bows sound as assertive as down bows). The fact that the bow remains on the string between the two notes stops the sound (and, in the 19th century, bow strokes of this kind were classified as 'muted *détaché*').

The application of Muffat's bowing rules (reinforced by a different under-standing of the implications of the time signature) makes any of the currently available period-instrument recordings sound very different indeed from 'conventional' performances.[19] Muffat advises that dotted groups (seen in their most straightforward form in bars 4–7 of ex. 8.2) should be taken on alternate down- and up-bows. In order to recover enough bow to make possible a succession of long (stressed) down strokes and short (unstressed) up strokes the bow spends quite a lot of time in the air while the string continues to resonate. Additionally, period-instrument players have settled empirically on a technique where (often) less effort is made to recover bow before a weak beat than before a strong one (indicated by my 'heel' and 'middle' markings in bar 5 of ex. 8.2). More than just an orchestral uniformity is achieved through all of this – the technique encourages a highly-articulate and vivacious style and imparts a strong sense of rhythmic hierarchy within the bar. Interestingly,

---

[18] The preface to *Florilegium Secundum* (Passau, 1698); modern edition in *Denkmäler der Tonkunst in Österreich* ii (4), ed. H. Rietsch (Vienna, 1895). An English translation of the preface is available in *Georg Muffat on Performance Practice*, ed. and trans. David K. Wilson (Bloomington and Indianapolis, 2001).

[19] Compare, for example, Christopher Hogwood and the Academy of Ancient Music (Decca 458 069–2) with Karl Münchinger and the Stuttgarter Kammerorchester (Decca 448 231–2). On the significance of the C time signature, see B. D. Sherman, 'Bach's Notation of Tempo and Early Music Performance: Some Reconsiderations', *Early Music* 28 (2000), 455–66. Sherman's observation that period-instrument performers tend towards tempi at the upper end of the band indicated by historical evidence is borne out in respect of BWV 1067. Of the currently available recordings, Hogwood's tempi are relatively moderate. (On the other hand, there is no obvious historical justification for tempi as slow as that adopted by Münchinger for the opening of the Overture.)

Ex. 8.2 J. S. Bach, B Minor Orchestral Suite in B minor, BWV 1067, Ouverture (flute, violin, and continuo lines only), bars 1–6

though, Muffat hands the responsibility for how to bow pairs or clusters of very rapid ornamental notes (the demisemiquavers present in either top or bottom voices in all but bar 5 of ex. 8.2) back to the performers. They can be bowed separately, or slurred in various ways depending on taste (see ex. 8.3):

Ex. 8.3 Georg Muffat, *Florilegium Secundum* (**Passau, 1698**), preface: examples **FF** and **GG**

When two little notes, such as semiquavers, are attached to some other note purely as decoration, they can sometimes be played with a separate stroke for each note (GG) and sometimes, for greater sweetness, they can be slurred into the preceding note with either one or two strokes (FF).[20]

Even the most detailed exposition of bowing rules cannot cover all eventualities.

While the rule of the down bow remained the basis of good orthodox bowing, it is nevertheless true that there is as much emphasis in violin treatises on not adhering to it slavishly as there is explanation of its principles. In 1693 John Lenton had prefaced his advice on bowing with the warning that 'It would be a difficult undertaking to prescribe a general rule for Bowing, the humours of Masters being very Various . . . what is approved by one would be condemned by another'.[21] Geminiani went out of his way to urge players away from regimentation in bowing: 'Here it must be observed, that you are to execute [these scales] by drawing the Bow down and up, or up and down alternately; taking Care not to follow that wretched Rule of drawing the Bow down at the first Note of every Bar.'[22] Tartini, in his 'Regole ['Rules', notice] per arrivare a saper ben suonar il Violino' advised that 'As regards bowing there are no definite rules for determining whether one should begin with a down-bow or an up-bow. On the contrary, all passages should be practised in both ways, in order to gain complete mastery of the bow in both up and down strokes.'[23] Towards the end of the century J.-B. Cartier (in introducing an edition of Corelli Op. 5), expanded on Geminiani's reservations about the down-bow rule: 'It is wrong to think that upbeats must always come on up-bows, or that down-bows must mark the beat. The school of Corelli never subscribed to this servile rule, and the French Corelli, Gaviniès, has never ever adhered to it. The bow must be free, and the beauty of the sound depends on the way in which it is used . . .'[24] It would not be too far fetched to claim that before *c.* 1750, most direct instruction in this area is too amateur in its focus to tell us much that is reliable about the practice of sophisticated violinists while in the later 18th century statements about the impossibility of giving definite rules probably outnumber the more straightforward enunciation of guidelines. Hence, even in an area like bowing, the treatises deny us the certainty they seem at first sight to have promised.

[20] '. . . quand deux petites notes, comme deux double crochues se joignent seulement pour l'ornement à quelqu' autre note, on les Joü quelque fois chacune à son trait; & quelque fois pour plus de douceur on les coule avec la note precedente d'un trait ou deux.' (*Florilegium Secundum*, p. 46.)

[21] John Lenton, *The Gentleman's Diversion, or the Violin Explained* (London, 1694), p. 7.

[22] Francesco Geminiani, *The Art of Playing on the Violin* (London, 1751), p. 4.

[23] 'Intorno all'Arco non vi è regola determinata del cominciare l'Arcata in giù, o in sù, anzi bisogna exercitarsi in tutti li passiper dritto, e per rovescio, per essere frahchi dell'Arco con la stessa prontezza tanto in giù come in sù . . .' (G. Tartini, *Traité des Agréments de la Musique*, ed. E. R. Jacobi (Celle and New York, 1961), p. 56).

[24] Corelli, *XII Sonates à violon seul et basse . . . Oeuvre V, Quinzième édition par J. B. Cartier* (Paris, *c.* 1800); quoted by R. Stowell, *Violin Technique and Performance Practice in the Late Eighteenth and Early Nineteenth Centuries* (Cambridge, 1985), p. 303.

The second aspect of treatises as potential providers of rules is that often they adopt what amounts to a policy of reticence. The notion that the past might impose rules on a credulous present turns out to be a chimera. In areas where the range of possibilities open to a performer is particularly wide or where the role of imagination is especially important, writers of musical treatises were often reluctant to participate in legislating for fellow musicians. How to ornament Italian music of the central baroque period, for example, is something on which surprisingly little help is given. Nicola Matteis, in his *False Consonances of Musick* (1782) advised musicians that 'To set your tune off the better, you must make severall sorts of Graces of your one [own] Genius, it being very troublesome for the Composer to mark them.'[25] Roger North (writing in 1728) put the reticence of 'the elder Italians' down to an unwillingness to patronise competent musicians: 'in their finest cantatas [they] have exprest no graces, as much as to say, Whoever is fitt to sing this, knows the comon decorums'.[26] Pierfrancesco Tosi, writing in 1723, seems to confirm this view: 'If the Scholar be well instructed in this, the *Appoggiatura's* will become so familiar to him by continual Practice, that by the Time he is come out of his first Lessons, he will laugh at those Composers that mark them, with a Design either to be thought Modern, or to shew that they understand the Art of Singing better than the Singers. If they have this Superiority over them, why do they not write down even the Graces, which are more difficult and more essential than the *Appoggiatura's*?'[27] Tosi dismissed as a 'foreign infantile practice' the tendency to indicate ornamentation in scores. Geminiani, who was unusually interested in giving performers a multitude of performance instructions both in his scores and through his treatises, was criticised for what seemed like patronisation. William Hayes, Professor of Music in Oxford, wrote in 1753 that Geminiani was 'paying his Brethren of the String but an ill Compliment, to compel them to the Observance of arbitrary Taste . . .'[28] Hence, many musicians backed away from providing 'rules', and those that did provide them were criticised for it.

Thirdly, even where our informants are willing to talk, they don't always agree. Statements about vibrato provide a striking case since 17th- and 18th-century opinions cover an extraordinary range. Muffat (in 1698) and Bremner (1777) advised against its use in orchestral music on the grounds that it interfered with good tuning. Galeazzi at the end of the 18th century hated it, complaining that it 'cannot possibly please anyone except those who are accustomed to it'.[29] He thought that anyone with good taste would want to

---

[25] Nicola Matteis, *The False Consonances of Musick* (London, 1682), p. 79.

[26] Roger North, *The Musicall Grammarian 1728*, ed. Mary Chan and Jamie Kassler (Cambridge, 1990), p. 167.

[27] P. Tosi, *Opinioni de' cantori antichi, e moderni* (Bologna, 1723); Eng. trans. by J. E. Galliard as *Observations on the Art of Florid Song* (London, 1742), pp. 38–9.

[28] William Hayes, *Remarks on Mr Avison's Essay on Musical Expression* (London, 1753), p. 123.

[29] Francesco Galeazzi, *Elementi teorico-pratici di musica* (Rome, 1791–96), i, 171.

ban it altogether. At apparently the other extreme, Geminiani famously recommended using it 'as often as possible' – though this very recommendation was then suppressed by Robert Bremner in his *c.*1777 edition of Geminiani's treatise.[30] It apparently passed in and out of fashion. Roger North called it a 'late invention' in the early 18th century; but it was not new.[31] In the 1630s Mersenne had described it as something used by the great violinists Bochan and Lazarin in a way which delighted the spirit. But he notes, too, that lutenists were not using as much vibrato (the *verre cassé*) as they had in the past.[32] Much of the advice about vibrato given from the 17th century until the early years of the 20th century consists of warnings not to over-use it. But, as always with such injunctions, they are a sure indication that – tasteless or not – vibrato has been a conspicuous element in some players' performance. Leopold Mozart ridicules players who tremble as if they had a nervous disease – and the joke is echoed by Georg Löhlein (1774) and again by Leopold Auer (1921).[33] Wolfgang Mozart also complained (in a letter to his father) about the singer Meisner's excessive use of vibrato – but then widened his criticism to include many instrumentalists.[34]

It will have been obvious from chapter 1 that vibrato has been a contentious issue. But it must be abundantly clear that we don't get anywhere by appealing to particular sources as authorities in a situation where other sources can be invoked to mount a counter-argument. I doubt whether it is even possible to come up with a clear picture of its use (or non-use) for a particular regional grouping, a restricted period, or a specific repertory. In the end, trying to guess how much constitutes 'as often as possible' (to pick up on Geminiani's phrase) is neither constructive nor, ultimately, very interesting.

There may, however, be quite a lot to be learned from the contradictions themselves. Each statement needs contextualising. Nobody holding the violin in the way that Geminiani describes, for example, is likely to be able to produce anything like a full-blooded, modern-sounding continuous vibrato. Second, his advice comes at the end of his section on ornaments in the violin treatise – not earlier where he describes how to produce a satisfactory tone. It needs to be read in the same way as his encouragement to use plain trills (which 'may be made upon any note') or appoggiaturas (which may also be 'added to any note you will'). But more than that, contemplating the diversity of views on this subject (and the situation which could produce such

[30] See R. Hickman, 'The Censored Publications of *The Art of Playing on the Violin*, or Geminiani Unshaken' *Early Music* 11 (1983), 73–6.

[31] J. Wilson, ed., *Roger North on Music* (London, 1959), p. 167.

[32] Mersenne trans. Chapman, *Harmonie universelle*, pp. 24 and 109.

[33] L. Mozart, *Versuch einer gründlichen Violinschule* (Augsburg, 1756); Eng. trans. by E. Knocker as *A Treatise on the Fundamental Principles of Violin Playing*, 2nd ed. (London, 1951), p. 203; G. S. Löhlein, *Anweisung zum Violinspielen* (Leipzig and Züllichau, 1774), p. 51; L. Auer, *Violin Playing as I Teach it* (1921; repr. New York, 1980), pp. 22–4. Interestingly, J. F. Reichardt's revision of Löhlein's treatise (1797) omits the line about the player shaking as if he had a fever and is generally better disposed towards vibrato.

[34] See Mozart, *Letters*, p. 552.

diversity) must surely encourage the performer to think across a much broader range of possibilities than the usual binary (whether or not to use vibrato). In some ways, the process of reading treatises – no matter how dogmatic any single volume might seem – throws more emphasis, rather than less, on a performer's judgement.

But 17th- and 18th-century sources can offer positive help about ways in which to use vibrato expressively. To begin with, it is striking how often vibrato is considered in conjunction with dynamic nuances. In the very passage that has been the subject of so much attention, Geminini stresses the variety of affects that the 'close shake' can be made to serve depending on its speed and intensity and the relationship of this to the character of the bowing: 'when it is long continued swelling the Sound by Degrees, drawing the Bow nearer to the Bridge, and ending it very strong it may express Majesty, Dignity, *&c*. But making it shorter, lower and softer, it may denote Affliction, Fear, *&c*.' In the early 18th century Roger North used a memorable image to evoke the expressive potential of vibrato introduced at the peak of a crescendo:

> The Italians have brought the bow to an high perfection, so that nothing of their playing is so difficult as the *arcata* or long bow, with which they will begin a long note, clear, without rubb, and draw it forth swelling lowder and lowder, and at the ackme take a slow waiver; not trill to break the sound or mix 2 notes, but as if the bird sat at the end of a spring [and] as she sang the spring waived her up and downe, or as if the wind that brought the sound shaked, or a small bell were stuck and the sound continuing waived to and againe – so would I express what is justly not to be shewn but to the ear by an exquisite hand.[35]

Though none do it as eloquently as Roger North, Tartini, Bailleux, Leopold Mozart, and Michel Corrette all suggest ways of introducing vibrato as a bow swell is dying away and most make the point that such a gesture can sound like a naturally occurring phenomenon.

Lastly, it is worth noting that a number of treatises that provide rules build in a certain latitude in their interpretation. Pincherle quotes de la Voye-Mignot writing in 1666, 'It is not that rules should be rejected, in such a manner that they may be used only according to one's whim, but there is always reason not to observe them when one wishes to do something better'; and Dupuits (1741), 'It does not matter if one deviates slightly from the rule, provided that the piece is rendered with as much feeling and as perfectly as if the rule had been followed.'[36]

With any luck, therefore, what the reading of historical sources will do for performers is stimulate musical imagination – opening up expressive possibilities that lie outside their standard vocabulary. From a performer's point of view, one way of coping with the ambiguities, contradictions, and inconclusiveness of so many areas of performance practice research is to recognise the

---

[35] Wilson, *Roger North*, p. 164.
[36] See Pincherle, 'On the Rights of the Interpreter', 165. De la Voye-Mignot's *Traité de Musique* (first edition, 1656) deals with composition rather than performance, however. The Dupuits quotation is from *Principes pour toucher de la vièle.*

value of being confronted with, not answers, but questions. The act of informed contemplation might function (like the sand in the oyster) as a way of stimulating a creative response to historical prompts.

Such an attitude to treatises is clearly a long way from the rather frightened conformity seen by Dreyfus in the attitudes of some performers of early music. But, as we have just seen, many treatises place a high value on imagination and emotional involvement. In a sense, those looking for authority from the rules for the engagement of their own imagination in what they do can have it. It is, in fact, a recurring topos in performance manuals.[37]

This brings me to a second major objection levelled at period-instrument performance. Even where they are not being accused of a slavish and unmusical adherence to rules, period-instrument performers and their singing colleagues are often accused of undervaluing passion. This is like having a charge of murder reduced to manslaughter. Many who acknowledge the expressive potential of using period instruments have nevertheless asserted that this privileges brightness, lightness, and a kind of vivaciousness over weight, seriousness, and strength. In other words, the argument is that period instruments may succeed in bringing out one dimension of a musical work at the expense of others which are better served by more conventional approaches.

Beethoven is the favoured example here – and, in particular, Roger Norrington's Beethoven recordings. Mark Everist writes that 'a symphony by Beethoven under the baton of Richard Strauss develops a rather different meaning from one under the direction of Roger Norrington'.[38] With characteristic vigour, Roger Scruton dismisses Norrington's Beethoven 9 recording as 'thinned with white spirit . . . and painted with fast brush-strokes on the air'.[39] Alain Frogley contrasts Furtwängler and Norrington as representatives of two totally distinct approaches.[40] Taruskin, ambivalent as always, declares,

---

[37] Edward T. Cone observed in *Musical Form and Musical Performance* (New York, 1968) 'the rules of performance of the past were never meant to be applied in a restrictive way. They were never meant to be *applied* at all: they were – so far as they existed – merely expressions of the necessary relationship between the musical form and its physical expression. To take them more literally than that today is to misread them' (p. 58).

[38] Everist, *Rethinking Music*, pp. 389–90.

[39] Scruton, *Aesthetics*, p. 449.

[40] Alain Frogley, 'Beethoven's Music in Performance: Historical Perspectives', in G. Stanley, ed., *The Cambridge Companion to Beethoven* (Cambridge, 2000), p. 256. (Note that the emphasis here is on tempo: 'If the slow movement of the Ninth Symphony takes just over eleven minutes in Roger Norrington's version, and close to twenty in Wilhelm Furtwängler's, in what sense are we still dealing with the same piece? In this context, formulations such as "Furtwängler's Beethoven" become more than verbal conveniences. While such questions are hardly restricted to this composer, they strike one here with unusual force: can the music of Beethoven, undisputed master of form, timing and compositional control at every level, really be this malleable if responsibly performed?') Rosen ('The Benefits of Authenticity', p. 221) also cites Norrington's Beethoven as an Early Music benchmark.

Table 8.1 Recordings surveyed of Beethoven, Symphony No. 7 in A major, Op. 92

BBC Symphony Orchestra, cond. Arturo Toscanini (BBCL 4016–2)

Wiener Philharmoniker, cond. Carlos Kleiber (447 400–2)

London Classical Players, cond. Roger Norrington (7243 5 61376)

Orchestre Révoluionnaire et Romantique, cond. John Eliot Gardiner (459 060–2)

Chamber Orchestra of Europe, cond. Nikolaus Harnoncourt (9031–75714–2)

Speeds! Norrington published Beethoven's tempo markings right on the back of his CD, where the movements are listed. It is not only an act of bravado, it is a *profession de foi*. It is from the tempos that his approach derives, the very tempos all the others flee. And it must be so, for no other givens are nearly so specific. He does not begin, then, by asking whether Beethoven's tempos are "suitable"; he *assumes* they are, for you have to start your strip-down somewhere. Everything else can go, but they must stay![41]

Is this really true? I have been comparing the five recordings of the Beethoven Symphony No. 7 in A major listed in table 8.1, and this, of course, includes the Norrington version. The second movement, 'Allegretto', has a metronome marking of crotchet = 76. The conductor who adheres most closely to this marking throughout the movement is (surprisingly, perhaps) Carlos Kleiber. Toscanini touches crotchet = 76 from time to time, but his basic tempo is below that at crotchet = 72. Despite his being known for leading the reaction against 'tempo rubato' conductors (see above, p. 100), he eases back to crotchet = 64 in the closing section of the movement (and then introduces a conspicuous *rit* in the final two bars). Norrington begins at crotchet = 84, well above tempo, and never comes down beneath crotchet = 79. In the approach to the fortissimo dominants at bar 149 (ex. 8.4), the tempo begins at crotchet = 84 and has actually got a notch faster by the time the piano semiquaver movement begins at 150. Those who find this rushed and would prefer Carlos Kleiber's 'mainstream' Beethoven, don't need to blame authenticity. Kleiber's tempo is exactly what Beethoven specified and Norrington's is not. Moreover, one knows how to breathe between phrases and the other appears not to – not here, anyway.

It is interesting to compare these with John Eliot Gardiner in the same passage with the Orchestre Révolutionnaire et Romantique (a group which surely should win a 'Diapason d'or' for the most pretentious name ever invented). Gardiner sticks quite closely to Beethoven's metronome marking throughout. He begins a couple of ticks below at crotchet = 74 and that is what we hear, too, at the start of ex. 8.4. By the time he reaches the semiquavers, it has slipped to crotchet = 73. This is all quite close to Beethoven's markings and, to my ears, musically more coherent. But my personal favourite in this symphony is Harnoncourt with the Chamber Orchestra of Europe. His Allegretto begins

[41] Taruskin, *Text and Act*, p. 232.

Ex. 8.4 Ludwig van Beethoven, Symphony No. 7 in A major, Op. 92, second movement, Allegretto, bars 139–50

Ex. 8.4 (*cont.*)

Ex. 8.4 (*cont.*)

slightly above the metronome marking at crotchet = 79 but the tempo is subtly modified throughout the movement. At the approach to letter E he broadens out to crotchet = 71 and he makes a more noticeable comma than Gardiner (Norrington had none whatsoever) before crossing over into the *p dolce* passage at E itself.

I am getting tired of the two-pronged argument which first gives Roger Norrington's Beethoven recordings normative status and then attacks the lightweight character of period-instrument performances on the basis of what we hear there. There are other conductors who are well informed about performance practice and who have a rather different view of these works – and there will be more to come.

There are a number of related issues that need disentangling. It is perhaps best to deal with the idea of historical listening first. According to this, our concepts of (for example) religious grandeur have been moulded by listening to later composers thus making it impossible for us to hear one of the Bach passions in the same way as a Leipzig audience in the late 1720s. Adorno again: 'No matter how it was done in the Church of St. Thomas, a performance of the *St. Matthew Passion*, for instance, done with meagre means sounds pale and indecisive to the present-day ear, like a rehearsal which a few musicians have by chance decided to attend, while at the same time it assumes a didactic-pedantic character.'[42]

Peter Kivy suggests that this forces us into a choice of authenticities: we can strive to recreate Bach's sound world and in so doing deny ourselves the opportunity to be affected by the work's emotional power in the way that original audiences, we suppose, must have been. Or we can go for an authentic impact while realising that this means giving up on attempting to recreate the work's original sound world. He writes,

> if our paradigm of 'large' music is Berlioz's Requiem, or the *Carmina Burana*, then the opening chorus of the *St. Matthew Passion*, with the numbers available to Bach, far from sounding like massed forces, is going to have a rather modest, almost chamber music-like sound. So if we want sensible authenticity in this regard, we cannot achieve it by performing this chorus in Bach-like size: doing so will merely give us sonic authenticity.[43]

This is inherently circular, presupposing as it does that we know what it is that the *St Matthew Passion* has to offer us emotionally. If it really is something like the Berlioz Requiem (or the Brahms, or any other later masterpiece written specifically for much larger forces) then why would we bother performing Bach at all, particularly when upgrading to the forces needed to make the big impact might do violence to other aspects of the composition (such as the transparency of rapid contrapuntal lines)? And is it really true that having experienced Bruckner we can never again hear grandeur and weight in, say, Bach without re-

[42] Adorno, 'Bach Defended', p. 144.
[43] Kivy, *Authenticities*, p. 53.

orchestrating his music to suit our reconstructed ears? Personally, I don't think so. Musical works establish, as it were, their own frame of reference. We are all perfectly capable of entering the sound world of musical works of vastly different characters. The factoid that previous generations didn't even try to do this is irrelevant and so, too, is the idea that composers in the 19th century found bigger (and supposedly better) ways of 'doing' strength, grandeur, sorrow (just about anything, it seems). I am not convinced that, when it comes to powerful emotional communication, size is necessarily of the essence. Just as Shakespeare was sure that the strength of his own conception entrusted to the talents of his actor colleagues was quite enough to transport his audience from the confines of the Globe to the fields of Agincourt, I suspect that our ears are capable of hearing what Bach has to say through Bach's own resources (assuming that we can ever establish precisely what they were).

Lightness, brightness, and a highly-articulated character are not the necessary consequences (virtues, if you like) of using period instruments and taking account of historical performance practice. In so far as most of the activity to date has focussed on attempts at reducing what are seen as late 19th-century instrumental colours and expressive strategies, it is inevitable that the efforts of period-instrument performers will be heard as anti-romantic. But in chapter 6 I suggested that it seems equally possible that a similar determination to question 'received pronunciation' applied to romantic writing might have the opposite effect. Since what is involved here is the capacity of an interest in historical performance practice to achieve a deviation from a norm – the most generally accepted way of doing things – it is at least possible that a greater receptivity to 19th-century performing practice would increase, rather than restrict, the extrovert expression of emotion in late romantic repertoire.

As a postscript to this chapter I want to mention one more permutation of the museum/art gallery image – this time, one that was vigorously taken up by advocates of period-instrument performance in the 1970s and has by now become one of the most tired clichés of justification. The effect of performing familiar repertory on period instruments has often been compared to the restoration of works of art and, in particular, the removal of layers of varnish that obscured the brilliance of the original. The prime example was the revelation in the 1960s that Rembrandt's 'Night Watch' was not a night scene at all and that it pulsated with contrasts of light and shade, brilliant and sombre colours.

The analogy seemed just in the 1970s. The use of period instruments brought to familiar masterpieces (such as the Brandenburg Concertos or *Messiah*) transparent textures and more astringent instrumental timbres. Dreyfus comments on the value placed on this re-lighting of the most significant works in the Baroque canon under the subheadings 'Early Music as Defamiliarization' and 'Early Music and the Aesthetic of Novelty'.[44]

---

[44] Dreyfus, 'Early Music Defended', pp. 306–8 and 314–15.

But in the end, the 'restoration' mentality could (or should) only ever have provided a temporary justification for the use of old instruments. Over the past three decades we have seen them become orthodox (and heard 'conventional' ensembles adapt their approach to baroque and classical repertory in ways that demonstrate that they have been taking note).

It is interesting that the 'art restoration' metaphor itself has been applied with a slightly different emphasis. In 1990 Christopher Hogwood wrote

> We have conditioned ourselves to extremes of stimulation incompatible with the code of intention of the creator. We have asked, as it were, for the Rembrandt to be relegated to the gallery store-room and a 12-times enlargement with 'colour enhancement' to be hung in its place . . . I have to confess to an old-fashioned preference for Handel the colour he started off. You may rightly ask how can one be so presumptuous as to 'know' what that was, but I would rather make some progress along such a line of thought, even with difficulty and experiment, than sell out to the school of obligatory italics and car-chases which presupposes that whatever colour he was, it wasn't good enough. The historical approach is far from limiting; it actually offers a greater freedom of choice, a multiple choice of 'correct' readings.[45]

This is an interesting statement since, although he does not say so directly, I suspect that those Hogwood is accusing of 'colour enhancement' are not the massive choirs and orchestras doing their annual *Messiah*, but performers who prioritise the shock of the new above all else, where outrageousness (sometimes paraded as insight) becomes the goal. (Nigel Kennedy and Fabio Biondi have more in common than their different orientation as performers would suggest.) Nicholas Temperley, in the 1984 *Early Music* 'discussion' alerted readers to this trend: 'If we are to believe that [the sound is authentic], then the sound must be conspicuously different from what we are used to. Here lies one of the greatest dangers of the movement. For it puts a stronger premium on novelty than on accuracy, and fosters misrepresentation.'[46]

The miracle of what great art has to offer is that its newness endures. Stravinsky described Beethoven's *Große Fuge*, Op. 133, as an 'absolutely contemporary piece of music that will be contemporary forever'.[47] And in 1972 he wrote 'It has been such a long time since I last heard the *Meistersinger* that I am unable to say what it would mean to me now. But I think I would still listen to it as an active composer listening to an active composition, for at the age of a hundred the *Meistersinger* is a very lively monument.'[48] In both cases, he was simply acknowledging the works' aesthetic presence and parallel statements

---

[45] Foreword to *Companion to Baroque Music*, ed. J. A. Sadie (London, 1990), pp. xii–xiii. Another recent discussion of the painting restoration metaphor occurs in Nicholas Kenyon's lecture *Tradition Isn't What it Used to Be* (London: The Royal Philharmonic Society, 2001), p. 12.

[46] Leech-Wilkinson et al., 'The Limits of Authenticity', p. 16.

[47] Quoted by Joseph Kerman, *The Beethoven Quartets* (London, 1967), p. 253.

[48] Stravinsky, *Themes and Conclusions*, pp. 206–7.

could be made about countless musical compositions. The important question here (as, indeed, in the previous chapter) is how to acknowledge (to enjoy) the fact that these works can speak very directly to modern audiences.

I would not deny the positive benefits of drawing an audience's attention to aspects of a work that may have gone unnoticed provided, of course, that that does not involve some more serious distortion. But finding novel elements to emphasise is not in itself a very worthwhile goal. Genuine and open analytical and historical enquiry must offer the performer the opportunity to understand what is going on in a musical work. The formalist defamiliarisation or controlled estrangement is not necessarily hell-bent on novelty. It simply asks for a readiness to learn what a work has to offer unclouded by preconceptions or easy assumptions about its structure, style, character, or performance demands. Even if the end result of such study were to be no more or less than a reaffirmation of what generations have recognised as that work's particular genius it would be worth doing. The only real enemy (as Mahler recognised in his maxim 'Tradition is laziness – in every performance the work should be born anew') is complacency.

9. In the meantime . . .

In the introductory chapter I took issue with the view that just about everything that needed to be said about the aesthetic issues surrounding historically-informed performance had already been well traversed. I have not attempted here a comprehensive treatment of the subject, nor a systematic rebuttal of the critics of historically-informed performance. My individual chapters might be seen as essentially a series of musings on related topics, musings that have deliberately stayed away from definite conclusions. But it might nevertheless be useful to reflect on the implications of these chapters for the six critical positions articulated in my introduction.

First, I have no difficulty in conceding that a comprehensive authenticity is an impossibility, a chimera. The concept of authenticity is ultimately not helpful. As for the charge that the 'past' evoked in period-instrument performances is a fundamentally modernist construction, it is evident that, like all historical enquiry, historical-performance practice is susceptible to being coloured by present prejudices (assumptions).That was the central point of the Bach case study in chapter 2. The challenge for anyone not prepared to accept a rather nihilist view of human knowledge is to engage in a continuous re-examination of inherited assumptions. Performance-practice research is concerned with establishing (and, in performance, implementing) truths about a real past in the confidence that this will increase our understanding and appreciation of great music.

There is no easy answer to the claim that, because a modern audience's experience has been modified by an awareness of later music, a sonically-exact recreation an original performance would no longer evoke the response it did when first heard. This seems unanswerable since we simply cannot put ourselves inside the minds and bodies of, say, Bach's original audiences. My own unprovable conviction, as I assert in chapter 8, is that we are perfectly capable of entering the sound world of a musical work and experiencing it in its own terms. In other words, musical compositions (and art works in general) establish their own frame of reference. One of the things that fascinate me about the historical listening argument is that it only ever seems to be advanced in relation to timbre and sonority. If we can't hear Bach's instrumentation as he expected it (the *St Matthew Passion* sounding, as Adorno speculated, like a small group of not-so-competent musicians who have got together to rehearse), why does this not prevent us from appreciating other parameters of the composition? Surely we ought to find the harmonic language or rhythmic organisation of 17th- and 18th-century music unsatisfyingly naive? There is, in any case, something inherently circular about the historical-listening argument since it embodies an underlying assumption that we know what the music of the past means or ought to mean.

The idea, too, that notions of fidelity to a work are inherently anachronistic seems dependent on an oversimplification of the history of aesthetic perception. The articulation of a Kantian aesthetic at the end of the 18th century is the product of attitudes that had been centuries in the making. Moreover, the intertwining of artistic appreciation with other functions remained a feature of musical life well after 1800, whether it be in the use of the Opéra Comique as a meeting place for the families of courting couples or the initiation of rugby matches with an opera star singing the national anthem.

Of all the charges laid at the door of period-instrument performers, this book has been most centrally concerned with the idea that an interest in historical research might somehow be at odds with the use of the imagination in performance. Historical-performance practice does not, and could not, supply a set of rules comprehensive enough to replace musical judgement. On the contrary, historical sources enrich our understanding of the music and stimulate the imagination. For performers to exploit fully this wonderful resource, it is crucial to maintain an awareness of the difference between historical research and the application of historical research. This distinction is important for lots of reasons. First, research must be carried out in a disinterested way – without the threat of it destabilising cherished performance habits, for example. (This is important, not because such habits should not be disturbed, but to prevent desired outcomes influencing too strongly the direction of the enquiry.) Secondly, it needs to be recognised that even if the application of historical research (perhaps as experiment) were a performer's primary aim, personal judgement and taste will inevitably loom large in the result.

It will be clear from the ground covered in chapter 7 that the interpretative margins surrounding any historically-transmitted advice are broad enough to produce quite different results from two players interested in exactly the same sources. One point of divergence in interpretation illustrates this in a particularly interesting way. Period-instrument string players are generally well aware of the insistence in historical sources on avoiding percussive attacks at the beginning of a bowstroke and that this is often expressed as a recommendation to begin each stroke softly and then to increase the sound.[1] But the degree to which old bowing styles presupposed an actual swell within a note has been a matter of dispute. In the 1970s and 80s particularly, the ways in which violinists tried to implement the advice of Geminiani, Leopold Mozart, Tartini and others in this regard differed. Because of the location of teaching institutions and professional period-instrument orchestras, this tended to

---

[1] See my entry on bowing in *New Grove II*, Bow §II.iii.

divide up along national lines. English and American violinists used less conspicuous dynamic inflexion as an element in the basic bowstroke than players trained in Holland or Belgium. The adherents of the first group (the 'English School') admired a straighter and less mannered sound and spoke dismissively of players in the second group as exhibiting 'Dutch swell disease'.[2]

Richard Taruskin, in his essay for the Kenyon volume, seized on the emergence of such schools to express scepticism about the way in which historical sources were being used by performers. Taking as his starting point Donald J. Grout's scorn for those who sought to revive 'dead' musical traditions, he gave a rather cynical picture of the construction of new orthodoxies:

> our conception of historical verisimilitude . . . remains just as speculative and contingent – and hence, just as specious – as it was in 1957. It is true that some performance styles that have arisen in the last quarter century under the banner of historical verisimilitude have proven extremely persuasive, influential, and (with the passage of time) authoritative – at least within the world of performance. One is . . . the Netherlandish style of baroque string playing associated with names such as Jaap Schröder, Anner Bylsma, and the brothers Kuijken.

It may be surprising that anyone could wish to yoke Schröder and Kuijken together in this way. Their approach to baroque violin playing is at least as different from each other as, say, Schröder is from Monica Huggett. But that is beside the point. What would the implications be if these Europeans all sounded identical to each other and decidedly different from their English or American confrères? Why deny performers of our own time their right to reflect the same kind of divergence that prevailed in the past? For just as individual violinists have always had personal styles, it is also obvious that 'schools' of playing (sharing a common vision for sound and style) have always existed. Leopold and Wolfgang Mozart were both quite critical of 'Tartini school' players, for example. When in 1778 Wolfgang reported to his father on the violinist Rothfischer's playing he wrote that he 'plays well in his way (a little bit in the old-fashioned Tartini manner)'. It seems that Tartini's pupils had a reputation for tidy but perhaps rather understated playing. Burney remarked that the Tartini school was 'rather remarkable for delicacy, expression, and high finishing, than for spirit and variety'. He several times comments on the gentle playing of Tartini's pupils – and so, too, do the Mozarts.[3] So, *if* there is – or was in the 1970s and 80s – such a thing as a Netherlandish style or school, that does not necessarily have any bearing whatsoever on the historical accuracy of what they were doing. History and basic observation of both diversity and

---

[2] See Daniel Leech-Wilkinson, 'The Limits of Authenticity', p. 13: 'In the Affettuoso of Bach's Brandenburg Concerto no. 5 . . . Leonhardt presides over a performance in which the sighing dynamics so often deplored by English critics are the principal means of articulation . . .'

[3] See my 'Mozart and the Violin', *Early Music* 20 (1992), 23.

trends in our own musical culture(s) should lead us to expect marked differences between (a) individual violinists and (b) 'schools' of players.

In another essay in the Kenyon volume, Howard Mayer Brown offered a rather less radical and less dismissive comment on the emergence of national schools:

> Their [Leonhardt and the Kuijkens'] style of playing, characterized by careful attention to detail, is sometimes criticized for its exaggerated mannerisms, and especially for its dependence on the effect of messa di voce (swelling and dying down on single notes) which, it is argued, has a tendency to destroy the listeners' sense of melodic line. But their manner of playing has been carefully developed from intensive study of what older writers on music had to say. The contrast between the way members of the Netherlands school and others play is therefore especially illuminating for the evidence it gives that musical results can differ widely even when two people base their performing style on the same assumptions, and even on the same treatises for their information.

This is undoubtedly true; but what are the implications of recognising this?

It would be interesting to try to construct a model of musical performance that quantified its various components. What I have in mind here is the extent to which any performance (1) contains elements that are historically verifiable, (2) depends on received and unquestioned traditions, and (3) relies on the performer's individual musical instincts. These three areas are inextricably interrelated. One flows into the other with the result that the boundaries separating them are inevitably (hopefully even) somewhat vague. The first category involves the conscious application of learned features (the 'Rules'). The second – received tradition – is in many ways the most complex and made up of a tangle of constituents. It is most obviously transmitted through orthodox teaching but must derive in part from the characteristics inherent in the nature of whatever instrument is being played. (Some techniques that could, if necessary, be empirically re-invented simply maximise the particular instrument's efficiency.) And some of the continuity with the past that we take for granted doubtless does extend back to the 17th or 18th century. The third component – imagination, inspiration, an interpretative ability – cannot exist in a vacuum. It is inevitably informed by study of some kind. One quite legitimate way of regarding inspiration is as the internalising of knowledge or learned skills.

If we could separate out these elements, I would guess that even amongst the most conscientious period-instrument performers, the conscious historically-aware segment is not going to get much above, say, 10%. And although it would be even harder to quantify the third segment (that which depends on the musician's own creativity and imagination) we can be sure that it is a constituent of any performance whatsoever. Again, it probably never gets above, say, 10% since, if it did, we would probably not recognise what was being played. Percentages in such an area are a nonsense but, however wrong-headed, they might provide a tool for thinking about what happens on stage.

The basis of every performance is bound to be my middle category – received tradition. But all three bands are in a state of flux – and what interests me most is the potential for the first category, conscious learning, to stimulate and eventually become dissolved in the third, inspiration. And – an act of faith here rather than scientific analysis – the more the first category is topped up the greater the benefits for the third.

In chapter 7, I used Dahlhaus's distinction between historicists and conservative traditionalists as a way of characterising the difference between performers who espouse historical awareness and those who regard such concerns as irrelevant, or even an impediment, to the communication of the essence of a musical work. In practice, there is not an absolute division between 'conservative traditionalists' and historicists.[4] John Eliot Gardiner is strongly associated with the historicist perspective. But when admiring the fuzzy half-truths of outdated musicology and arguing that there are more important things in performing Bach than doing it with the means the composer said he wanted (see above, p. 47), Gardiner is for the time being allying himself with conservative traditionalist views. It is perhaps unfair to single out such an obvious case of a blurred attitudinal stance. There is bound is to be something of the conservative traditionalist in every performer, even those in whom the anxiety of influence rages so strongly that they would do almost anything to break free of the fetters of tradition.

Step 1 in being historically informed is to try to answer the question 'How was this music performed?' That question is the province of the music historian and must be recognised as one which precedes and is distinct from the question 'How should this be performed?' The value of tackling the first question is, initially, quite independent of the need to answer the second. Like other forms of historical enquiry, performance-practice research is worth doing for the light that it throws upon music of the past regardless of its possible application in contemporary performance. It is available alike to those who wish to strive for historical authenticity and to unrepentant conservative traditionalists. It is, though, the *sine qua non* of the second question, 'How should this be performed?'

In view of the incompleteness of the record, the inherent difficulties of describing subtleties of performance, variations in style between schools of players (and even individual performers) within the same milieu, and so on, it would rarely, if ever, be possible to approach a single, comprehensive, and definitive answer to the first question. (That realisation in no way undermines the value of pursuing it, though it gives some indication of the scope of the responses it will produce.) This in turn means that the second, contingent question is even less susceptible to simple answers since it introduces additional

---

[4]   Rosen alludes to the different ideals of historicist and conservative traditionalist approaches by positing two opposing performance ideals: of 'authenticity' on the one hand and 'fidelity' on the other. (See 'The Benefits of Authenticity', p. 202.) As a binary set of terms this seems appealingly simple, but the notion of 'fidelity' is as fraught with problems as that of 'authenticity'.

complications of its own. First, there is the difficulty of bringing 'inherited' assumptions into a realm where conscious choice can be exercised (the difficulty of escaping tradition). Then there is the nature of performance itself which depends on a commitment from moment to moment to just one of a range of historically-possible options. Accepting the obvious – that complete authenticity is ultimately not achievable – is not, however, the same thing as conceding that striving for historical authenticity is a futile, unworthy, or unmusical aim – though that, as we have seen, has often been implicit in much of the critical writing.

Historical sources, even when they use the language of prescription, cannot restrict creativity. There is inevitably too wide a gap between what they can tell us and an actual performance for that to be so. But they will help us to understand the works we wish to perform and they may offer creative musicians an imaginative resource. Moreover, musicality, imagination, and a commitment to communicating the emotional content of the music we perform were as much valued in the past as they are now. I leave the last word to Francesco Geminiani: 'I would besides advise . . . the Performer who is ambitious to inspire his Audience, to be first inspired himself; which he cannot fail to be if he chuses a Work of Genius, if he makes himself thoroughly acquainted with all its Beauties; and if while his Imagination is warm and glowing he pours the same exalted Spirit into his own Performance.'[5]

---

[5] Geminiani, *Art of Playing on the Violin*, p. 8.

Bibliography

ADORNO, T. W. 'Bach Defended against his Devotees.' In *Prisims*. Trans. S. and S. Weber. London, 1967. 133–46.

ALLSOP, P. *Arcangelo Corelli: New Orpheus of our Times*. Oxford, 1999.

—— *The Italian 'Trio Sonata' from its Origins until Corelli*. Oxford, 1992.

ARNOLD, F. T. *The Art of Accompaniment from a Thorough-Bass as Practised in the XVIIth & XVIIIth Centuries*. London, 1931.

AUER, L. *Violin Playing as I Teach it*. New York, 1921; repr. 1980.

BARNARD, J. *The First Book of Selected Church Musick*. London, 1641.

BASOLI, A. G. 'Paganini's Violin Encounters Jazz'. *New York Times* 2 January 2002 (on line).

BAUMGARTNER, J. B. *Instructions de musique, théorique et pratique à l'usage du violoncelle*. The Hague, *c.* 1774.

BÉRIOT, C.-A. de. *Grande Méthode de violon*. Paris, 1858.

BIZET, Georges. *Lettres*. Ed. Claude Glayman. Paris, 1989.

BLOOM, Harold. *The Western Canon*. New York, San Diego, and London, 1994.

BORGIR, T. *The Performance of the Basso Continuo in Italian Baroque Music*. Ann Arbor, MI, 1987.

BOWEN, José A. 'Can a Symphony Change? Establishing Methodology for the Historical Study of Performance Styles.' In *Musik als Text: Bericht über den internationalen Kongress der Gesellschaft für Musikforschung* ii. Kassel, 1998. 160–72.

—— 'Mendelssohn, Berlioz and Wagner as Conductors: The Origins of the Ideal of "Fidelity to the Composer".' *Performance Practice Review* 6 (1993), 77–88.

—— 'The Conductor and the Score: The Relationship between Interpreter and Text in the Generation of Mendelssohn, Berlioz and Wagner.' PhD thesis. Stanford University, 1994.

BRAHMS, J. *Johannes Brahms: Life and Letters*. Selected and annotated by S. Avins. Oxford and New York, 1997.

BROWN, C. 'Bowing Styles, Vibrato and Portamento in Nineteenth-Century Violin Playing.' *Journal of the Royal Musical Association* 113 (1988), 97–128.

—— *Classical and Romantic Performing Practice 1750–1900*. Oxford, 1999.

BROWN, H. M., and S. SADIE, eds. *Performance Practice: Music after 1600*. London, 1989.

BURNEY, Charles. *Music, Men and Manners in France and Italy 1770*. Ed. E. H. Poole. London, 1974.

BUTT, John. *Playing with History*. Cambridge, 2002.

CAMBINI, G. G. *Nouvelle méthode théorique et pratique pour le violon*. Paris, 1803; repr. 1972.

CARERI, Enrico. *Francesco Geminiani (1687–1762)*. Oxford, 1993.

CAVICCHI, A. 'Corelli e il violinismo bolognese.' In *Studi Corelliani. Atti del Primo Congresso Internazionale (Fusignano 5–8 settembre 1968)*. Florence, [1972]. 33–46.

CHAPPLE, Geoff. *Rewi Alley of China*. Auckland, 1980.

CONE, E. T. *Musical Form and Musical Performance*. New York, 1968.

Cook, Nicholas, and Mark Everist, eds. *Rethinking Music*. Oxford and New York, 1999.

Corrette, Michel. *Méthodes pour apprendre à jouër de la contre-basse à 3, à 4. et à 5 cordes*. Paris, 1773; 2nd ed. 1781; repr. Geneva, 1977.

Dahlhaus, Carl. *Grundlagen der Musikgeschichte*. Köln, 1977. Trans. J. B. Robinson, as *Foundations of Music History*. Cambridge, 1983.

Dart, Thurston. *The Interpretation of Music*. London, 1954.

David, H. T., and A. Mendel, eds. *The Bach Reader*. New York and London, 1945; rev. with supplement 1972. Revised and expanded by Christoph Wolff as *The New Bach Reader*. Norton, New York, and London, 1998.

Davies, Fanny. 'Some Personal Recollections of Brahms as Pianist and Interpreter'. In *Cobbett's Cyclopedic Survey of Chamber Music*. London, 1929. 184.

Dean, Winton. *Bizet*. The Master Musicians. London, 1948.

—— 'The Corruption of *Carmen* and the Perils of Pseudo-Musicology'. *Musical Newsletter* 3/4 (1973), Oct. 7–12, 20.

—— 'The True *Carmen*'. *Musical Times* 106 (1965), 846–55.

Dolmetsch, Arnold. *The Interpretation of Music of the 17th and 18th Centuries*. London, 1915.

Donington, Robert. *Baroque Music: Style and Performance*. London, 1982.

—— *The Interpretation of Early Music*. London, 1963; rev. 1989.

—— *A Performer's Guide to Baroque Music*. London, 1973.

—— *String Playing in Baroque Music*. London, 1977.

—— *The Work and Ideas of Arnold Dolmetsch*. Haslemere, 1932.

Dreyfus, Laurence. 'Early Music Defended against its Devotees: A Theory of Historical Performance in the Twentieth Century.' *Musical Quarterly* 49 (1983), 297–322.

Edwards, Owain. 'The Response to Corelli's Music in Eighteenth-Century England.' *Studia musicologica norvegica* 2 (1976), 51–96.

Fabbri, Paolo. *Monteverdi*. Trans. Tim Carter. Cambridge, 1994.

Frogley, A. 'Beethoven's Music in Performance: Historical Perspectives.' In G. Stanley, ed. *The Cambridge Companion to Beethoven*. Cambridge, 2000.

Galeazzi, Franceso. *Elementi teorico-pratici di musica*. Rome, 1791–96.

Gasparini, Francesco. *L'armonico pratico al cimbalo*. Venice, 1708. Trans. F. S. Stillings as *The Practical Harmonist at the Harpsichord*. Ed. D. L. Burrows. New Haven and London, 1963.

Geminiani, Francesco. *The Art of Playing on the Violin*. London, 1751.

Giudice, Gaspare. *Pirandello: A Biography*. Trans. A. Hamilton. London, 1975.

Gluck, Christoph Willibald. *Sämtliche Werke* vol. 4, ed. R. Gerber. Kassel, 1954.

Goehr, L. *The Imaginary Museum of Musical Works: An Essay in the Philosophy of Music*. Oxford, 1992.

Grimm, Friedrich Melchior (Baron von). *Le Petit Prophète de Boehmischbroda. Le correcteur des bouffons et la gurée de l'opéra*. Paris, 1753.

Groos, Arthur, and Roger Parker, eds. *Reading Opera*. Princeton, 1988.

Harnoncourt, N. *Baroque Music Today: Music as Speech*. Trans. Mary O'Neill. London, 1988.

Haskell, H. *The Early Music Revival: A History*. London, 1988.

Hawkins, Sir John. *A General History of the Science and Practice of Music (1776)*. 2 vols. London, 1963.

Hayes, William. *Remarks on Mr Avison's Essay on Musical Expression*. London, 1753.

Hickman, R. 'The Censored Publications of *The Art of Playing on the Violin*, or Geminiani Unshaken.' *Early Music* 11 (1983), 73–6.

HOLLOWAY, J. 'Corelli's Op. 5: Text, Act . . . and Reaction.' *Early Music* 24 (1996), 635–40.

HOLMAN, Peter, and Richard MAUNDER. 'The Accompaniment of Concertos in 18th-Century England.' *Early Music* 28 (2000), 637–50.

HUDSON, Richard. *Stolen Time: The History of Tempo Rubato.* Oxford, 1994.

JOHNSON, J. *Listening in Paris, a Cultural History.* Berkeley and Los Angeles, 1995.

KENYON, N., ed. *Authenticity and Early Music.* Oxford and New York, 1988.

—— *Tradition Isn't What it Used to Be.* London: The Royal Philharmonic Society, 2001.

KERMAN, Joseph. *The Beethoven Quartets.* London, 1967.

—— 'The Byrd Edition – in Print and on Disc.' *Early Music* 29 (2001), 109–18.

KIVY, Peter. *Authenticities: Philosophical Reflections on Musical Performance.* Ithaca and London, 1995.

KOOPMAN, Ton. 'Recording Bach's Early Cantatas.' *Early Music* 24 (1996), 604–19.

KOTT, Jan. *Shakespeare Our Contemporary.* Trans. Bodeslaw Taborski. London, 1964.

KOURY, D. J. *Orchestral Performance Practices in the 19th Century: Size, Proportions, and Seating.* Ann Arbor, 1986.

LA LAURENCIE, Lionel de. *L'École Française de Violon de Lully à Viotti.* 3 vols. Paris, 1922–24.

LANG, P. H. *Music in Western Civilization.* New York, 1941.

—— 'Performance Practice and Musicology.' In M. Bent, ed. *Musik, Edition, Interpretation: Gedenkschrift Günter Henle.* Munich, 1980. 314–18.

LEECH-WILKINSON, D., R. TARUSKIN, and N. TEMPERLEY. 'The Limits of Authenticity: A Discussion.' *Early Music* 12 (1984), 3–25.

LENTON, John. *The Gentleman's Diversion, or the Violin Explained.* London, 1694.

LINDGREN, L. 'The Accomplishments of the Learned and Ingenious Nicola Francesco Haym (1678–1729).' *Studi musicali* 16 (1987), 247–380.

—— 'Nicola Cosimi in London, 1701–1705.' *Studi musicali* 11 (1982), 229–48.

LÖHLEIN, G. S. *Anweisung zum Violinspielen.* Leipzig and Züllichau, 1774.

LONG, M. *At the Piano with Maurice Ravel.* London, 1973.

LUBBOCK, Tom. 'The Early Early Show.' *The Independent,* 20 September 1988.

MACCLINTOCK, Carol, ed. *Readings in the History of Music in Performance.* Bloomington and London, 1979.

MANGSEN, S. 'The Trio Sonata in Pre-Corellian Prints: When Does 3 = 4?' *Performance Practice Review* 3 (1990), 138–64.

MARSHALL, Robert L. 'Bach's Chorus: A Preliminary Reply to Joshua Rifkin', *Musical Times* 124 (1983), 19–22.

MATTEIS, Nicola. *The False Consonances of Musick.* London, 1682.

MERSENNE, Marin. *Harmonie Universelle.* Paris, 1636–37; Eng. trans. of the book on instruments by R. E. Chapman. The Hague, 1957.

MÉRIMÉE, Prosper. *Carmen, suivi de Les Âmes Du Purgatoire.* Paris, 1999.

MITCHELL, Donald. *Mahler: The Wunderhorn Years.* London, 1975.

MONTEVERDI, C. *The Letters of Claudio Monteverdi.* Trans. D. Stevens. Oxford, 1995.

MORTENSEN, L. U. ' "Unerringly tasteful"?: Harpsichord continuo in Corelli's Op. 5 Sonatas.' *Early Music* 24 (1996), 665–79.

MORPHET, Richard, et al. *Encounters: New Art from Old.* London, 2000.

MOSER, A. 'Zu Joh. Seb. Bachs Sonaten und Partiten für Violine allein.' *Bach-Jahrbuch* 17 (1920), 30–65.

MOZART, Leopold. *Versuch einer gründlichen Violinschule.* Augsburg, 1756. Eng. trans. by E. Knocker as *A Treatise on the Fundamental Principles of Violin Playing.* 2nd ed. London, 1951.

Mozart, W. A. *Briefe und Aufzeichnungen: Gesamtausgabe.* Eds. W. A. Bauer and O. E. Deutsch. 7 vols. Kassel, 1962–75.

—— *The Letters of Mozart and his Family.* Trans. Emily Anderson. 3rd ed. London, 1985.

Muffat, Georg. *Florilegium Secundum.* Passau, 1698. In H. Rietsch, ed. *Denkmäler der Tonkunst in Österreich* ii (4). Vienna, 1895.

Muffat, Georg. *Georg Muffat on Performance Practice.* Ed. and trans. David K. Wilson. Bloomington and Indianapolis, 2001.

Musgrave, Michael, ed. *The Cambridge Companion to Brahms.* Cambridge, 1999.

Nattiez, Jean-Jacques. *Music and Discourse: Towards a Semiology of Music.* Trans. Carolyn Abbate. Princeton, 1990.

Neumann, Frederick. *New Essays on Performance Practice.* Ann Arbor and London, 1989.

—— *Ornamentation and Improvisation in Mozart.* Princeton, 1986.

North, Roger. *The Musicall Grammarian 1728.* Eds. Mary Chan and Jamie Kassler. Cambridge, 1990.

Parrott, Andrew. 'Bach's Chorus: A "brief yet highly necessary" Reappraisal.' *Early Music* 24 (1996), 551–80.

—— 'Bach's Chorus: Who Cares?' *Early Music* 25 (1997), 297–302.

—— *The Essential Bach Choir.* Woodbridge, 2000.

Pascall, Robert. 'The Editor's Brahms.' In Michael Musgrave, ed. *The Cambridge Companion to Brahms.* Cambridge, 1999. 250–67.

Peirce, Charles Sanders. *Collected Papers,* ed. C. Hartshorne, P. Weiss and A. W. Burks, 8 vols. Cambridge, Mass., 1931–66.

Penna, L. *Le primi albori musicali.* Bologna, 1672.

Pfeiffer, R. *History of Classical Scholarship from the Beginnings to the End of the Hellenistic Age.* Oxford, 1968.

Philip, Robert. *Early Recordings and Musical Style.* Cambridge, 1992.

Pincherle, Marc. 'On the Rights of the Interpreter in the Performance of 17th and 18th-Century Music'. *The Musical Quarterly* 44 (1958), 145–66.

Plantinga, L. *Beethoven's Concertos: History, Style, Performance.* New York and London, 1999.

Playford, J. *An Introduction to the Skill of Musick.* London, 1664.

Quantz, J. J. *Versuch einer Anweisung, die Flöte traversiere zu spielen.* Berlin, 1752. Trans. E. R. Reilly as *On Playing the Flute.* London, 1966.

Rasch, Rudolph. 'Corelli's Contract: Notes on the Publication History of the Concerti Grossi . . . Opera Sesta [1714].' *Tijdschrift van de Koninklijke Vereniging voor Nederlandse Muziek Geshiednis* 45.ii (1996), 83–136.

Rifkin, Joshua. 'Bach's Chorus: A Preliminary Report.' *Musical Times* 123 (1982), 747–54.

—— 'From Weimar to Leipzig: Concertists and Ripienists in Bach's *Ich hatte viel Bekümmernis.*' *Early Music* 24 (1996), 583–603.

Rosen, Charles. 'The Benefits of Authenticity.' In *Critical Entertainments.* Cambridge, Mass., and London, 2000. 200–21.

Rousseau, J. J. *Dictionnaire de Musique.* Paris, 1768.

Sadie, J. A., ed. *Companion to Baroque Music.* London, 1990.

Sadie, Stanley and John Tyrell, eds. *The New Grove Dictionary of Music and Musicians.* 2nd ed. 29 vols. London, 2001.

Saint-Saens, Camille. 'The Execution of Classical Works: Notably Those of the Older Masters.' *The Musical Times* 56 (August 1915); repr. *The Musical Times* 138 (October 1997), 31–5.

SCHERING, A. *Aufführungspraxis alter Musik*. Leipzig, 1931.

—— 'Verschwundene Traditionene des Bachzeitalters.' *Bachjahrbuch* 1 (1904), 104–15.

SCHRÖDER, Jaap, and Christopher HOGWOOD. 'The Developing Violin.' *Early Music* 7 (1979), 155–65.

SCHWEITZER, A. *J. S. Bach*. Trans. E. Newman. 2 vols. Leipzig, 1911; repr. New York *c.* 1966.

SCRUTON, Roger. *The Aesthetics of Music*. Oxford, 1997.

SHERMAN, B. D. 'Bach's Notation of Tempo and Early Music Performance: Some Reconsiderations.' *Early Music* 28 (2000), 455–66.

—— 'Tempos and Proportions in Brahms: Period Evidence.' *Early Music* 25 (1997), 463–77.

SMITHER, Howard. '*Messiah* and Progress in Victorian England.' *Early Music* 13 (1985), 339–48.

SPITTA, P. *Johann Sebastian Bach*. Trans. C. Bell, and J. A. Fuller-Maitland. 2 vols. New York, 1951.

SPOHR, L. *Violinschule*. Vienna, 1832.

STEVENS, D. *Musicology: A Practical Guide*. London, 1980.

STEWART, A. 'Sir John in Love.' *Early Music Today* 8.4 (2000), 18.

STOWELL, R. *Violin Technique and Performance Practice in the Late Eighteenth and Early Nineteenth Centuries*. Cambridge, 1985.

—— *The Early Violin and Viola*. Cambridge, 2001.

STRAVINSKY, Igor. *Autobiography*. New York, 1936; repr. 1962.

—— *Themes and Conclusions*. London, 1972.

STRUNK, O., ed. *Source Readings in Music History*. Revised edition ed. Leo Treitler. New York and London, 1985.

STUCKENSCHMIDT, H. H., ed. *Three Classics in the Aesthetic of Music*. New York, 1974.

TALBOT, Michael. *The Musical Work: Reality or Invention?* Liverpool, 2000.

—— 'Tenors and Basses at the Venetian *Ospedali*.' *Acta Musicologica* 66 (1994), 123–38.

TARTINI, G. *Traité des Agréments de la Musique*. Ed. E. R. Jacobi. Celle and New York, 1961.

TARUSKIN, R. *Text and Act*. New York and Oxford, 1995.

TOSI, P. *Opinioni de' cantori antichi, e moderni*. Bologna, 1723. Eng. trans. by J. E. Galliard as *Observations on the Art of Florid Song*. London, 1742.

TREITLER, L. *Music and the Historical Imagination*. Cambridge, Mass., 1989.

URMSON, J. O. 'The Ethics of Musical Performance.' In *The Interpretation of Music: Philosophical Essays*. Oxford, 1993. 156–64.

VERGO, Peter, ed. *The New Museology*. London, 1989.

WAGNER, Richard. *Three Wagner Essays*. Trans. R. L. Jacobs. London, 1979.

—— *Sämtliche Briefe*. Ed. G. Strobel and W. Wolf. 11 vols. Leipzig, 1993.

WALLS, P. 'The Baroque Era: Strings.' In H. M. Brown and S. Sadie, eds. *Performance Practice: Music after 1600*. New York and London, 1989. 44–79.

—— 'Geminiani and the Role of the Viola in the Concerto Grosso.' In Warren Drake, ed. *Liber Amicorum John Steele: A Musicological Tribute*. New York, 1997. 379–413.

—— '"Ill-compliments and arbitrary taste"? Geminiani's Directions for Performers.' *Early Music* 14 (1986), 221–35.

—— 'Mozart and the Violin.' *Early Music* 20 (1992), 7–29.

—— 'Performing Corelli's Violin Sonatas, Op. 5.' *Early Music* 24 (1996), 133–42.

—— 'Violin Fingering in the 18th Century.' *Early Music* 12 (1984), 300–315.

—— *Music in the English Courtly Masque 1604–1640*. Oxford, 1996.

WATKIN, D. 'Corelli's Op. 5 Sonatas: "Violino e violone *o* cimbalo?" ' *Early Music* 24 (1996), 645–63.

WEBERN, Anton. *The Path to the New Music.* Ed. Willi Reich, trans. Leo Black. Bryn Mawr, Pa., 1963.

WILLIAMS, Peter. 'BWV 565: A Toccata in D Minor for Organ by J. S. Bach?' *Early Music* 9 (1981), 330–7.

—— 'Performance Practice Studies: Some Current Approaches to the Early Music Phenomenon.' In J. Paynter et al., eds. *Companion to Contemporary Musical Thought.* London and New York, 1992. 931–47.

WILSON, J., ed. *Roger North on Music.* London, 1959.

WIMSATT, W. K., and M. C. BEARDSLEY. 'The Intentional Fallacy.' *Sewanee Review* (1946), 466–88.

WRIGHT, L. A. 'A New Source for *Carmen.*' *19th-Century Music* 2 (1978), 61–71.

ZASLAW, Neal. 'In Vino Veritas.' *Early Music* 25 (1997), 568–9.

—— 'Ornaments for Corelli's Violin Sonatas, Op. 5.' *Early Music* 24 (1996), 95–118.

ZOHN, Steven. 'When is a Quartet not a Quartet?: Relationships between Scoring and Genre in the German Quadro, ca. 1715–40'. In *Johann Friedrich Fasch und sein Wirken für Zerbst.* Fasch-Studien 6. Dessau: Anhaltische Verlagsgesellschaft, 1997. 263–90.

Index